The Holy Sp.
Renewal of All Things

Pneumatology in Paul and Jürgen Moltmann

T. David Beck

James Clarke & Co

James Clarke & Co
P.O. Box 60
Cambridge
CB1 2NT
United Kingdom

www.jamesclarke.co.uk
publishing@jamesclarke.co.uk

ISBN: 978 0 227 17332 9

British Library Cataloguing in Publication Data
A record is available from the British Library

Copyright © T. David Beck, 2007

First published by James Clarke & Co, 2010

Published by arrangement with Wipf and Stock

Contents

Acknowledgments

Although I hope to have conveyed significant theological content in the following pages, much of the meaning that this book holds for me stems from the experience of following the project through to its completion. Because I have received endless support from many people, this experience has been one of growth, both as a scholar and as a person.

Whatever virtues I have developed as a teacher and scholar can be traced to the influence of excellent role models. In my days at Fuller Theological Seminary, Professors Nancey Murphy and James McClendon demonstrated the combination of scholarship and personal care that marks the very best teachers. At Southern Methodist University, Professor Victor Furnish is exemplary in his standard of scholarly excellence and fairness with the biblical texts. Professor Ellen Charry has convinced me that all activities of a teacher, even handing out grades, can be done in a way that carries positive pastoral value. I thank Professors Furnish and Charry for serving on my dissertation committee. Finally, my advisor, Professor William Abraham, has given me persistent and gentle guidance and encouragement, the influence of which will remain with me throughout my career. In many ways, I am only beginning to appreciate the mark he has left on me as a theologian and a philosopher. My aspiration for the coming years is to carry on the legacy of these scholars, teachers, and people of faith.

There are friends too numerous to name who have helped me and my family through this doctoral degree. However, I would like to especially thank a handful of them. Our small group and other friends at Christ Episcopal Church have always been there to cheer us on. John Wright's long-distance phone calls and visits to our house have provided many laughs as well as much needed encouragement. Jon-Martin Crowley has been unwavering in his support of me and my family. Two of my fellow doctoral students, Don Smith and Darrell White, came alongside me at the beginning of my first year in the program and have remained there ever since. I deeply appreciate all these people.

Utmost in importance is the steadfast affection and encouragement given by my family. I thank my parents, my brother and sister, and my wife's parents and family for their care, their concern, and their prayers. They have all helped in more ways than they know. My children, Lauren and Spencer, have brought me laughter, fulfillment and a new sense of what is important in life. Finally, I have immense gratitude and admiration for my wife, Susan. Despite the considerable sacrifices demanded by the doctoral program, she has remained faithful and cheerful, quietly inspiring me and everyone else who knows her.

1

An Eschatological Orientation in Pneumatology

Pneumatology in the Protestant Tradition

THROUGHOUT the history of Western Christian thought, one of the most persistent difficulties has been the role of the doctrine of the Holy Spirit within theology. Consistent with the logic of the *filioque* clause, the Holy Spirit has been overshadowed by the preeminent figure of the Son. Consequently, the Holy Spirit has been "the forgotten Person of the Trinity," and pneumatology has become a backwater of Western theology. It is not without reason that the Eastern tradition has accused the Western tradition of subordinationism and neglect of the Third Person of the Trinity.

Considering the tendency toward pneumatological imbalance in the West, it should come as no surprise that the theology of the Holy Spirit within Protestantism has been marked by a tendency toward bipolarity. The theology of the Holy Spirit has swung back and forth between what I will call an "institutional" tendency and an "experiential" tendency.

On one side stand Luther, Calvin, and the institutional churches of the Reformation. Whereas the Catholic church had located the work of the Spirit mainly in the sacramental function of the church, the Reformers emphasized its location not only in the sacraments but also in the Word. In addition, they also tied the Spirit to Christ. They identified the Holy Spirit as the agent through whom atonement in Christ is applied to all believing human beings. As it has worked out in the institutional churches of the Reformation, pneumatology has taken on a subordinationistic tone. The Spirit's work has tended to be confined to ecclesiology (Word and sacrament) and christology. It has become a function of the church and Christ.

On the other side of the Protestant tradition is the long line of protest movements—the "enthusiasts," Anabaptists, pietists, Methodists,
Pentecostals, and charismatics—which have reacted to the institutional
church's subordination of pneumatology with a corresponding elevation
of pneumatology. In particular, these movements have stressed the necessity of personal experience of the Spirit as a component of the authentic
Christian life. They have been perceived as "enthusiasts" by the institutional churches for failing to exert proper controls on manifestations of
the Spirit, and for seeking experience of the Spirit with what is seen as
imprudent eagerness. In return, they have on occasion been highly critical of the institutional churches' overly restrictive conception of the work
of the Spirit. One can reference, for instance, the vituperation in Thomas
Müntzer's treatise directed against Luther: *Highly Provoked Defense and
Answer against the Spiritless, Soft-living Flesh at Wittenberg, Which has
Befouled Pitiable Christianity in Perverted Fashion by its Theft of the Holy
Spirit.*

Thus, the doctrine of the Holy Spirit has swung back and forth between an institutional tendency and an experiential tendency. I will argue
that both of these tendencies make significant offerings to the ongoing understanding of the person and work of the Holy Spirit, but they also come
with unwanted baggage. Rather than trying to rehabilitate one of these
models, the burden of this dissertation will be to propose and explicate a
third option that comes not out of the Protestant tradition but out of the
original language of pneumatology: Christian eschatology.

The Institutional Tendency in Protestant Pneumatology: Karl Barth

One of the paramount figures in twentieth-century theology is Karl
Barth. He is known for opposing Protestant liberalism with a theological vision defined by the sovereignty and otherness of God, and God's
gracious outreach to humanity in the person of Jesus Christ. Concerning
the Holy Spirit, Barth serves as an illustration of the institutional tendency in Protestant pneumatology. To illustrate this point, I will discuss
the pneumatological dimensions of two key doctrines: reconciliation and
revelation.[1]

---

[1] Barth's pneumatology has received divergent interpretations. Philip Rosato takes a
unique position, viewing Barth as a thoroughgoing pneumatologian. Rosato attempts to
give pneumatocentric interpretations to all major themes of Barthian theology (*The Spirit
as Lord*). The weaknesses of Rosato's work have been raised by John Thompson in the last

Reconciliation between human beings and God comes through divine grace as enacted in the life, death and resurrection of Christ. It is the history of Christ, being epitomized in Calvary and the empty tomb, but also continued in Christ's presence in the church through the Holy Spirit and in his second coming. All of this takes place on behalf of humanity (and all of creation); it is the divine plan of redemption. In the history of Christ, God confronts humanity with the truth of humanity's need for salvation and the gracious offer of it. The saving work of God in Christ is the objective side of reconciliation. It is only by the objective work of Christ that human beings can be saved; not by their own efforts.

Corresponding to the objective side of the reconciliation of human beings with God there is a subjective side. Salvation involves the free and intentional act of believing in Christ by faith. But Barth is clear that the freedom and ability to believe are strictly gifts from God—specifically the Holy Spirit (*CD* IV.1: 645). The Spirit comes as the awakening power of the believing person.

The revelation of God to humanity, which is closely connected with the divine ministry of reconciliation, consists in large part of the unveiling of the mystery of Christ dying in shame on the cross and rising again for the sake of all human beings. This mystery is not accessible by means of human discovery; it must be revealed by God to human beings. Revelation takes on a three-fold form corresponding to the Trinity. It is a process involving God the Revealer making known to human beings his Word, the Revealed, the content of the revelation. Because sinful humanity is unable to independently comprehend the mystery of Christ, it is necessary for God to instill in human beings the power to grasp divine truth. This power is the Holy Spirit, who is referred to in this scheme as God's Revealedness. Thus, the Holy Spirit is the revelatory bridge between human beings who are predisposed to misunderstand God and that same God reaching out to them in mercy. In the Spirit, God empowers people from within to acknowledge divine truth.

Although Barth does not equate divine revelation with the written Word of God, he strongly believes that revelation happens in conjunction

chapter of his book *The Holy Spirit in the Theology of Karl Barth*. Thompson and Thomas Smail ("The Doctrine of the Holy Spirit") both acknowledge the christocentric nature of Barth's pneumatology, although Smail tends to see Barth as being more radical in this regard. Whereas Smail argues that Barth so thoroughly subordinates the work of the Spirit to the work of Christ that pneumatology is in danger of being merged into christology, Thompson claims that such criticism is too harsh. He does not shy away from identifying the christocentric nature of all of Barth's theology, but he does not see the danger toward a functional binitarianism that Smail describes.

with the Bible. Natural theology is both superfluous and impossible, for God is unknowable unless he chooses to reveal himself to us. Revelation is an event in which the message of Scripture, either read or proclaimed, becomes the dynamic and effectual Word of God. The Word of God, in turn, is centered in the person of Christ. That is, Christ is revealed in the activity of the Holy Spirit, through the occasions of the reading or proclamation of Scripture.

Like reconciliation, revelation has an objective side and a subjective side. The objective side of revelation is its source and content. The subjective side is the ability given to human beings by the Holy Spirit to receive revelation. Since revelation is given to and for human beings for their reconciliation to God, and since they are incapable of receiving it on their own, it is necessary that God fill in the noetic gap for them by giving them the gift of the Spirit. Thus, revelation is not complete without both its objective and subjective sides operating together. In other words, only through God is God known.[2]

I have made an effort in these descriptions of Barth's notions of reconciliation and revelation to highlight the trinitarian dimensions of his thought. Both reconciliation and revelation are events involving Father, Son and Holy Spirit. On the other hand, Barth's understanding of reconciliation and revelation are fundamentally oriented toward christology. In fact, his christocentric orientation overshadows his trinitarian thought. John Thompson states that whereas Barth's theology is trinitarian from start to finish, "it is from the center in Christ—and the cross and resurrection in particular—that [Barth] begins and continues" (3).

Philip Rosato asserts that for Barth there can be no question of primary or secondary when it comes to the being and work of God in any of its aspects (112). This is correct, insofar as Rosato's point in the argument surrounding this assertion is that one cannot remove or reduce the role of the Holy Spirit in the process of redemption. Barth's intention is to give the Holy Spirit an "indispensable function" in his theology (111). In other words, reconciliation requires the full action of the Holy Spirit on humanity's behalf. This is a theologically safe assertion. However, the truth remains that Barth assigns to the Holy Spirit the subjective side of

---

[2] Thompson refines this point by arguing that for Barth God is known in two ways. First, the Word has a rational nature which is necessary in order for us to apprehend and interpret it. Second, God enables us by the Holy Spirit to accept the Word. Thus, human knowledge of the divine revelation, like Christ himself, has both a human and a divine character. Properly understood, human knowledge of the divine is neither exclusively rational nor pneumatic, but both (9).

reconciliation, and *the subjective side depends on and assumes the objective side.* The Holy Spirit makes subjectively real in the being of Christians "what is already objectively real in the being of Jesus Christ" (113). Barth is clear that the church community is not made the body of Christ nor its members the members of the body of Christ by the pentecostal gift of the Spirit or any works of the Spirit. Rather, "it became his body and they became its members in the fulfillment of their eternal election on the cross of Golgotha, proclaimed in his resurrection from the dead . . . There can be no doubt that the work of the Holy Spirit is merely to 'realize subjectively' the election of Jesus Christ and his work as done and proclaimed in time, to reveal and to bring it to men and women" (*CD* IV.1: 667). It is the work of the Spirit to bring to historical expression the eternal hiddenness of the prior election of Christ. Thus, the church—the reconciled community—cannot exist as such apart from the action of the Holy Spirit. Nevertheless, for Barth the church is first and foremost the body of Christ, which indicates that whatever its pneumatic aspects, the church is a christological phenomenon (Thompson: 105).

Revelation is also christologically driven. Barth differentiates between the Spirit and Christ—the two cannot be collapsed into one. However, while the Spirit and not Christ is the agent who activates revelation within human beings, "He is still to be regarded wholly and entirely as the Spirit of Christ, of the Son, of the Word of God" (*CD* I.1: 452). This means that all revelation in which the Holy Spirit participates is oriented toward the Word as its content. Jesus is the revelation of God to humanity, and the Spirit is the power of Christ which actuates that revelation within people. Similarly, when someone comes to faith, it is the Holy Spirit who unites that person to Christ in faith. Christ is the object of faith, and the Holy Spirit is the awakening power of faith.

Barth's primary understanding of the Holy Spirit is reflected in this statement: "But fundamentally and generally there is no more to say of Him than that He is the power of Jesus Christ . . ." (*CD* IV.1: 648). For Barth the Holy Spirit is the Spirit of Christ. This is not to say that the Spirit is not also the Spirit of the Father, but preeminently for Barth he is the Spirit of Christ. He is the voice of Christ speaking to the church, he actuates faith in Christ, and he unites Christians to Christ. The Spirit's work is constantly oriented toward Christ. This is the identifying mark that distinguishes the Holy Spirit from other spirits.

Barth regularly expresses himself in ways that reveal a strong christocentric orientation in his pneumatology. He assigns certain actions to the Spirit, but he often describes these actions as being carried out *by Christ* in the Spirit. For instance, Barth can sum up the Spirit's role in reconciliation by saying that "Jesus Christ attests his own reconciliation to us and does so by the Spirit" (Thompson: 92). The Spirit's power is the power of Christ (182). The Spirit's role in calling Christians to their vocation is Christ calling by the Word and the Spirit. The picture one gets is of Christ calling and using the Holy Spirit as the voice or breath by which he calls. The Spirit is a necessary part of the process of calling, but what agency can we attribute directly to him? In a similar vein, Barth describes the Spirit as the arm of Christ in his self-revelation to humanity (CD IV.2: 332). Once again the Spirit appears as an extension of Christ rather than a divine agent. These points can be summed up in Barth's statement, "And in great things and in small the presence and gift of [Christ's] Holy Spirit are directly [Christ's] own work" (CD IV.1: 694). It is remarks like this that draw Smail's criticism that the danger of Barth's pneumatology is "to fail to assert the distinction between [the Spirit and the Son] which formally he wishes to maintain, so that pneumatology is in danger of being merged in to Christology. . ." (108).

In conclusion, Thompson points out that in Barth's treatment of Christian faith there are trinitarian, christological, eschatological and pneumatic aspects that are all interrelated (134). Be this as it may, for Barth Christian doctrine primarily revolves around Christ. In general, Thompson correctly holds that the Spirit is integrated into Barth's total theological perspective, but this integration comes via christology (209).[3]

In evaluating Barth's christocentric orientation in pneumatology, we can begin by taking notice of his insistence that the agency of the Holy Spirit is absolutely essential to the processes of revelation and reconciliation. No fallen human being can understand God or gain a proper relationship with him without divine help. This help comes through the entire Trinity, but the subjective side of it is the work of the Holy Spirit. Thus, Barth incorporates the work of the Spirit into the grace of God and the action of the Trinity.

We can also appreciate the effort to which Barth has gone to give adequate treatment of the relationship between Christ and the Spirit. He rightly interrelates the activities of these two persons of the Trinity and further relates them to the Father. One question, however, is whether he has worked out such relations in a satisfactory manner. For if the Spirit

---

[3] A more extreme form of Barth's christocentric paradigm for pneumatology comes in Hendrikus Berkhof's book, *The Doctrine of the Holy Spirit*. Berkhof follows Barth's lead, but he argues for a more strict functional identity between the risen Christ and the Holy Spirit. The result is a theology that is more binitarian than trinitarian.

is functionally identified with Christ, thereby becoming little more than an extension of Christ or a mode through which Christ is present and active in the world, the relation between the Spirit and Christ becomes less characterized by cooperation and more by subordination. Additionally, the Spirit tends to evaporate as the third person of the Trinity, appearing instead as a thin veneer for Christ. This diminishment of the Spirit's identity is the chief danger of the christocentric pneumatology of Barth.

A second danger with Barth's christocentric pneumatology is the nature of the personhood one posits with regard to the Spirit. As reflected in the previous paragraph, in the theology of Barth the Spirit tends to take on the character of an extension of Christ. This is illustrated in the consistency with which he refers to the Spirit as a force through which Christ works or as the power of Christ. Barth also refers to the image of the Spirit as the arm of Christ. Treatments like this only serve to increase the difficulty Christians have conceiving of the Holy Spirit as being in some way personal.

Although Barth's theology is exceedingly christocentric, it nonetheless provides an example of the direction pneumatology can take in the stream of Protestantism that I have called "institutional." In keeping with the trajectory of mainstream Western theology, Barth makes Christ the centerpiece of theology and subordinates the Holy Spirit to Christ in the process. Such subordination creates difficulties with the trinitarian balance of Barth's notions of reconciliation and revelation, as well as other doctrines. As we have seen, it results in the vanishing of the Spirit as a divine person who is the equal of Christ, and in the relegation of the Spirit to being little more than an impersonal extension of Christ.

The Experiential Tendency in Protestant Pneumatology: John Wesley

The experiential tendency in Protestant pneumatology can be illustrated in the work of John Wesley. As Wesley pursued a "vital piety," he was drawn into sharp debate with leaders in the Anglican church, and much of the controversy revolved around Wesley's understanding of the role of the Holy Spirit in the Christian life. When he pushed the experiential aspects of interaction with the Spirit, Wesley drew the charge of "enthusiast" from his opponents. The debate between Wesley and his opponents illustrates the bipolarity of Protestant pneumatology.

As he worked his way through the issues of the Spirit's influence in the life of the Christian, Wesley developed a theological vision that has resonated with millions of believers over the years. Donald Dayton has argued that the theological roots of holiness Christianity and modern Pentecostalism can be traced back to the influence of Wesley.[4] Therefore, it is no exaggeration to state that Wesley's mark on twentieth-century theology is every bit as indelible as is Barth's. Although Wesley's pneumatology occasionally reflects the christocentric pattern of institutional pneumatology, his doctrine of assurance provides an apt illustration of the experiential tendency in Protestant pneumatology.

Characteristic of Wesleyan theology is the distinction between justification and sanctification. Justification is the pardon of the guilty sinner. Wesley writes that justification is "not the process of making a person just and righteous. This is *sanctification*, which is, indeed, in some degree, the immediate *fruit* of justification, but nevertheless is a distinct gift of God and of a totally different nature. The one implies what God *does for us* through his Son; the other, what he *works in* us by his Spirit" (Outler: 201). Thus, Wesley assigns justification to the agency of the Son, and sanctification to the agency of the Spirit, qualifying these claims with the medieval doctrine of appropriations (Staples: 93).

At the moment of justification the process of sanctification begins. Believers undergo a change of relation in terms of their status with God. At the same moment they undergo a change of being in terms of the new presence of the Holy Spirit within them. The process of inner renewal commences (Outler: 274). Simultaneously, and as a result of the presence of the Spirit within believers, their inner struggle begins between the conflicting principles of "flesh" and "spirit." Wesley holds that "spirit" can eventually win this struggle; the believer can reach a state of "perfection." By the word 'perfection,' Wesley means "loving God with all our heart, mind, soul, and strength," which in turn means that "a Christian is so far perfect as not to commit sin" (267). By 'sin' in this statement, Wesley means imperfections in thought or action other than those produced by simple mistakes in judgment. If every thought and action stems from perfect love, as it does for the perfected believer, then her mistakes along the way are not properly counted as sins (285).

Thus, the center of Wesley's pneumatology is the Holy Spirit's work of sanctification.[5] The Holy Spirit indwells believers and impels them from

---

[4] *Theological Roots of Pentecostalism.*

[5] The Spirit is also the agent of the prevenient grace by which human beings are convicted of sin and made aware of their need for God's forgiveness. However, in Wesley's writings this theme is not as important as that of the sanctification which begins when one actually confesses faith in Christ.

within toward greater holiness of life. Within the process of sanctification there are specific functions of the Spirit. One of these is the assurance produced by the inner witness of the Spirit. Wesley believed that the unique understanding of the nature and importance of the witness of the Spirit was a "grand part" of the testimony the Methodists could contribute to all of humanity (211).

The witness of the Spirit comes in two main forms for Wesley—direct and indirect. The direct witness of the Spirit can be either a testimony to the believer's initial salvation or to her entire sanctification. The direct witness to salvation is given by the Holy Spirit to and with the spirit of the individual believer. Specifically the Spirit testifies that not only does God will to redeem the world to himself through Christ, but that God loves *me—the individual believer*—in this way. Accompanying this assurance is a "sweet calm" and satisfaction that God has forgiven the believer's sins (212). This is the direct testimony of the Spirit to salvation—a direct awareness of the indwelling Spirit which communicates assurance that God's grace is being applied to the individual believer.[6]

Regarding the direct testimony of the Holy Spirit to entire sanctification, Wesley teaches that, by the grace of God, some Christians reach such mastery over their own motives that their will is in regular conformity with the will of God. These Christians do not commit intentional and deliberate sins. At the point of entire sanctification believers experience "a death to sin and an entire renewal in the love and image of God . . ." (293). Accompanying this experience is the witness of the Spirit to the entire sanctification of the believer, once again taking the form of a direct awareness of the effects of the Spirit. This testimony is a necessary part of the process; no Christian should claim to have reached the state of perfection until such testimony has come (293).

The second main form of the witness of the Holy Spirit is the indirect testimony to salvation. It is the result of reflection on what is felt in the soul about one's conduct. More specifically, it is the application of a logical progression drawn from Scripture to the qualities of one's life. The argument is this. Scripture says that everyone who has the Spirit is a child of

---

[6] Maddox describes the background to Wesley's insistence on the direct witness of the Spirit: "Wesley championed the importance of the Spirit's witness in conscious contrast to two alternatives more common in his day: (1) that the ultimate basis of our assurance is our clear conscience; and (2) that this basis is the presence of Christian virtues (the 'fruit of the Spirit') in our lives. Wesley did allow for these alternative factors a subsidiary role in assurance, confirming the Spirit's direct witness . . . However, he denied that they were more reliable than, or foundational to, the direct witness" (129).

God. But how can the believer know whether she has the Spirit? Scripture also teaches that the Spirit produces certain "fruit" in the believer's life. Therefore, the fruit of the Spirit can function as signs of the Spirit's presence. The indirect witness of the Spirit is thus the rational conclusion that if the fruit of the Spirit is present, then the Spirit is also present, and thus the individual is a child of God (212). It is important to note that the fruit of the Spirit is not to be equated strictly with good works. It also has to do with affections such as joy and peace. Thus, the fruit of the Spirit that serves as the evidence of the presence of the Spirit is a reflection of the overall transformation going on within the believer. To put the matter in another way, if a believer reflects on her life and sees the signs of sanctification, she can be sure that she is filled with the Holy Spirit and therefore a child of God.

The prominence of personal experience in all three of Wesley's forms of the witness of the Spirit is striking. Assurance comes from the experience of the peace given by the Spirit that one is a child of God (direct assurance of salvation) or has conquered willful sin (direct assurance of complete sanctification). Wesley makes it clear that the direct witness of the Spirit is a cooperative affair between the Holy Spirit and the individual's spirit, for "the Spirit bears witness with our spirit." This insistence on the necessary role of the believer's spirit in the event of assurance ensures that the experience will be distinct and recognizable. Wesley defends his doctrine of the witness of the Spirit by asserting that it is founded on both Scripture and experience. One element does not diminish the other.

Likewise, in the indirect witness of the Spirit the consciousness of one's own transformation serves as grounds for the conclusion that one is a Spirit-indwelt child of God. There are three ways in which experience is a part of the indirect witness of the Spirit. First is that the believer is aware that she has grown in the fruit of the Spirit. Her transformation is noticeable enough that she is able to use it as grounds from which to make an inference that the Holy Spirit is active in her life.[7] Second is the inference itself. The believer experiences herself forming the argument. Third is the degree of assurance derived from the strength or weakness of the inference. The extent to which the believer is lastingly assured of her salvation depends on the confidence with which she can draw the conclusion of the presence of the Spirit based on the qualities of her life. If she understands her attitudes and behavior to consistently display the fruits of the Spirit,

---

[7] This inference is made on the assumption that true love, joy and peace are not qualities which human beings have or can produce on their own.

then she gains a great deal of confidence that she has received redemption. By the same token, if she perceives only moderate correspondence between her attitudes and behavior and the fruits of the Spirit, the degree of assurance she gains will drop considerably.

Randy Maddox indicates that in the mid-1740s Wesley exchanged correspondence with one "John Smith," and a central issue between them was the perceptibility of God's grace as shown in believers' hearts by the Holy Spirit. Wesley maintained that it cannot happen that a person be filled with the Holy Spirit and the gracious affections of peace, joy and love without perceiving it. He stopped short of claiming that all actions of the Holy Spirit are perceptible, but it remains true, says Wesley, that many episodes of God's gracious work in the believer typically are (Maddox: 128–9). Throughout his career Wesley continued to insist on the perceptibility of the works of the Spirit, despite repeated charges of enthusiasm.

In summary, the basic orientation of pneumatology for Wesley is salvation as worked out and experienced in the day-to-day lives of Christians. Experience of God's grace at work in oneself is what prevents Christianity from lapsing into a formal religion in which a living relationship with God is either lost or hampered. "Because of this fear of formalism there is in Wesley's writing a constant stress on experience" (Williams: 33).[8] It is experience that forms the test of whether believers are living in the promises of which Christian doctrine speaks (104). That is, when believers learn from Scripture that a Christian is filled with the Holy Spirit and transformed by the same Spirit into the image of Christ, they can search the patterns of their own lives to determine if God's truth and presence is reflected in them. All along the journey which is the Christian life the believer should be experiencing the presence and work of the Spirit. This emphasis on experience is distinctive of Wesley's approach to theology, and pneumatology is the arena in which the works of God directly affect human experience.

Wesley has had immense influence in the Protestant tradition in several ways. One of them is his concentration on the experiential aspects of one's encounter with the Spirit. The contributions of such an approach are many, among them the attitude among believers that they can (and should) expect the presence of God to be an experience-able phenomenon. They gain confidence that God is truly present in their lives, and they anticipate that he will work in distinct and powerful ways.

---

[8] Williams brings out this emphasis in Wesley's writings, but he also presents the other side of the story—that Wesley also feared "any reliance upon experience which left the question of truth to the vagaries of individual or collective feeling" (34).

Furthermore, they understand these events to be brought about by the agency of the Holy Spirit. The Spirit's work is viewed as distinct from the work of Christ and the Father, but oriented toward the Father's will that all be saved and the Son's work in securing the conditions of redemption for the world. In other words, Wesley and those who follow him typically perceive the Holy Spirit to be acting in his own right—not as an extension of Christ. At the same time, the Holy Spirit never acts alone, but always in conjunction with the agency of the Father and the Son.

Unfortunately, just as there are strengths to Wesley's experiential orientation in pneumatology, so are there weaknesses. One of them is the tendency of Wesley to relate the Holy Spirit's work mainly to the individual believer. This is not a strict association, but it is the association that predominates when Wesley discusses the Holy Spirit. The most appropriate way to organize the pneumatological writings of Wesley would be in the form of an *ordo salutis* beginning with prevenient grace and continuing through justification, sanctification, and on into eschatology. What is significant about such an organization is that it is ordered according to aspects of the faith journey of the individual believer. Just as religious experience is primarily a matter for the individual, so is Wesley's experientially oriented pneumatology.

Another weakness of Wesley's pneumatology is that the work of the Spirit is tied almost exclusively to the present time. When the emphasis is on experiencing the works of the Spirit, the focus is on recognizing and enjoying those experiences in the present. The works of the Spirit in past historical periods or in the eternal future fade into the background behind those in the past, present and immediate future of the individual person.

There is a third weakness in the experiential orientation that does not show up in Wesley but sometimes does in those who share the experiential orientation. It is a tendency toward pneumatocentrism. One can occasionally see pneumatocentrism showing up in Pentecostalism.[9] The driving force behind Pentecostal movements has been a perceived lack of spiritual power when the modern church is compared to the apostolic church as described in the book of Acts. The church of today lacks the zeal and power of the early church. What is needed is a "Holy Ghost revival," and many perceive that it has become a reality in Pentecostalism. Although the Pentecostal movement has made significant contributions to twentieth-century Christianity, its concentration on the Holy Spirit as the key to the

---

[9] Donald Dayton makes the case that modern Pentecostalism derives theologically from Methodism in *Theological Roots of Pentecostalism* (Peabody, MA: Hendrickson, 1987).

restoration of the power of the earliest church does not reflect the type of balance which was also a part of the earliest church. The New Testament portrays the church as assuming the miracle-working presence of the Holy Spirit; there was never a lack of "power" to which the apostles needed to react. Thus, Paul recognizes the practice of speaking in tongues, but he subordinates this to the practice of Spirit-empowered *agapē* and service (1 Corinthians 12–14). Pentecostal leaders, on the other hand, struggle with the absence of overt signs of the Spirit and desire to see them restored to the church.[10] This task leads them to seek the Holy Spirit as the key to the restoration of the form of the early church. The expectation is that as the Holy Spirit falls on the church in power, Christians will encounter the Spirit in particular experiences such as the manifestation of the spiritual gifts. In practice, Pentecostalism sometimes takes the form of a pneumatocentric search for experiences of the power of God.[11] It is natural for Christians to desire experiences of the Spirit, but when this desire elevates the Spirit above the Father and the Son the effects on theology are deleterious. In addition, when experiences of God become too prominent in the practice of Christianity the result is usually a lapse into the very fanaticism that many Pentecostal leaders rightly fear. Two centuries earlier, Wesley himself warned against such developments. His way of differentiating the persons of the Trinity was in terms of their most defining work: creation/providence (Father), redemption (Son), and sanctification (Spirit). On such terms "a 'unitarianism of the Spirit' could become enamored with

---

[10] Aimee Semple McPherson, founder of the Foursquare Church, repeatedly uses two metaphors when discussing the Holy Spirit. One is 'power.' The church lacks it (as is evidenced by the dearth of holiness, miracles, and soul-winning zeal of many modern-day churches), but the Holy Spirit is waiting to supply it. The other is 'fire.' The earliest church was characterized by having hearts that burned with the fire of the Spirit. Not long after the New Testament era that fire burned out and was replaced with the coldness of worldly satisfaction. McPherson describes those hostile to the Pentecostal movement as "cold" or "frozen," and refers to ecclesiastical formalism as "the refrigerator" (McPherson: 189). Combining the two metaphorical concepts of power and heat, McPherson writes, "The church has grown cold and backslidden, having a form of godliness and denying the power thereof" (173). Fortunately, starting with the Reformation and now especially in movements such as the Foursquare Church, she sees that fire as returning to significant portions of the church (172ff.).

[11] It is no coincidence that Pentecostalism tends to appeal to Christians who want more out of their relationship with God. They want more power to overcome sin and to evangelize, and they want to experience that power, just as Peter and the disciples did. Thus, the people drawn to Pentecostalism are those who realize that the church has set its expectations too low and has become content to live with a very small portion of the Spirit's anointing, and who desire to live in the fullness of the power of the Spirit.

the Spirit's power per se, forgetting its purpose of effecting our recovery of the moral Image that the Father intended for us and Christ displayed to us" (Maddox: 140). Like Paul, Wesley placed more emphasis on the fruit of the Spirit than on the gifts of the Spirit (135–36).

In summary, the experiential tendency in pneumatology yields many valuable offerings for theology. This orientation recognizes that the Spirit indwells each individual Christian, and it seeks to examine thoroughly the phenomena associated with individual endowment by the Spirit. It also leads Christians to expect that the Spirit is indeed present and active in the church. On the other hand, an emphasis on experience of the Spirit typically is accompanied by individualism, a focus on the Spirit's work in the present time, and occasionally pneumatocentrism.

We have briefly reviewed two prominent orientations in Protestant pneumatology: the institutional and the experiential. In evaluating these orientations there are two criteria we can use. One is to take a telic approach, inquiring about what effects a given orientation has on pneumatological development. This is the approach we have taken in this section. Examining each of the orientations, we found that they make important contributions to pneumatology, but they also tend toward significant difficulties in how the Spirit is conceived within Christian life and doctrine.

The other primary criterion to consider when evaluating pneumatological orientations is how they reflect the content of the biblical witness to the Holy Spirit. We will see that what drives the institutional and experiential orientations is a departure from what drives pneumatological reflection in the New Testament. For the New Testament witness to the Holy Spirit is not driven by matters of ecclesiology, christology or religious experience. These are important themes, but they are secondary to the primary theme, which is eschatology. The New Testament pneumatological orientation (inasmuch as there is such a thing) is an eschatological orientation. That is, all reflection on the Holy Spirit in the New Testament takes place within an eschatological framework. It is the thesis of this dissertation that adopting an eschatological orientation in pneumatology is not only possible, but highly beneficial for the study of the work of the Holy Spirit in this age and the age to come.

Eschatology in the New Testament and in Systematic Theology

In order to set the stage for adopting an eschatological orientation for pneumatology, it is necessary to first discuss eschatology in more general terms. Therefore, in this section I will argue the following two major points. First, of the three major competing conceptions of eschatology, an inaugurated model emphasizing both the "already" and the "not yet" does the best job of handling all the New Testament evidence. Second, despite the fact that the locus of eschatology has tended to be defined in terms of the "not yet," there are good reasons to adopt the stance of inaugurated eschatology in systematic theology.

It is a fundamental position in New Testament studies to identify eschatology as not only the matrix within which early Christianity developed, but also an indispensable feature of early Christianity itself.[12] I will accept this position without argument. What is debatable is how 'eschatological' is to be understood.

In Christian theology the term 'eschatology' refers to beliefs concerning death, the after life, judgment and the resurrection of the dead. In biblical studies as well, eschatology is commonly associated with events which include and follow the consummation of history (cf. Mowinckel: 149). However, there are difficulties stemming from the use of this definition that affect the interpretation of early Old Testament prophetic writings, later apocalyptic writings, and the New Testament material. First, by this definition 'eschatological' would be an inappropriate description of the element of hope and restoration in Israelite prophecy subsequent to Amos and Hosea, for they did not operate with the concept of an end of history with further events beyond it (Aune: 596). Such ideas are, however, characteristic of later apocalyptic writings. The problem here is that ideas about history coming to an end do not appear in apocalypticism with absolute precision (von Rad, II: 114). Finally, the New Testament does contain many apocalyptic claims about the return of Christ at the end of the age, but New Testament eschatology can hardly be limited to its apocalyptic predictions. For these reasons it is important to consider alternative conceptions of eschatology to gain a proper appreciation of Israel's hope in the Old Testament Scriptures, as well as the combination of fulfillment and hope in the New Testament.

Working within Old Testament scholarship, Gerhard von Rad opens up the notion of the eschatological to include not only the later apocalyptic writings, but also those of the classical prophets as well. The conception of eschatology which he develops is of a new state in which the break with

---

[12] One hardly needs to cite sources for this, but a good example is David Aune's opening statements when introducing the subject of New Testament eschatology for his article in the *Anchor Bible Dictionary*. Since he frames the issue well, I have adopted some of his wording from p. 597.

the present state is so deep that it cannot be understood as the continuation of what has gone before (II: 115). At the same time, the determining factor for both states is the action of Yahweh; this is the primary element of continuity between the noneschatological and the eschatological (115). Regarding eschatological events, "the new is to be effected in a way which is more or less analogous to God's former saving work" (117). For instance, the prophets speak of a new Zion, a new covenant, a new David, and the like. For the classical prophets these anticipated realities do not happen outside of history, but as events in future history. The key is not a scheme of time but the type of divine saving action under consideration. "The prophetic teaching is only eschatological when the prophets expelled Israel from the safety of the old saving actions and suddenly shifted the basis of salvation to a future action of God" (118).[13] The language of prophetic expectation gradually took on the characteristics of later apocalypticism, which looks to a definite break between history and events beyond history. Despite this fundamental difference between pre-apocalyptic and apocalyptic thought, both types of writing can be set within von Rad's broad definition. Both pre-apocalyptic and apocalyptic writers conceived of God's saving actions as the pivotal impetus for events which can be classified as eschatological. For the pre-apocalyptic prophet, God's saving actions alter the order of redemption through events in history. For the apocalyptic prophet, God brings history to an end, but the apocalypse is brought on by God as part of his plan of salvation and judgment.

Consistent Eschatology

Throughout the twentieth century biblical scholars have highlighted the profoundly eschatological character of New Testament theology. However, there have been several different construals of New Testament eschatology. Chief among them are consistent eschatology, realized eschatology and inaugurated eschatology. Consistent eschatology was championed by Albert Schweitzer in his two books, *The Mystery of the Kingdom of God* (1901) and *The Quest for the Historical Jesus* (1910).[14] Schweitzer parted ways with the Ritschlian school in emphasizing that the kingdom of God is not to

---

[13] Aune follows von Rad: "The term eschatology can be meaningfully applied to the perspective of the 8th- and 7th-century Israelite writing prophets when the term is broadly defined as the expectation of imminent events brought about by the action of God in history accompanied by the dissolution of the old salvation history" (596).

[14] The other main representative of consistent eschatology is Johannes Weiss, *Jesus' Proclamation of the Kingdom of God.*

be equated with ethical conduct, but rather with a future apocalypse that Jesus worked to bring about. Jesus' views on the kingdom were completely shaped by first-century Jewish apocalyptic thought, and thus his message about the kingdom of God is exclusively about an apocalyptic age to come (Ladd, 1974: 5).

Schweitzer's work, along with that of Johannes Weiss, turned a corner in New Testament studies, for the two succeeded in recovering the significance of eschatology for understanding the proclamation of the kingdom in the Gospels. Many scholars followed Schweitzer and Weiss in advocating a consistent eschatology. Although the conception of the kingdom of God took on many different forms in these presentations, they all share the basic stance that the kingdom is strictly a future and apocalyptic reality.[15] Still, all the advocates of consistent eschatology are compelled by the New Testament evidence to assert that something is happening in the present. Typically they understand the kingdom to be so near that it casts its shadow of influence on the present time.

Realized Eschatology

C. H. Dodd reacted strongly against the consistent eschatology of Schweitzer and Weiss. Dodd argued that the Gospel evidence shows that the kingdom of God is not an apocalyptic expectation, but rather a present reality. In the parables of the kingdom Jesus lays bare the eternal issues at stake. "It is the hour of decision. It is realized eschatology" (Dodd: 148). Thus, the kingdom of God is a reality presently impacting the souls of believing human beings. It is God reigning in the human heart (Hiers: 18).[16] Because the kingdom is an eternal reality, it really has no past, present or future. It is timeless. "Thus, by definition, there could be no future coming of the kingdom of God, Son of man, judgment, or other eschatological events" (22).

Richard Hiers notes that Dodd's impact on Western theology has been significant. "Nevertheless, few other scholars have subscribed to Dodd's proposal that Jesus regarded the kingdom as *entirely* present. Instead, most have maintained that Jesus expected and proclaimed *both* that the kingdom of God was already present *and* that it (or its consummation) was

---

[15] For an extensive discussion of various forms of consistent eschatology, see Ladd, 1974: 5ff.

[16] Along similar lines, Bultmann interprets the eschatological in terms of what is ultimate or final in significance. Thus, the individual's confrontation with the gospel message is an eschatological moment for him/her—it is the moment of ultimate decision.

yet to come, whether in the near or indeterminate future" (24). The main problem with Dodd's interpretation of the Gospels is that there are passages in which Jesus clearly proclaims a future coming of the kingdom of God, the Son of man, or a time of judgment. Dodd bypasses many of these passages, often by relegating them to inauthentic status. However, Dodd also retains a number of futuristic passages as authentic sayings of Jesus. These he either construes as references to historical crises of some sort or as symbolizing more transcendent but nontemporal meanings (21). Unfortunately for Dodd, these strategies have not convinced the majority of New Testament scholars.

Another consideration counting against realized eschatology has been uniquely expressed by John Macquarrie: "I think we must frankly say that if that was the end and this is the new age, and if it has all happened, then it does not seem to amount to very much. If eschatology has been realized, well, it is rather a damp squib" (117). A damp squib is a wet firework that looks great, promises to make a big bang, but when it is lit it simply fizzles out and does nothing. Both a damp squib and realized eschatology are disappointments. If eschatology is God's plan for redemption, then surely he is capable of more.

Thus, realized eschatology contains two major faults: dealing unsatisfactorily with all of the New Testament data, and mischaracterizing the kingdom of God. By the same token, consistent eschatology commits its own versions of the same errors. It dismisses passages in the Gospels where Jesus speaks of the kingdom as being present (an important example is Mt 12:28), and it underestimates the experiential significance of the changes which the New Testament writings testify to have taken place in this, the messianic age.

Inaugurated Eschatology

For reasons like these, the majority opinion in New Testament studies is that Jesus proclaimed the kingdom of God as both a present and a future reality. This position is known as inaugurated eschatology. One of the foremost representatives of this kind of approach is George Ladd.[17] In an autobiographical reference, Ladd revealed that his own interest in the problem of New Testament eschatology arose during his undergraduate

---

[17] Other scholars who articulated their own versions of the inaugurated position that emerged in the post-World War II years were Oscar Cullmann, W. G. Kümmel, Ernst Käsemann, and Norman Perrin.

studies when he found that "no available interpretation of the kingdom of God seemed to square with the biblical data" (quoted in Epp: 46–47).

For Ladd, the rule of God was active in the Old Testament in the events of the Exodus and the captivity in Babylon where God was at work liberating and judging his people. At the same time, the kingdom was still to come, and it did in the person and ministry of Jesus (1993: 60–67). Ladd's central thesis is that the Kingdom of God is the redemptive reign of God dynamically active to establish his rule among men, and that this Kingdom, which will appear as an apocalyptic act at the end of the age, has already come into human history in the person and mission of Jesus to overcome evil, to deliver men from its power, and to bring them into the blessings of God's reign. The Kingdom of God involves two great moments: fulfillment within history, and consummation at the end of history. (1974: 218)

The reign of God is present in the human heart (cf. Dodd), but also in the person of Jesus Christ and in human history. The way in which the kingdom can be understood as both present and future is by taking a functional view of it—understanding it as the active rule of God rather than as a realm over which God rules (121). More properly, the kingdom is primarily God's kingly rule and secondarily the realm of blessing inaugurated by the divine act of ruling (Epp: 50).

Thus, Ladd both incorporates and corrects the insights of realized eschatology and consistent eschatology. The kingdom of God is not only near; it is actually present in the person of Jesus and the ongoing ministry of the Holy Spirit. By the same token, those living in the blessings of the present kingdom still look forward to the time of apocalyptic consummation in the future (cf. Ladd, 1974: 120).

Finally, Epp notes that whereas Kümmel interprets the kingdom of God as including promise and fulfillment, Ladd includes promise, fulfillment and consummation (52). Thus, Ladd's notion of the kingdom of God incorporates deep historical ties between the past, present and future. The present eschatological age is at the same time a fulfillment of past promises and also an anticipation of future consummation.

This is a summary of Ladd's view of the kingdom of God, which is an important theme in the Synoptic Gospels, but what about the rest of the New Testament? He asserts that the source of unity of New Testament thought is that it is "all about the divine mission to the world." The center of this mission is Jesus, the Spirit-filled Messiah and Son of God, who inaugurated the saving rule of God (1993: 712). Since the mission of Jesus is the center of the New Testament message, for Ladd an inaugurated eschatology is fundamental to New Testament theology as a whole.

Inaugurated Eschatology and Systematic Theology

Ladd mounts a powerful argument that New Testament theology revolves around an inaugurated eschatology. Turning to contemporary theology, we make the noteworthy observation that there is a fundamental difference between eschatology as conceived in the New Testament and eschatology as taught in current systematic theology. In systematic theology since the early nineteenth century when the term was coined, eschatology has included the study of the parousia, the resurrection of the dead, heaven and hell—all events occurring at the future consummation. That is, systematic theology tends to view eschatology as pertaining to the end of the age, and not to the present age. As Stephen Travis puts it, eschatology "is concerned with things which have not yet happened" (13). On the other hand, according to Ladd and many other biblical scholars, the New Testament authors understood the new age to include things that have happened and have been happening since the earthly ministry of Jesus, and will continue with and beyond his parousia. The contrast between a New Testament inaugurated eschatology and systematic theology's consistent eschatology is striking.

There is basic agreement between New Testament scholarship and systematic theology that eschatology deals with future events that consummate God's universal rule. The disagreement is over their differing conceptions of the present. In biblical studies, the general understanding is that the early Christians viewed the time in which they lived as the beginning stages of the new age. This is because they experienced several events, centering in and around the coming of the Messiah, that constituted fulfillment of eschatological promises recorded in Scripture. In systematic theology, there is a persistent failure to think of the present age as an eschatological age. Inasmuch as the present age is eschatological, it is so in only a secondary sense as compared with the "real" eschatological age to come. For all practical purposes, it is not eschatological at all. There are several unfortunate effects on theology from taking this perspective.

First, there is an alienation of present-day believers from the thought world of the New Testament writers. The strong sense of fulfillment that characterized early Christian experience is largely lost on us today. Some of this is natural, for nearly two thousand years stand between us and them, and the excitement of the Messiah having just burst onto the scene has faded. However, when theology disconnects eschatology from fulfillment that has already taken place, it does not offer assistance in fostering a sense of fulfillment in modern Christians. As a result, there is that much less connection between present-day believers and the thought-world of a good portion of their canonical writings.

Second, in Ladd's terms, consummation becomes severed from promise and fulfillment. That is, the continuity between promise, fulfillment and consummation disappears. Inasmuch as contemporary Christians hold out hope for the resurrection of the dead and the renewal of all things, they are not inclined to view these events as extensions of the blessings of the present age. In contrast, Paul refers to Christ as the first fruits of the resurrection (1 Cor 15:20, 23) and the Holy Spirit as the first fruits of our complete redemption (Rom 8:23), suggesting in both cases deep continuity between the present and the future that is constitutive of the understanding of each age.[18] This perspective on Christ and the Holy Spirit arises from the apostle's "already/not yet" view of the present age.

Third, there is an inclination in systematic theology to treat eschatology as an addendum relegated to the end of theological treatises,[19] because it is mired in exegetical difficulties surrounding the interpretation of the Bible's apocalyptic passages. What the "already/not yet" scheme means for eschatology is that the new age contains both historical and apocalyptic components. On the other hand, when eschatology is limited to events at the end of history, the eschatological is divorced from the historical, and eschatology is limited to apocalyptic phenomena. It becomes a theological category for the "not yet." Whereas most other theological loci can appeal to some extent to historical research and analysis of present experience, eschatology must rely on interpretation of cryptic divine revelation about the end of time.

Fourth, in Western systematic theology there is a correlation between this restrictive view of eschatology and a generally anemic pneumatology. The Western tradition has long focused its attention on the person of Christ. The theology of the Holy Spirit has been neglected by comparison, and when it has been worked out, it has typically taken on subordinationistic overtones. These tendencies have led to a conception of the present age as the time between the two appearances of Christ. It has been

---

[18] See chapter 2 for a thorough discussion of the notion of first fruits in Pauline thought.

[19] Not only did a particular understanding of eschatology cause it to take its place at the end of dogmatic treatises, but the organizational impetus of being placed at the end contributed in turn to an understanding of eschatology as referring to things yet to come. The two phenomena support each other.

viewed as inferior to these two highpoints in history—the rickety bridge between two strong towers. The negative view of this age and underdeveloped pneumatology coincide, for the influence of the Holy Spirit is the key to experiencing the present age as eschatological. This is true if we take seriously Paul's understanding that the Holy Spirit is the first fruits of our complete redemption. It means that we are already experiencing the beginning phases of our complete transformation. Thus, there is a great deal of continuity between what goes on in this era and what will go on in the consummation. Continuity between the already and the not yet lends an eschatological character to the present age.

Because of these considerations, I shall argue that theology would be healthier operating with a notion of eschatology that is more consistent with what is reflected in the New Testament—a comprehensive vision of the divine plan of eschatological salvation as beginning with the first coming of Christ and carrying on through and beyond his second coming. Present eschatological realities are in continuity with promises received in the past, just as they are in continuity with events of the future consummation. At the same time, just as there is a strong theme of continuity between the present age and the age to come, there is also an equally strong theme of discontinuity. For the age of consummation will feature the complete establishment of God's rule over all of creation.

What this stance means for pneumatology is that the gift of the Spirit in this age can be set within a framework that includes Old Testament promises regarding the Spirit, present fulfillments of those promises as reflected in New Testament writings and Christian experience, and anticipations of the future work of the Spirit in the consummation. All of these elements can be interwoven with each other in a great tapestry that will enlarge the scope of much current pneumatological work being done today.

An Eschatological Orientation for Pneumatology

To review this opening chapter, I began by identifying the two opposing tendencies of Protestant pneumatology—the institutional and the experiential—and noting that each of them has important contributions to make but is also hampered by significant weaknesses. I then asked whether there is another orientation we might adopt that will feature significant strengths while avoiding a good deal of the difficulties of the other orientations. The preliminary answer to this question is affirmative. An eschatological orientation (inaugurated eschatology to be specific) is one that will satisfy two important criteria by which we can judge theological positions—the eschatological orientation is closer to the biblical witness to the Holy Spirit, and it is theologically salutary. It will be the burden of this dissertation to provide support for this two-pronged claim.

I will begin to develop the themes of an eschatological model for pneumatology by examining the writings of the apostle Paul. Of the three major pneumatologies in the New Testament—the Pauline, the Lukan and the Johannine—it is the Pauline which provides the broadest conception of the work of the Spirit in the life of the individual Christian and in the Christian community. James Dunn claims that Paul has been referred to as the New Testament's "theologian of the Spirit," because "he gives a more rounded and more integrated teaching on the Spirit than we find in any other literature of that time . . ." (1986: 700). Similarly, J. Christiaan Beker holds that "it is the merit of Paul to have been the first theologian of the Spirit in the New Testament, that is, to have thought through the implications of the experience of the Spirit. Luke and John, the other two distinctive theologians of the Spirit, each in their own way stand in Paul's debt" (1958: 3). Alisdair Heron writes, "Everything from justification to the final manifestation of the children of God, from faith to prayer, from ethical behavior to calling God 'Abba! Father!,' is enabled by the Spirit. This is a far wider canvas than in the Synoptics. Paul (a) discerns an integral connection of the Spirit's work with the activity of God in Christ, and (b) depicts it as extending across the whole spectrum of Christian life, and as driving dynamically toward the *eschaton*" (46).

Not only is Paul's contribution to pneumatology profound, it is also pervaded by intimate connections between the Holy Spirit and eschatology. Geerhardus Vos notes the irony that most Christians do not appreciate these connections.

> The lack of recognition of this fact [that pneumatology and eschatology are intertwined], so common among even doctrinally informed Christians is mostly due to the eclipse which the Spirit's eschatological task has suffered on account of his soteric work in the present life. The ubiquitousness and monergism of the Spirit's influence in the gracious processes we now experience have, as it were, unduly contracted our vision, so that after having emphasized the all-inclusiveness of this work, we forget that we have forgotten, or merely counted in *pro forma* the other hemisphere pertaining to the Spirit, that dealing with the introduction into and the abode in the life to come. Paul has not left us in uncertainty or unclearness in regard to this part of the Spirit's working. (1952: 159)

Although Vos is using the word 'eschatology' as referring strictly to the "not yet," the situation he describes would point the inquirer who is interested in the connections between the Holy Spirit and eschatology to the writings of Paul. Consistent with Vos' claim, in Chapters Two and Three, we will find that Paul's reflection on the Holy Spirit is shot through with eschatological sensibilities, and his eschatological views depend in part on the present activity of the Spirit. Paul's conception of the Christian faith is formed from within an understanding of eschatological redemption as having begun but not been completed. This foundational view of God's activity in the world shapes the way Paul understands the gift of the Spirit, since the latter is essentially an eschatological reality for the apostle and others in the early church.

As valuable as Paul's insights are, a contemporary construction needs to draw on later developments in trinitarian theology, pneumatology and eschatology. Of the theologians working in the present day, there is no one who is stronger in all three of these areas than Jürgen Moltmann. Chapters 4–8 will comprise a detailed examination of Moltmann's work in eschatology and pneumatology.

With his *Theology of Hope* in 1964, Moltmann brought eschatology to center stage in systematic theology. Richard Bauckham observes, "One of the most important contributions of Moltmann's theology has been to rehabilitate future eschatology" (1995: 8). Unfortunately, especially in his early theology, Moltmann emphasized future eschatology to the degree that the present age became less than eschatological. He was mainly operating with an eschatology that consisted of the "not yet." As his theology has progressed, he has gained more appreciation for the role of the Holy Spirit in redemption and for the eschatological nature of the present. Still, the relation between the Spirit and eschatology remains inconsistent in Moltmann's theology. It is precisely this gap that Pauline theology fills. Therefore, between the work of Paul and Moltmann, there are strong contributions in New Testament eschatology and pneumatology, and in contemporary eschatology, pneumatology and trinitarian theology. The two figures complement each other well. In chapter 9, drawing on both of them, I will lay out proposals for a contemporary formulation of eschatological pneumatology. Finally, I will return to the two dominant pneumatological orientations of the Protestant tradition—the institutional and the experiential—and argue that an eschatological model is both more faithful to the biblical texts and more salutary for theology than either of them.

2

The Holy Spirit and the Pauline Eschatological Framework

The Pauline Eschatological Framework[1]

Eschatological Tension

"So if anyone is in Christ, there is a new creation: everything old has passed away; see, everything has become new! All this is from God, who reconciled us to himself through Christ . . ." (2 Cor 5:17–18). These words concisely express core commitments in the Pauline understanding of Christianity. Like other New Testament writers, Paul perceives himself

---

[1] It is necessary to take note of two issues upon beginning this study in Pauline pneumatology. First is the matter of authenticity. As illustrated by the stance of the Pauline Theology Group of the Society of Biblical Literature, the most common approach to the Pauline corpus among scholars is to consider the following seven letters as authentic: Romans, 1 Corinthians, 2 Corinthians, 1 Thessalonians, Galatians, Philippians, and Philemon. The following letters are believed to have been written by followers of Paul: 2 Thessalonians, Colossians, Ephesians, 1 Timothy, 2 Timothy, and Titus. I do not intend to engage textual arguments, but I wish to inform the reader that I will be following this view of the authenticity of the Pauline letters. Second is the issue of the divinity of the Holy Spirit. My primary interest is not in Paul's ideas about the divine status of the Spirit, but rather in his ideas about the eschatological dimensions of the work of the Spirit. Certainly these issues have mutual implications, but rather than spending numerous pages hashing out the arguments on both sides of the thorny issue of the divinity of the Spirit in Paul's theology, I will simply state my position: Paul considered the Holy Spirit to be the active, personal presence of God working cooperatively with the Father and Son to bring the divine plan of redemption to completion. Of course, Paul was not a trinitarian per se; but his comments on the Holy Spirit reflect the incipient beginnings of what would later develop into trinitarianism. In other words, Paul considered the Holy Spirit to be divine in some way, but he did not work out the implications of this commitment for the doctrine of God. In carrying out the following study I will assume the basic (and slightly open-ended) position summarized here about the divinity of the Spirit in Paul's theology.

to be living in a dynamic new age of salvation, marked by the action of God in sending his Son and his Spirit. By his death and resurrection Christ has secured a new covenant with humanity that surpasses the old covenant based on the Law. God has also sent the Holy Spirit to dwell within believers, binding them to Christ. When Paul asserts in this particular passage that "everything old has passed away," and that "everything has become new," he is speaking about viewing people from a new perspective as a result of the eschatological act of God. In Christ, God has begun the age of salvation, so that when Paul looks at believers he sees not only people, but the beginnings of the new creation of all things. The conversion to new life experienced by any person is a part of the great and comprehensive eschatological move of God, the scope of which includes individual believers, the communities into which they gather, the world in which they live, and ultimately the entire creation of God, seen and unseen. This age, which is inaugurated by the coming of Christ and the Holy Spirit, is an eschatological age. It is the age anticipated by the Old Testament prophets and hoped for by the Jews.

Pauline scholars are in general agreement that the apostle's eschatology is fundamental to his entire theological outlook. A central argument of J. Christiaan Beker in his book *Paul the Apostle* is that the triumph of God forms the coherent theme of Paul's entire gospel. What Beker means by the 'triumph of God' is the dawning victory of God and the redemption of the created order, which God has inaugurated in Christ (1980: ix). Beker's claim is that Paul's apocalyptic eschatology constitutes the coherence of the gospel message which Paul then tailored to meet the particular needs of his congregations. Geerhardus Vos voices the same basic view when he says that "to unfold the Apostle's eschatology means to set forth his theology as a whole" (11). Victor Furnish also identifies eschatology as the best heuristic key to Paul's theology as a whole (1968: 114). Paul's very concept of salvation is determined by his eschatological perspective (122).

Vos asserts that the primary structure of Paul's eschatology is the duality of this age and the age to come (1952: chapter 1). Combined with this epochal duality is a sense of the succession of history toward a goal, a sense inherent in the Jewish way of looking at history. Thus, Paul's pre-Christian way of thinking about eschatology was that the Messiah would come in the future at the time when God would consummate all things in his kingdom.

With the coming of the Messiah and the Spirit the age to come had already begun. Paul himself was living in it. Yet he recognized that the present messianic age is not the complete consummation of the kingdom of God. Thus, the age to come had split, much like the division of one cell into two (36). The present Messianic age is the new age, but in an incomplete form. The age to come represents the completion of all that God is establishing in the present. Put in another way, the kingdom of God has come in the present age, but it will not be consummated until we inherit it with Christ in the age to come. Thus, Paul's hope in the age to come goes hand in hand with his apocalyptic talk about the two ages, the age of the consummation still retaining the status of "the age to come." In this way his sense of the successiveness of history remains intact (36).

However, alongside the retention of old eschatological notions came the new notion that the states corresponding to the two ages co-exist in the present. It is not that the ages co-exist (for this is impossible within in a scheme of temporal successiveness), but that the states of being do (36–38). Thus, Vos's interpretation of Paul is that the sense of temporal sequence in which the present age will someday give way to the future age remains intact. In this way Paul remains consistent with apocalyptic theology of his day. However, he was not restricted to a rigid apocalyptic separation between this age and the age to come, for he also holds that the state of being that belongs to the future age is already manifest to some degree, and in some ways, in the present.

The line of interpretation which Vos represents, that Paul's eschatological views feature the inbreaking of future states of being in the present, is shared—in various forms—by many Pauline scholars. For instance, Victor Furnish argues that Paul combines ideas of temporal successiveness and qualitative interpenetration.[2] The future age will someday follow the present. At the same time, the qualities of the future age have already penetrated into the present. The point Furnish makes is that Pauline thought is characterized through and through by the eschatological tension produced when the apostle characterizes this age as an eschatological one, while at the same time looking to a future age for the consummation of all that God has begun in the present. Theologians have labeled this eschatological tension in Pauline theology as the tension between the "already" and the "not yet." If one is to gain a proper understanding of Pauline theology, or New Testament theology in general, one has to keep this tension in mind when interpreting New Testament writings. For it is, in fact, distinctive of early Christian thought to conceive of the present and future ages in this way. Furthermore, to fail to retain the tension between the already and the not yet will result in a distortion of New Testament theological positions.

---

[2] *Theology and Ethics in Paul*, part III, ch. 1.

The Example of Salvation

Returning to Paul in particular, let me illustrate the present point by examining his views on a most fundamental theological concept: salvation. The Jewish view of Paul's day was that salvation is a thoroughly eschatological reality. It is God's final eschatological saving of his people. But for Paul the eschatological process has already begun, although it has not been completed. Implicit in his teaching about salvation is the tension between the already and the not yet. This tension leads him to talk about salvation in different ways at different times.[3] In certain contexts Paul speaks of salvation as a future reality. If we have been reconciled to God through justification, then surely we will be saved (Rom 5:9–10). Salvation is nearer to us now than when we first believed (Rom 13:11). We belong to the day which is coming, not to the night which has passed. For this reason, let us put on the helmet of the hope of salvation, for salvation is our destiny in God (1 Thess 5:8–9).

At the same time, Paul also refers to salvation as something that is already happening. The message about the cross is power to those who are *being* saved (σωζομένοις) (1 Cor 1:18). This same present participle, σωζομένοις, occurs again in 2 Cor 2:15 as a label for Christian believers. As long as the Corinthian believers hold firmly to the message of good news which Paul conveyed to them, they are being saved (σώζεσθε) (1 Cor 15:2). Thus, Paul apparently understands salvation to be a process.

Furnish adds that salvation has both a negative and a positive aspect. Negatively it means deliverance from bondage to the world. Positively it is the total transformation of the believer's life (1968: 122–23). Clearly, both of these aspects have begun in the present, but they will not reach fruition until the "day of salvation" in the future. Salvation cannot be reduced to present occurrences, for it has not yet been manifested in its entirety. However, "the decisive aspect of salvation—the death and resurrection of

---

[3] Beker observes that Paul argues from different perspectives depending on which audience which he is addressing and the context of the situation. Judaizers and Jewish Christians most often need to hear the eschatological "now" of the gospel—that God's intervention in Christ eradicates "the works of the Law" and any fearful striving for acceptance by God in the last judgment, as if the Messiah had not already come. This approach is illustrated in such passages as Romans 1–4 and Galatians 1–6, where Paul stresses the importance of the Christ-event without equally stressing the apocalyptic future. On the other hand, Hellenistic Christians tend to celebrate their participation in Christ to the exclusion of the "imperatives" of Christian life. In these cases Paul typically argues the "not yet" of the gospel in conjunction with a specific ethic. In addressing the Corinthians, for instance, who thought that all the blessings of the future had already appeared in the present, Paul operates with what Beker calls an "eschatological reservation" (1980: 255).

Christ—has already occurred and is already effective" (126–27). On the other hand, salvation "is not unambiguously 'future,' and it is not only a 'hope.' Even in the present age the 'first fruits' of salvation may be savored and the authenticity of hope confirmed" (126). As Dunn so aptly puts it, salvation is an ongoing process which "has begun and begun decisively" (1975: 310).

Thus, we can see that for Paul salvation has aspects of the "already" as well as the "not yet." It is not an exaggeration to say that Paul's teachings about even the fundamental notion of salvation cannot be understood unless one keeps a proper eschatological tension in place. The same general points could be made about Paul's understanding of the crucifixion of Christ, the resurrection of Christ, righteousness, justification, adoption, and the like. The eschatological tension between the already and the not yet runs throughout all of Pauline theology.[4]

Eschatological Tension and the Holy Spirit

The Spirit as Eschatological Fulfillment

We have seen that for Paul the qualities of the new age are already penetrating this age. One key element of the new age that Christians enjoy in the present is the gift of the Holy Spirit. The focus of this section will be on the "already" aspects of the work of the Spirit.

"In Paul's view it was precisely the coming of the Spirit which set up the already—not yet tension in the believer's life" (Dunn, 1975: 310). This is so because the Spirit is the "future good" which has already become a reality in the present life of the person of faith.

As with most Jews, especially those with rabbinic training, Paul understood the outpouring of the Holy Spirit to be one of the "end events." He developed this interpretation of the gift of the Spirit against the backdrop of certain Old Testament texts. In the following paragraphs I will briefly discuss four main themes of Old Testament prophecy regarding the Spirit which Paul understood to be fulfilled in the present age. Paul's description of the Holy Spirit becomes more intelligible when seen against the background of these texts and the eschatological hopes which they inspired.

---

[4] Each New Testament scholar will put his or her own nuance on what he or she believes Pauline eschatology to be. The point I wish to make is a general one: virtually all Pauline scholars are in agreement that there is an eschatological tension between the already and the not yet in Pauline theology. In particular, I will work on the way this tension is played out in Paul's understanding of the Holy Spirit.

THE OUTPOURING OF THE SPIRIT

First, Isa 44:3 and Joel 2:28–29 promise the outpouring of the Spirit upon the descendants of Israel. Although Paul does not explicitly refer to these passages, the fulfillment of these promises appears to be reflected in his statements that God gives his Holy Spirit to believers (1 Thess 4:8), and that anyone who is led by the Spirit of God is a child of God (Rom 8:14). More explicit is 1 Cor 12:13, in which all believers "drink of one Spirit," a verse which both James Dunn and George Beasley-Murray interpret to refer to Old Testament prophecies about the Spirit being poured out in the golden age to come. The new age is a time in which God's Spirit is given not only to kings and prophets, but to everyone who becomes a disciple of Christ. Thus, since the church is the community of the new age in which God pours out his Spirit, it is a pneumatic community. There is a landmark distinction between the community of the previous age which was visited by the presence of God on certain occasions and in certain individuals, and the community of the new age in which God distributes his Spirit at all times and in all people.

THE INDWELLING OF THE SPIRIT

Second, Ezekiel associates the promise of a new heart of flesh with the gift of the Spirit within God's people. "I will put my Spirit within you, and make you follow my statutes and be careful to observe my ordinances" (37:27). Ezek 37:14 states that God will put his Spirit within his people, and they shall live. These passages are probably behind Paul's teachings that the Spirit of God indwells believers (Rom 8:9) and that they are temple of God's Spirit (1 Cor 3:16). Paul's position that the Spirit now dwells within Christian believers individually and the body of Christ corporately has far-reaching implications. The indwelling of the Spirit is a vehicle by which he can assert that the Spirit is active in all aspects of Christian life—in "the entire circle of believers, and within the life of every believer over the entire range, subconscious and conscious, religious and ethical, of this life" (Vos, 1952: 58).

THE NEW COVENANT

Third, the idea of God empowering his people from within to keep the commandments of his Law brings to mind Jeremiah's prophecy of a new covenant in which, says the Lord, "I will put my Law within them, and I will write it on their hearts; and I will be their God, and they shall be my people" (v. 33). In Rom 8:1–4, Paul emphasizes that the written Law, which symbolizes the old covenant, has been replaced by a new "law of the Spirit." Ironically, although the written Law is made obsolete by the law of the Spirit, its requirements are fulfilled in a Christian living by the Spirit. In this way the Holy Spirit replaces the written Law. The covenant of which Christians are ministers is a covenant not of letter but of Spirit (2 Cor 3:6; cf. Rom 7:6). Thus, as Jeremiah foresaw, there is now a new covenant in place. The new covenant replaces the old, but it also fulfills the old. Thus, the covenant which marks the new age is both discontinuous and continuous with the covenant of the previous age.

The Coming of the Messiah

A fourth expectation of the new age was that it would bring the promised Messiah, who would be the bearer of the Spirit of God. The Messiah would be permanently endowed with the Spirit, and his pneumatic ministry would be characterized by wisdom, power, knowledge of God, fear of God, justice, gentleness and faithfulness (Isa 11:2–3; 42:1–4). Paul knows Jesus as the Christ, and the Holy Spirit as the Spirit of Christ. Although he does not speak much about Jesus in his earthly ministry, Paul definitely views Jesus' present ministry as pneumatic, for our bond to Christ in faith is the means by which we receive the gift of the Holy Spirit. In Rom 8:9–10, Paul makes a strict association between belonging to the Messiah and having the Spirit dwell within oneself. Furthermore, the presence and activity of the Spirit within the church is the vehicle by which Christ is present to his people. Paul can even say that Jesus in his resurrection became "a life-giving Spirit" (1 Cor 15:45). The Spirit and Christ are the two main actors in the drama of the new age. Their work is mutually interdependent and intertwined. It consists of the salvation and sanctification of believers in this time and continuing on into the eternal future. It is eschatological work.

Summing up, Old Testament prophecies associate the following events with the new age (though they do not restrict the new age to these events): the outpouring of the Spirit, the indwelling of the Spirit, the formation of a new covenant associated with the Spirit, and the appearance of the Spirit-bearing Messiah. Dunn asserts that for Paul the gift of the Spirit was an essential and distinctive element which served to differentiate the Christian from the Jew and the new age from the old (1986: 701). The Spirit "constitutes that immediacy of personal relationship with God which Moses had fitfully enjoyed (2 Cor 3:3–18) and which Jeremiah had only foreseen from afar (2 Cor 3:3 referring to Jer 31:33–34; cf. Eph 2:18)" (701). With the gift of the eschatological Spirit, the new age has begun. To quote Dunn again, "The Spirit then is that power which earlier men of faith had assumed must be reserved for the age to come. The first Christians' experience of an inner power that transformed and made new was such that they could only conclude: This is the power of the new age, this is the eschatological Spirit" (1975: 311).

The Spirit as Pointing toward the Future

We have seen that according to Paul the coming of the Holy Spirit is an essential mark of the eschatological age. The excitement of those days when the early Christians began to realize that God was moving powerfully to set in motion his final plan for salvation must have been overwhelming. Indeed, the excitement was too much for congregations like that at Corinth. Paul had his hands full convincing the Corinthian believers that God's promises had not been completely fulfilled. The transforming and empowering Spirit has been given to us, but we still must wait for the resurrection of our bodies. Only then will our redemption be complete.

Paul's position with the Corinthians, and with his congregations in general, is that the Holy Spirit represents both fulfillment and promise. The appearance of the Spirit signals that the end is here, for the end includes the coming of the Spirit upon all of God's people. But the end is not yet complete, since we still await the total transformation of ourselves inside and out, and the transformation of the world to the point where all resistance to God is squelched. Paul teaches that such a future awaits us. What we now enjoy of the blessings of the new age are wonderful, but they are fragmentary and thus deficient without their *telos*. Salvation that does not include the future resurrection of the dead and the consummation of the kingdom of God remains incomplete. It is no salvation at all.

Hope is an essential feature of the Christian faith. But hope needs a basis upon which to be founded. Paul teaches that there is such a basis: a pair of indicators that the remainder of God's promises will be fulfilled. One is a past event—the resurrection of Christ from the dead—and the other focuses on current events—the presence of the Holy Spirit.

In 1 Corinthians 15, Paul makes a case for the future resurrection of all believers, and he does so on the basis of the resurrection of Christ. He begins by reciting a credal formula, what he "had received": "that Christ died for our sins in accordance with the Scriptures, and that he was buried, and that he was raised on the third day in accordance with the Scriptures, and that he appeared to Cephas, and then to the twelve" (15:3–5). Paul then adds that Christ appeared to more than five hundred believers, then to James, then to all the apostles, and last of all to Paul himself (vv. 6–8).

This accounting of the appearances of Christ functions as historical evidence for the resurrection of Christ.

Then the argument shifts as Christ's resurrection becomes the grounds upon which Christians can base a hope for their own resurrection. Paul asks, "Now if Christ is proclaimed as raised from the dead, how can some of you say there is no resurrection of the dead?" (v. 12). He then answers, "But in fact Christ has been raised from the dead, the first fruits of those who have died" (v. 20). Christ is the first fruits of the resurrection. He is the first among us to be raised. Counting on the true humanity of Christ (death and resurrection both come through a human being, v. 21) and the resulting continuity between the resurrection of Christ and our own resurrection, we have absolute confidence that we too will be raised.

Thus, the resurrection of Christ is one indicator that points toward the eschatological future. If all our eschatological hope rested exclusively on the past event of the resurrection of Christ, then the case for an eschatological future would be limited to historical proofs that the resurrection of Christ really happened, like the argument we see in brief form in 1 Cor 15. But this is not the case. For the other indicator pointing toward the eschaton is the presence of the Holy Spirit—a matter of events encompassing both the past and the present.

Just as Christ is the first fruits of the resurrection, the Holy Spirit is the first fruits of our complete redemption (Rom 8:23). What we now savor of the Spirit's gracious activity is only a foretaste of the feast we will relish on that day. In addition, Paul describes the Spirit as the first installment which God has made toward our complete salvation (2 Cor 5:5). As such, the present gift of the Holy Spirit is the guarantee that God will complete what he has begun. According to Rom 5:1–5, the hope of sharing God's glory survives because of the Holy Spirit. "Precisely because God's love is already powerfully present and active in his Spirit, there is hope for something more, namely, the fulfillment of salvation, the completion and perfection of God's redemptive activity" (Furnish, 1968: 132).

Thus, the Spirit serves as a promise in and of itself—"the absolute guarantee of [the future's] final consummation" (Fee: 806). It is worth noting for us in the twentieth century that inasmuch as Paul's ideas can be construed in terms of an argument from experience of the Spirit, it is not an argument for the existence of God or the truth of Christianity; it is an argument for the reality of the eschatological future.

For Paul the gift of the Holy Spirit is a specific ground of hope. But it is important to note that we need not experience the Spirit in a certain way in order for the Spirit to serve as a vital foundation for our confidence in the future. All that is necessary is that the Spirit be present in our lives. In Gal 5:5 it is through the Spirit, by faith, that we "eagerly wait for the hope of righteousness." In this verse hope is well founded because it is based on faith rather than on obedience to the Law. Salvation by faith is the defining character of life in the new age—in the light of Christ's work on the cross (cf. v. 11). Thus, to rely in faith on God's grace includes not only the reality of salvation now, but also the hope of salvation in the future. What believers experience in this case is an eager anticipation growing out of a context of faith—faith which is the work of the indwelling Spirit. In other words, the Holy Spirit produces faith, and faith produces hope. This means that the experience of hope assumes the work of the Spirit, but it does not necessarily include a conscious awareness of the Spirit. The fact that believers may or may not identify hope as resulting from the work of the Holy Spirit does not invalidate the hope itself. Thus, the Holy Spirit may function as the basis for hope without necessarily being consciously identified in the experience of hope.

The Pauline Metaphors

Paul uses many metaphors, drawn from several sectors of life, to speak of different aspects of the Christian life. From the law court he takes justification, from the slave market redemption, from warfare reconciliation. From everyday life, which includes wholeness and health, he draws salvation as well as waking up, putting on new clothes and being invited to a banquet. Agriculture supplies the images of sowing, watering, grafting and reaping. Out of the world of commerce and trade Paul takes the ideas of seal, down payment, accounting, refining and building. From religion come circumcision, baptism, purification, consecration and anointing. Finally, drawing on the major events of life and history, Paul adapts the notions of creation, birth, adoption, marriage, death and resurrection (Dunn, 1975: 308–9).

In this section we will look specifically at three metaphors he uses in connection with the Holy Spirit: first fruits, down payment and seal. These metaphors all function in two ways with regard to eschatology. They each characterize the Spirit both as what we already enjoy of our future redemption, and as a divine pointer toward the not yet. Because these metaphors so aptly integrate the present and future aspects of the gift of the Holy Spirit, they are ideal vehicles to reflect the *eschatological tension* of Pauline pneumatology (cf. Fee: 806–8). Besides eschatological tension, two other themes that will appear in these metaphors are the *continuity* between what believers experience now in the gift of the Spirit and what they will experience in the eschaton, and the Spirit as *guarantee* that what God has begun he will finish.[5]

First Fruits (ἀπαρχή)

Gerhard Delling notes that ἀπαρχή has three basic meanings: "(a) the first fruits of natural products but also (b) the 'proportionate gift' from the earnings or possessions of the giver, then 'thankoffering' for any success, and finally (c) any 'offering' to the deity or to the servants or sanctuary of the deity, whether as a special or a regular offering" (484). The question for our purposes is what meaning or meanings are attached to Paul's use of the metaphor in connection the Holy Spirit.

There is one instance in the Pauline letters in which the apostle refers to the Holy Spirit as first fruits. In Rom 8:23 he writes that "we ourselves, who have the first fruits of the Spirit, groan inwardly while we wait for adoption, the redemption of our bodies." Here Paul reverses the relationship of giver and recipient that is customary with the giving of first fruits. We are not giving a thank offering of first fruits to God; he is giving to us the first fruits of our complete redemption. Since it would not make sense for God to be presenting us with a thank offering, or an offering of any kind, we can conclude that by referring to the Spirit as first fruits Paul intends Delling's first definition, not the second or third. That is, the Spirit is the first fruits of our redemption in a similar way that the crop which is harvested earliest in the year is the first fruits of the harvest.

Paul's use of the metaphor of first fruits reveals important eschatological dimensions of his understanding of the Holy Spirit. Along these lines I will draw out four points. First, harvesting the first fruits implies a temporal process of which the reaping of the ἀπαρχή, is the beginning. The rest of the harvest is sure to take place. For the concept of 'first fruits' has no meaning apart from the greater harvest which follows. Just as

---

[5] Janet Martin Soskice has argued effectively that metaphorical language plays a vital role in human speech about God. Theists can use metaphorical language to depict reality and therefore express knowledge of God, while also adding the qualification that such knowledge is not definitive or final (*Metaphor and Religious Language*). Such a thesis is highly appropriate for Paul's claims about the Holy Spirit and eschatological realities. These claims take on the character of depicting the realities of God and eschatology, while stopping short of circumscribing such realities within a definition. Soskice also argues that the use of certain metaphors develops within linguistic communities because they communicate aspects of experience that are common to the members of those communities. Thus, Paul's use of the metaphors of first fruits, down payment and seal as referring to the Holy Spirit reflects an eschatological aspect of experience within the believing communities of which he was a part.

Christ's resurrection is the guarantee that our resurrection will follow, the Spirit's presence is the guarantee which God has given us that he will see us to our final redemption. As Paul teaches in Rom 8:11, if the Spirit of the one who raised Christ from the dead dwells in us, we can rest assured that the same God will also raise us.

Second, the ἀπαρχή, is the first of the crop to be harvested, but it is identical in kind with the general crop. The first fruits "are more than blossoms and leaves and green fruit; they are the fruit come to full growth, ready for harvest . . ." (Ladd, 1993: 408). Thus, what believers now experience of the Spirit's blessings is continuous with that which they will experience at the full harvest, the consummation of their redemption. The Spirit is not a mere pointer toward the eschaton, but is the actual first fruits of it. The notion of 'first fruits' supports Paul's entire interpretation of eschatology as being inaugurated but not consummated (408).

Third, it is significant that Paul uses ἀπαρχή to describe both Christ and the Spirit. Although the metaphor carries a different significance in each case, it serves to reveal the interrelation of Christ and the Spirit in the eschatological plan of God. Christ is the first fruits of the resurrection because he is the first among all of God's people to be resurrected (1 Cor 15:20, 23). Just as Christ was resurrected, so too will we be resurrected. Not only can we be sure that we will be raised, but also that we will have the same kind of "spiritual" body that Christ has (1 Cor 15:44–49). Our resurrection is of one piece with his; the two are continuous. But we await our resurrection, whereas his has already happened. It is as if there is a vast field of corn, from which one ear has been plucked in advance of the others.

The Holy Spirit is the first fruits because what we experience now in the fellowship and power of the Spirit is of one piece with what we will experience at the consummation of our redemption. Paul's point here is that the pneumatic aspects of our present existence and of our future existence are continuous, not fundamentally different. Therefore, just as Christ is related to the general resurrection, so the Holy Spirit is related to the complete redemption of humanity and the coming glory of God (cf. Beker, 1990: 32).

Since it carries the element of continuity between the first fruits and the rest of the harvest, ἀπαρχή makes a significant statement about the completion of our redemption. There is continuity between us and the risen Christ, for Christ is the first fruits of the resurrection-event, the first human being to be raised. There is also continuity between the present work of the Spirit in us and his future work. The present gift of the Spirit is the first fruits of the resurrection-life; our experience of the Spirit is a foretaste of our own future pneumatic existence. To say that we will be raised like Christ and that we will enjoy a fully pneumatic existence are two ways of describing the same future state. Like Christ we will have a "spiritual body," as Paul calls it. What this implies is not just a change in our physical make-up, but also a fully pneumatic existence in which we live in complete harmony with the Spirit. This, in turn, is what it means to be conformed to the image of Christ. The first fruits which we now enjoy are a proleptic appearance of our future resurrection-life: complete transformation inside and out that is accomplished by the Holy Spirit and shaped after the person of Christ. The resurrection-life is the eschatological Spirit forming us to be like the eschatological Man.

Fourth, the metaphor of first fruits expresses the eschatological tension of Pauline thought. In Rom 8 this tension comes to light in the close association between believers having the first fruits of the Spirit and their groaning in anticipation of redemption. In Rom 8:1–16 Paul has been talking about the triumphant victory of the Spirit who is present within the believer and the church. But in vv. 17–27 the triumphant tone disappears. There is a basic shift from present triumph to future hope in 8:17b, because the Spirit compels the Christian to look outside the walls of the church into the created world, a world subject to death and decay (Beker, 1980: 364).

In Rom 8:22–23 Paul teaches that the whole of creation has been groaning in labor pains. We groan along with creation, but we groan as those who have the first fruits of the Spirit. Because we enjoy the presence of the Spirit now, we have an idea of the glory to be revealed to us and in us at the redemption of our bodies, and of all of creation. The contrast between our present life with its mixture of joy and suffering, and the future glory of which we have an inkling, fills us with a longing so intense that it hurts. We groan because we have an idea of what we are missing as we live in present conditions. Paul says hyperbolically, "I consider that the sufferings of this present time are not worth comparing with the glory about to be revealed to us" (v. 18). At the same time, Paul knows that we cannot help but compare the two states of being—we must compare them, for hope itself rests on such a comparison, in which what is hoped for surpasses what is now the case (vv. 24–25).

We groan (στενάζω), but we do not groan on our own, for the Spirit helps us pray by interceding "with sighs [στεναγμοῖς] too deep for words" (v. 26). The appearance of cognate words translated as our "groaning" and the Spirit's "sighing" indicates that, whereas v. 23 tells us that we groan, v. 26 tells us how the Spirit actually participates in our groaning (cf. Fee: 576). We can thus understand Paul's position to be that since the Spirit groans in us and with us, and we groan along with creation, the Spirit must also groan along with all of creation.[6]

Therefore, the Spirit as first fruits of our redemption functions in a double-edged way. "We do not groan because we long for the Spirit; rather, the Spirit itself is the agent that makes us 'sigh' and 'groan' (Rom 8:23) and gives us endurance to wait for the final redemption of the body (Rom 8:23, 25). It is remarkable that in the same chapter (Romans 8) the Spirit both conveys present eschatological peace and joy (vv. 1–16) and yet makes us sigh restlessly (vv. 17–27)" (Beker, 1980: 279). In these two dimensions of rejoicing and groaning, the metaphor of first fruits conveys the eschatological tension of Paul's pneumatology. We rejoice because we already experience the eschatological Spirit in our hearts, but we also groan as we wait for God to complete his redemptive purposes.

DOWN PAYMENT (ἀρραβών)

The term ἀρραβών comes from the language of business and trade. "It is used only rarely . . . and means: (1) an installment, with which a man secures a legal claim upon a thing as yet unpaid for; (2) an earnest, an advance payment, by which a contract becomes valid in law; (3) in one passage (Gen 38:17ff) a pledge. In each case it is a matter of payment by which the person concerned undertakes to give further payment to the recipient" (Becker: 39).

A. J. Kerr argues that since the metaphor of ἀρραβών is used in 2 Cor 1:22; 5:5; and Eph 1:14, it most likely carries the meaning it would have in a Greek contract for services. In this type of contract the ἀρραβών is given from the one for whom the work is to be done, to the one who will do the work. What would it mean for God to give us an ἀρραβών in this sense? He would be using the ἀρραβών to secure the legal obligations of both sides of an agreement, much like the way two sides enter into a covenant with each other. Kerr envisions Paul teaching that God gives human beings an ἀρραβών, thereby ratifying their obligation to believe in him and serve him.

The problem with Kerr's interpretation is that such a picture of the relationship between God and human beings is not consistent with Pauline soteriology. Kerr follows J. B. Lightfoot in specifying that in receiving the

---

[6] It is worth noting that according to Rom 8:23, whereas all of creation groans, it is not all of creation that groans because it has the first fruits of the Spirit. This is true only of believers.

ἀρραβών, the recipient "pledges himself to accomplish his side of the contract" (97). As Luther made so clear, it is fundamental to Paul's gospel that our redemption does not depend on our accomplishments. In 2 Cor 1:21–22, in the same sentence in which Paul uses the metaphor of ἀρραβών for the Holy Spirit, he states, "But it is *God* who establishes us with you in Christ . . . ." It is difficult to imagine that in the same breath that Paul says this, he turns around and implies that salvation depends on our upholding our end of a contractual obligation. In this case, Paul should have said that it is *God and we* who have accomplished our establishment in Christ.

There is no doubt that Paul's gospel includes the expectation that Christians be characterized by faith that is manifested in service of God and others. However, the apostle is clear that none of this is possible without the enabling power of the Holy Spirit. Therefore, inasmuch as we can say that the Holy Spirit is part of a contract of mutual obligation between God and us, he is much more than a commodity that serves merely to ratify the agreement in the form of a down payment. He is the power that makes the fulfillment of the agreement possible. Thus, Paul's use of the metaphor of down payment again underscores the grace of God, as he not only enters into an agreement with us, but also provides the means by which we may participate in the agreement. The empowering dimension of the ἀρραβών of the Holy Spirit is a vital implication that Kerr has left out of his analysis.

Another aspect which we must consider in interpreting Paul's use of both of the metaphors of first fruits and down payment is that these terms appear in the form of a genitive—e.g., "δοὺς τὸν ἀρραβῶνα τοῦ πνεύματος" (giving the down payment of the Spirit) (2 Cor 1:22). This genitive is not partitive, as if believers only received a part of the Spirit as an installment on a future full indwelling. Instead, the genitive is appositional. When Paul speaks of the first installment of the Spirit, he is referring to the first installment which is the Spirit. It is not an installment of some of the Spirit's gifts to be followed by the full measure of gifts; rather, the installment is the Spirit himself. "The forward looking emphasis in both metaphors [first fruits and down payment] does not imply further givings of the Spirit, simply the increasing control of the believer by the one Spirit already given" (Dunn, 1975: 443 n49; cf. Beker, 1980: 279).

While the down payment of the Spirit represents the full gift of the eschatological Spirit and not a partial endowment, the concept of down payment indicates that in quantity an installment is not the same as a full payment. With this thought in mind, what is the difference between the sums, if the Spirit is our down payment? We have already seen that the answer cannot lie in the quantity of Spirit-endowment we are given. Rather, the answer, as hinted at by Dunn in the previous paragraph, lies in us who are the recipients of the down payment. In this age, even if we are indwelt by the Holy Spirit, we are still prone to live according to the flesh at times. Only after we are resurrected—and undergo the total transformation entailed in resurrection—will we be able to enjoy the full benefits of the gift of the Holy Spirit, because only then will we be living in complete harmony with the Spirit. Thus, the difference between the down payment and the total sum is not the quantity of Spirit-endowment, but rather the extent of our submission to the Spirit.

We have seen that Paul associates the Spirit as the first fruits of the eschatological future and our groaning in the present age. There is also a connection between the Spirit as down payment and our groaning. Paul writes in 2 Corinthians 5 that while we live in these bodies we groan in frustration. But in criticism of Corinthian ideas, Paul states that "while we are still in this tent we groan under our burden, because we wish not to be unclothed but to be further clothed . . ." (2 Cor 5:4). That is, we do not wish to be *freed* from our bodily existence but to have a *new* bodily existence. In the meantime we groan. Then Paul adds, "He who has prepared us for this very thing is God, who has given us the Spirit as a guarantee [ἀρραβών]" (v. 5). In this passage, unlike Romans 8, Paul does not specify the Spirit's role in our groaning. But he does link the Spirit to our groaning. We long for the resurrection, but we have the guarantee of the Spirit, so we are confident in our longing (v. 6).

The metaphor of down payment communicates the sense in which the Holy Spirit is God's guarantee that we will have complete redemption. Having the ἀρραβών of the Spirit gives us utter confidence that what God has promised to us will come to pass. In 2 Corinthians 5, Paul describes the benefits of the presence of the Spirit in terms of confidence that our hopes for the future will be fulfilled. He does the same in 2 Cor 1:21–22. Behm affirms that the common thrust of the ἀρραβών passages is: "The Spirit, which God has given them, is security to the Christians in the future, complete possession of salvation" (474). It is not that the Spirit *gives* believers a guarantee of complete salvation; it is that the Spirit *is* the guarantee. His very presence is the source of Christian confidence in the future.

Our confidence in the future is based on the expectation that what we will enjoy at our resurrection is continuous with the gift of the Spirit which we now enjoy. For if the Spirit is a "first installment" or "down payment" on our redemption, then what we have in our present possession as the gift of the Spirit is of one piece with the totality of our future inheritance. In other words, as the first installment payment on our inheritance the present gift of the Spirit is a part of the future whole. An ἀρραβών "is deposited money that both promises the full payment in the future and gives a partial payment in the present" (Ladd, 1993: 409).

The theme of continuity is further underscored in 2 Cor 5:5, when Paul equates—or at least closely links—two divine actions: preparing us for our future resurrection and giving us the Spirit as an ἀρραβών. The giving of the down payment of the Spirit is a way of preparing us for the consummation of our redemption. It is a foretaste of things yet to come.

With the metaphor of down payment we again see the familiar pattern of a tension between the already and the not yet. In the use of the terminology of down payment, Paul is indicating that we are already in possession of a part of our total redemption. However, we are waiting to receive the full amount, indicating that we will not enjoy the Spirit's full blessings until the future age.

SEAL (σφραγίς)

It is common for New Testament scholars who are treating the eschatological aspects of Pauline pneumatology to discuss the metaphors of "first fruits" and "down payment." However, not many scholars also treat the metaphor of the "seal" of the Spirit. Gordon Fee is an exception to this rule, including all three metaphors as vehicles to express the eschatological significance of the gift of the Holy Spirit. He accurately claims, "In contrast to 'down payment', there is nothing inherently eschatological in this image; nonetheless, when Paul uses it as a metaphor for the Spirit it carries a decidedly eschatological overtone" (807).

Geoffrey Lampe points out that there is remarkable diversity in the use of the words σφραγίζω and σφραγίς in the New Testament (1967: 7). Our concern is not with the entire range of uses, but specifically with the uses that link the idea of sealing with the Holy Spirit. At the same time, it will be profitable to fill out the uses of the idea in the Old Testament and apocryphal literature that serve as background to Paul's connection of the Spirit with the image of a seal.

The original application of σφραγίζω / σφραγίς was to the practices of branding cattle and branding or tattooing slaves. Later, after the apostle's day, soldiers were also tattooed to mark them as the emperor's men. In any of these cases the idea was to mark the animal or person as the property of a specific owner (9).

When this basic concept of marking animals or people as possessions was transferred into the religious realm, the seal became either a
physical mark or an inner token by which the follower is identified with
his or her god (12). We find the idea of a seal in several places in the Old
Testament. In Ezek 9:4–6, God's people are marked on the foreheads and
thus spared from judgment. In the story of the Exodus the Israelites are
instructed to put blood on their doorposts as a sign to the angel of death
that their firstborn sons are to be passed over (Exod 12:13). Lampe asserts
that the Old Testament writers did not always understand the marking of
God's people to be an exterior one. The prophets looked forward to a new
covenant, when God's people would bear a "circumcision of the heart."
This inner circumcision was linked with the endowment with the Spirit
of God (16).

The metaphor of a seal also occurs in the apocryphal literature. 4 Ezra
6:5 mentions the sealing of those who have stored up treasures of faith.
Psalms of Solomon 15:6–10 speaks of two types of seal on human beings.
When God's judgment goes forth, the unrighteous, who will have the
mark of destruction on their foreheads, will fall under the wrath of God.
The righteous, on the other hand, have the mark of salvation. They will
escape judgment and enjoy redemption.[7] Lampe concludes, "This conception of a sign set by God upon His elect to mark them as His own and
protect them from destruction is a frequent motif in Hebrew eschatology,
and it exercised a profound influence upon the Christian theory of the
sealing of the faithful 'for a day of redemption' . . ." (15).

Moving to the thought of Paul, Lampe writes, "It is against this background of the sealing of God's people with a sign which marks them as
His own, assures them of salvation in the day of wrath and judgment, and
protects them from divine condemnation and from the malignant powers
of evil, that we must set St. Paul's reminder to his converts that they have
been 'sealed for a day of redemption'" (16). In other words, the background to Paul's use of the metaphor of seal for the Holy Spirit is loaded
with eschatological connotations. But this fact in itself does not make the
case that Paul intended the metaphor of seal to be taken eschatologically.

---

[7] George Nickelsburg, in *Jewish Literature between the Bible and the Mishnah*, expresses
uncertainty whether this psalm is speaking of an eschatological judgment or a perennial
judgment (212). Indeed, when issuing warnings about the lot of sinners, the writer shifts
back and forth between the devastation that follows sinners from generation to generation
(v. 11) and the everlasting destruction which will be their inheritance on the day of the
Lord's final judgment (v. 12). Since the psalmist toggles so freely between the two types of
judgment, it is probable that he understood the seal which marks people for one destiny or
the other can be understood in both an non-eschatological and an eschatological sense.

To complete the argument, let us examine the verses in which Paul uses the metaphor. Upon doing this it will become plain that seal is an eschatological metaphor when Paul uses it in connection with the Holy Spirit.

The metaphor of the seal of the Spirit appears three times in the letters of the Pauline tradition, once in 2 Corinthians and twice in Ephesians. Paul writes in 2 Cor 1:21–22 that God has established believers in Christ "and has anointed us, by putting his seal on us and giving us his Spirit in our hearts as a first installment." In this passage the anointing believers receive from God consists of both a seal and the gift of the Holy Spirit. Does this mean that the seal and the gift of the Spirit are two different endowments? Probably not, since Paul uses them both to describe an anointing, which is often a pneumatological concept.[8] On this interpretation God bestows on believers the Holy Spirit, who functions as a seal and also as a down payment. As we will see next, this is the interpretation taken by the author of Ephesians.

The author of Ephesians makes the eschatological connotations of the seal of the Spirit more straightforward and explicit than does Paul. Early in the letter the Ephesian believers are reminded that when they had heard the word of truth and believed in Christ, they were marked with the seal of the Holy Spirit, who is the "pledge [ἀρραβών] of our inheritance toward redemption as God's own people" (1:13–14). This passage carries forward the basic position given in 2 Corinthians 1 in two ways. First, in both passages the Spirit is described as a down payment (ἀρραβών). Second, there is development from Paul's linking of the seal with the gift of the Spirit in 2 Corinthians 1, and his disciple's use of the Spirit as an actual explication of what kind of seal believers are receiving. That is, Paul does not explicitly say that the Spirit is the seal which believers are receiving, but the author of Ephesians does. This slight alteration of Paul's wording is a significant move, but, as I argued briefly in the preceding paragraph, not an improper one. Therefore, both Paul and the author of Ephesians appear to understand the Holy Spirit to be a seal that marks us for redemption and the down payment toward that redemption—two closely related eschatological notions.

The author of Ephesians again uses the metaphor of Holy Spirit as seal in Eph 4:30, where he states that believers have been marked with the Holy Spirit "with a seal toward the day of redemption." Therefore, they must not grieve the Holy Spirit. The idea of grieving the Spirit is an echo

---

[8] For instance, when the Judaic and Christian communities speak of the Messiah as the "anointed one" they mean that he is the unique Spirit-bearer. Here being anointed and bearing the Spirit are synonymous.

of Isa 63:10, in which the prophet explains that the Israelites grieved the Holy Spirit, and God then chastised them. With this verse in the background, the warning to the Ephesians takes on a new light. The Holy Spirit is the mark which God has put on Christians. As a seal, the Spirit functions in two ways. In a negative sense, he protects Christians from judgment—unless they grieve him, in which case their protection will be removed and God will discipline them, just as he did the Israelites. In a positive sense, the Holy Spirit is a sign of God's ownership. But the author makes it clear that God's ownership is not a static state of affairs. It is ownership toward a specific end: the total redemption of his people. God's seal is bound up with his love and grace, which is teleological and will only be fulfilled on "the day of redemption."

With the metaphors of first fruits and down payment we have seen the recurring themes of continuity, guarantee and eschatological tension. The metaphor of the seal of the Spirit does not communicate continuity, but it does connote the sureness of a guarantee and the tension of the already and the not yet.

The idea of God putting a seal on people to mark them as his own, protecting them from judgment and distinguishing them for salvation, includes the notion of a divine guarantee. If it is God who marks his people, then it is God who will be faithful to preserve them. This is the force of Eph 4:30, which states that the Ephesian believers were "marked with a seal for the day of redemption." However, it is not necessary to take this verse as a complete guarantee that believers will be marked with the Spirit no matter what they do. In Isa 63 the Israelites grieved the Spirit with their rebellion, and they were kept from the promised land for it. Inasmuch as the author of Ephesians follows the logic of Isaiah 63, he could be saying that the seal of the Spirit can be taken away from the most rebellious Christians, thereby leaving them open to God's wrath. In this case the Spirit is a seal guaranteeing their redemption as long as they do not grieve him to the point of departure. Of course, it is also possible that the verse means that when the Spirit is grieved and God becomes the enemy of his people, he does so in order to discipline them in love, not to reject them. In this case, the Holy Spirit is God's seal, guaranteeing that he will do whatever is necessary to see them to their full redemption.

The seal of the Spirit reflects the eschatological tension of Pauline thought because the Holy Spirit is a seal which represents the alive, dynamic and active presence of God which is given to believers now but points toward the future. The Spirit is one whom we should not *grieve*, implying that he is a personal presence. And if Isaiah 63 can be trusted as a source for the ideas in Ephesians 4, then the Spirit is the personal presence *of God*. For the prophet makes it plain that the presence who was with the Israelites was not a messenger or an angel, but God himself. In both cases—Israelites in the desert and now Christians—the presence of God with his people was/is moving and working to bring them to the fulfillment of the divine promises made to them. The great difference between the two cases is that only for the followers of Christ is the presence of God identified as the eschatological Spirit. The tension involved in being sealed with the eschatological Spirit is that Christians are now blessed with the living and active seal of the Spirit, but they wait to reach the goal toward which this seal is aligned.

Conclusion

In this chapter I have argued that eschatological tension between the already and the not yet is an essential element of Pauline theology, and in particular of Pauline pneumatology. I have hinted that this eschatological tension has two aspects, a theological one and an affective one. In this concluding section I will elucidate these two aspects of the eschatological tension of Paul's understanding of the Holy Spirit.

As soon as one claims, as Paul does, that we are living in an eschatological age, a theological tension arises. For Paul makes this claim in the light of an apparent contradiction. On the one hand, he and other Christian believers experienced the gift of the eschatological Spirit, enabling them to do what they could not do before: believe the gospel, recognize the Messiah, love others, prophesy, preach, heal the sick, and so on. Paul expressed the experience of the early Christians with the words, "everything old has passed away; see, everything has become new!" (2 Cor 5:17).

On the other hand, Paul is surely speaking in hyperbole. Not *everything* has become new in the believer, let alone the world. Just as believers have come "out of the world," so to speak, they all too often continue to live according to old patterns of life. The world is characterized by death, sickness, oppression, dishonesty, selfishness and other kinds of vice. Paul himself refers to Satan as "the god of this world" (2 Cor 4:4), implying that the rule of God has not yet been made completely manifest. Even in the church—the eschatological community—there is much to lament. Paul confronts the Corinthian congregation for harboring divisions among themselves. He asks the rhetorical question, "As long as there is jealousy and quarreling among you, are you not of the flesh, and behaving according to human inclinations?" (1 Cor 3:3). In other words, the Corinthians are conducting themselves as if the realities of the new age had not impacted them at all. Therefore, Paul himself recognizes that whereas from a certain perspective we can say that all things have become new, from a different perspective not much has changed. This is the theological tension inherent in claiming that the present age is the age of fulfillment. For as soon as one makes such a claim, one must add that this is not the age of *complete* fulfillment. That will come in the eschaton.

In order to avoid complete theological incoherence, Paul chose metaphors like the ones we have studied to nuance his eschatological claims. The Holy Spirit is the eschatological Spirit, but we experience him now only as the first fruits of a greater harvest, or an installment payment put down on a greater sum. It is not that we only experience a partial indwelling of the Spirit. No, the promise of an outpouring of the Spirit has been completely fulfilled. What is partial is our submission to the Spirit in this age. This is precisely the reason why Paul chose metaphors like first fruits and down payment. The meaning of these images includes continuity between the part and the whole, and also distinction between the part and the whole.

In order for the claim that we are living in the age of fulfillment to make sense, there must be continuity between eschatological realities in this age and those in the age to come. In the indwelling of the eschatological Spirit the qualities of the resurrection-life have penetrated into this age, defining the content of the life of the reborn Christian. The presence of the Spirit manifests itself in impulses to love God and other people, worship, cry out to the Father as "Abba," rejoice in our adoption, groan in anticipation, and defeat the long-regnant powers of the flesh. Our experience of these realities is eschatological experience. The qualities of these impulses is continuous with the qualities of our future resurrection existence, just as the crop gathered in the first fruits is continuous with the crop gathered in the general harvest, and as the currency given in a down payment is continuous with the currency given in a full payment.

Nevertheless, there is a distinction between the first fruits and the general harvest, and between a down payment and the full payment which follows. In both cases it is a distinction of quantity. In the same way, the quantity of the fullness in which we live according to the Spirit represents an element of discontinuity between our existence in the two ages. In this age, whereas we have the Spirit-given impulse to overcome our old destructive ways and live a new life, and we also have the empowerment of the same Spirit to follow these impulses, we still often behave in ways discontinuous with the Spirit's leadings. The Spirit empowers but does not coerce. In the age to come all impediments to complete submission to the Spirit will be removed from us, and we will live in complete accord with the Spirit's impulses.

Therefore, there is a distinction between quality and quantity in the character of our life in the Spirit. There is continuity in the pneumatic impulses, but there is discontinuity in the level of our cooperation with these impulses. This distinction is confirmed by Paul's use of the metaphors of first fruits and down payment, images which stress a distinction of quantity (cf. Shires: 152).

The combination of continuity and distinction embedded within the meaning of Paul's pneumatological metaphors is a powerful way of expressing the tension inherent in the claim that we live in an eschatological age. Paul has taken the apparent contradictions which cause eschatological tension and explained them in such a way that this tension becomes essential to his theological outlook. As Vos explains, for Paul the new age became split into two ages, a little like the way a cell divides into two. Both of the ages—this age and the age to come—retain an eschatological status, but there is a distinction in fullness between them.

Living in the tension between the already and the not yet impacts Christians theologically, and it also impacts them affectively. The affective dimensions of an eschatological tension are twofold. As we saw earlier in the chapter, Christians both rejoice and groan at the same time. We rejoice because the new age has dawned. The enemies of God have been defeated. His kingdom has come. The eschatological Spirit has been poured out. However, there is another side of the present age that causes us to groan in a mixture of frustration and anticipation. The new age has dawned, but it has not been consummated. The enemies of God have been defeated, but only in principle—the final enemy of God is death itself, and this foe will endure until the resurrection of the dead. The kingdom of God has come, but we must wait to inherit it in its full measure. The eschatological Spirit has been poured out on us, empowering us to live according to the Spirit, but all too often we still live according to the flesh. Thus, we groan and sigh in a world of contradiction, and a life of inconsistency.

However, it is precisely at this point that understanding the Spirit as guarantee meets us. The ways in which the Spirit is a guarantee come to light in Paul's use of the metaphors of first fruits, down payment and seal. Since the Spirit is the first fruits of our redemption, we have confidence that the rest of the harvest will surely follow. For the notion of first fruits has no meaning apart from the general harvest to which it is a prelude. Likewise, the very concept of a down payment includes a guarantee that the amount given as a deposit will be followed by the payment of the total sum. We have also seen that the idea of a seal, when used in religious contexts, is always oriented toward judgment and salvation in the future. The mark of God on his people functions as a guarantee that he will spare them from judgment and preserve them for salvation.

When we understand that the presence of the Spirit is a guarantee of greater things in the eschaton, the present blessings of the Spirit intensify our anticipation, and mollify us in the midst of our angst. The presence of the Spirit heightens our expectation of greater glory, for our hope for total deliverance is accompanied by the certainty that it really will come to pass. Likewise, we receive assurance that the contradictions of the present age will not last forever, even though it often seems they will. We still feel discomfort and we groan, but we have peace and confidence in our groaning.

There is an often-overlooked connection between the guarantee of the Spirit as first fruits, down payment and seal, and the inner witness of the Spirit of which Paul speaks in Rom 8:16. In both cases the Spirit is our source of assurance. In both cases the comfort we now receive gives us confidence that we have a future with God ("and if children, then heirs" [Rom 8:17]). In the midst of experiencing the sorrows of our present life, we need comfort. This comfort comes in the person of the Holy Spirit, who is God's guarantee that he will fulfill our deepest longings. God's presence in the indwelling of the Holy Spirit is the source of both our longing and the assurance that it is not just wishful thinking.

In the next chapter we will explore the eschatological dimensions of Pauline pneumatology in greater detail, examining a selection of loci of the Spirit's work in believers, both corporately and individually.[9] In all areas of Paul's teachings about the Holy Spirit, the theme of the tension between the already and the not yet will reappear consistently, reflecting the centrality of this type of eschatological vision in the apostle's pneumatological thought. Just as the Holy Spirit is fundamental to Paul's eschatological outlook, so is his eschatology fundamental to his conception of the Holy Spirit.

---

[9] Obviously, Paul does not present a systematic treatment of pneumatology in his letters. Rather, the reader finds insights related to the literary context and the specific situation he is facing with relation to a particular letter's addressees (cf. J. Christiaan Beker's arguments regarding the contingency of Paul's thought in *Paul the Apostle* and Victor Furnish, "Where Is 'the Truth' in Paul's Gospel?"). At the same time, the task of systematic theology requires some degree of synthesis of Paul's various remarks about the Holy Spirit, even while keeping in mind the contingent character of his writing.

3

Eschatological Characteristics of Pauline Pneumatology

IN organizing this chapter I have divided up the Spirit's work into that which is individual-oriented and that which is community-oriented. In some cases a locus of pneumatic activity fits neatly into one category. For instance, the links between the Spirit and the new covenant, or the Spirit and the inclusion of the Gentiles, obviously belong to the category of the Spirit and the human communities. On the other hand, in many cases there is a great deal of overlap between the two categories. I have included a discussion of spiritual gifts under the category of the Christian community, because even though the individual is the one who makes the wheels turn, the operation of the gifts is primarily a corporate affair within the functioning Christian community

In Paul's theology the gift of the Holy Spirit is primarily corporate and secondarily individual. Early Christians, Paul included, perceived that the turn of the ages had come. The Messiah had appeared, a new covenant had been formed, the Spirit had been poured out, and the Gentiles were being included in the eschatological blessings of God. It is into this all-embracing network of end-time divine activity that individual experience of the Spirit fits. For this reason, I will treat the community-oriented work of the Spirit first and the individual-oriented work of the Spirit second.

The Holy Spirit and the Believing Community

The Spirit and the New Age

THE NEW COVENANT

According to Pauline thought the establishment of a new covenant between God and humanity is a key ingredient of the new age. Paul is clear that there is such a new covenant, which fulfills the old Mosaic covenant.

There are two passages, 2 Corinthians 3 and Gal 4:21—5:1, in which Paul distinguishes the two covenants in a number of ways. In all cases, the Holy Spirit plays a pivotal role in his understanding of the dynamics of the new covenant.

In 2 Corinthians 3 the first distinction Paul makes between the old and new covenants is that the former is a covenant of letter, and the latter is a covenant of spirit (v. 6). Paul clearly associates the old covenant with death and the new with life, in large part because the old covenant did not feature the life-giving presence of the Holy Spirit within human beings. In contrast, under the new covenant the indwelling Spirit is freely given, enabling people to live a new life of true righteousness, even though obedience to the Law is not required to earn salvation. Gordon Fee argues that what Paul means when he says that "the letter kills" is that the Law of the old covenant "can arouse sin but is powerless to overcome it; the Torah lacks the one essential ingredient for life, the Spirit" (306). In other words, the Holy Spirit delivers under the new covenant what the Law could not deliver under the old covenant: abundant life.

Paul's notion of the new covenant in 2 Corinthians 3 is keyed by the gift of the Spirit in association with that covenant. This association becomes more clear when we identify the Old Testament prophetic passages which presumably form the background for such ideas. First, the promise of a new covenant is rooted in Jer 31:31–34, which states that under the new covenant God will write the Law on the hearts of his people. Paul uses and adapts the image of letters being written on the heart in 2 Cor 3:2–3. The appearance of this imagery in Paul's argument points to the likelihood that Jeremiah's prophecy was in his mind when he crafted his thoughts about the new covenant in this chapter of the epistle.

Second, the promise of comprehensive personal transformation in the eschaton is given in Ezek 36:26–27, where the prophet foresees a time when God will put his Spirit within his people, making them careful to obey his statutes and observe his ordinances. The prophet describes these changes with the metaphor of a new heart of flesh replacing an old heart of stone, which signals a transformation of God's people from the inside out. This idea is very similar to Jeremiah's prediction that God will write his Law on the hearts of his people. For both Ezekiel and Jeremiah, God is promising to place within his people someday an internal impulse and empowerment to obey and follow divine statutes. For Ezekiel, and later for Paul, this impulse and empowerment is identified as the Holy Spirit. The apostle and his converts were experiencing the change of heart for which Jeremiah and Ezekiel hoped. This Spirit-enabled transformation is a fundamental element of life under the new covenant.

Fee argues that v. 6 is the key to the rest of the third chapter of 2 Corinthians. This means that the ways in which Paul describes the new covenant in vv. 7–18 are explications of what it means for the new covenant to be a covenant of spirit (299). In vv. 7–11 Paul extols the glory of the new covenant, because it far surpasses the glory of the old. The ministry of the Spirit is so much greater than the ministry of Moses that by comparison the latter has lost its glory (v. 10). Furthermore, adding to its superiority, the ministry of the Spirit is permanent, unlike the temporary ministry of Moses (v. 11).

Not only was the glory of the old covenant limited and temporary, it was also misunderstood. For the minds of the Jews have had a veil over them, but this veil is lifted whenever one comes to Christ and is filled with the Spirit (vv. 14–16). At this point there is liberation—freedom *from* hardness of the mind, and freedom *for* transformation from one degree of glory to another (vv. 17–18).

Summing up Paul's thoughts in 2 Corinthians 3, under the new covenant there is a "ministry of the Spirit" which far surpasses the "ministry of condemnation" under the old covenant. Although the old covenant had glory, the new has a much greater glory—the glory into which all believers are being transformed from one degree to another. The key to this transformation is the Holy Spirit. This process of unending ascent, first from condemnation to glory, and then from glory to greater glory, is wrapped up in the idea of the Spirit as life-giver.

Turning to Galatians 4, we see Paul again using a contrast between the covenants to make the point that the new covenant of the Spirit is marked by liberation. He allegorizes the story of Hagar and Sarah, identifying the former with the old covenant of slavery and the latter with the new covenant of freedom (4:24–26). The Galatian believers are called to drive out the slave woman, for they are children of the free woman, and they should resist those who would attempt to place them under a yoke of slavery once again (4:30—5:1). The contrast between slavery and freedom underscores the division between the age of the old covenant and the age of the new. In doing so, it highlights the eschatological nature of the new covenant. As we would expect, the eschatological aspect of the new covenant contains within it a tension between the already and the not yet. For in the allegory the children of the free woman share an awaited inheritance. This view toward an anticipated future indicates that not all the blessings of belonging to the line of Sarah have been realized. There is an inheritance yet to come.

Once again, the Spirit takes a pivotal role in Paul's description of the new covenant, for he states that the children born to the free woman are "born according to the Spirit" (4:29). What Paul is saying is that membership in the community of the new covenant comes about through the Holy Spirit.

The Spirit is the agent of liberation for all who come to new life under the new covenant. The slavery from which the children of Sarah are emancipated is their bondage to "elemental spirits" (4:3), or "beings that by nature are not gods" (4:8), to which Paul refers in the beginning verses of chapter four. The emancipation from these powers involves the transference of believers from bondage to adoption into God's family, a process which is accompanied by the gift of the indwelling Spirit of Christ. The Spirit participates in the victory of God over opposing powers and the liberation of believers from them. He also bears witness to the adoption by God which accompanies that liberation (4:6).

THE SPIRIT AND THE LAW

As we have seen, a fundamental way Paul differentiates between the old covenant and the new is to describe the former as a covenant of letter and the latter as a covenant of spirit (2 Cor 3:6). Part of what Paul is alluding to in this distinction are the roles of the Torah in the old covenant and the Holy Spirit in the new covenant. In important ways, these roles overlap. In fact, Fee argues that the key to understanding Paul's view of the Law is found in his eschatological pneumatology (813).

Fee starts out by acknowledging a significant difficulty—Paul sometimes speaks of the Law in negative terms and other times in positive terms (814). For instance, the Law led to condemnation (2 Cor 3:9), it brings knowledge of sin (Rom 3:20; 7:7–12), and actually arouses sin (Rom 7:5). It has imprisoned human beings (Gal 3:23), keeping them as slaves (4:1). They were helpless to do anything about it, no matter how hard they tried (Rom 7:14–25). For these reasons the Law led to death, not life (Rom 7:9–10; 2 Cor 3:6). Therefore, with the coming of Christ and the Spirit the time of the Law came to an end (Rom 10:4; Gal 5:18). On the other hand, Paul can also describe the Law as "holy" and "spiritual," its commandments being "holy and just and good" (Rom 7:12, 14). Faith does not overthrow the Law; on the contrary, it upholds the Law (Rom 3:31).

The problem is how to reconcile such diversity. Fee leads us toward a solution. In developing his argument, Fee turns first to Paul's letter to the

Galatians, since it is the epistle that deals most explicitly with the relation between the Law and Christians. As Paul explicitly states in Gal 5:18, "if you are led by the Spirit, you are not subject to the Law." In other words, the Spirit marks the effective end of the Law. That is, the Spirit is able to do what the Law was not able to do by giving us the power to fulfill the Law's commandment of righteousness. Furnish and others make the point that Paul's problem with the Law is that people living by the Law are trying to earn salvation, and this is a patently hopeless task. Fallen human beings, in and of themselves, do not have the personal strength to follow the Law, even if they desire to (Romans 7). But, thankfully, this is not the end of the story as Paul tells it. "For God has done what the Law, weakened by the flesh, could not do: by sending his own Son in the likeness of sinful flesh, and to deal with sin, he condemned sin in the flesh, so that the just requirement of the Law might be fulfilled in us, who walk not according to the flesh but according to the Spirit" (Rom 8:3–4). Thus, there are two changes in the function of the Law in the present age. First, the avenue to salvation does not lead through the Law. Second, the requirements of the Law are not to be disdained. Rather, they are being fulfilled by those who are filled with the Spirit and follow his leadings.

The association of the Law with the old covenant and the inability of the Law to produce the kind of righteousness which it demanded are the keys to understanding Paul's tendency to speak of the Law in a negative fashion. The positive statements are based on the fact that the Spirit fulfills the Law's intent, leading and enabling people to live in true righteousness. Fee explains that Torah is fulfilled, but in such a way as to make it practically obsolete. However, since it is an integral part of the Old Testament story, of which the Christian story is a continuation, the Law is never completely obsolete (816).

We can conclude our discussion of the Law by noting that eschatological convictions drive Paul's entire understanding of the Law's current function. The Law is associated with an old covenant which has been overshadowed by a new covenant—a thoroughly eschatological event, according to Jeremiah. Furthermore, the new covenant is a fulfillment of what the old covenant was intended to be, in the sense that the righteousness expected under the old covenant is only now being realized under the new covenant. And it is being realized apart from the Law. Under the new covenant, the Law is now being written on believers' hearts by means of the eschatological Spirit, whose permanent habitation within the hearts of believers is also a fulfillment of Scripture. The eschatological Spirit is thus the cornerstone of the function of the Law in this age.

The Spirit and the Inclusion of the Gentiles

Another component of the new age is the inclusion of the Gentiles into the family of God. According to the account given in Acts, the inclusion of the Gentiles came as quite a surprise to the early Christian church. Peter would surely not have visited the house of Cornelius if he had not received specific revelation from God to cease considering Gentiles unclean. Regarding it as an act of obedience, Peter preached the gospel to Cornelius and his family, but still the report is that "the circumcised believers who had come with Peter were astounded that the gift of the Holy Spirit had been poured out even on the Gentiles . . ." (Acts 10:45). The same sort of shock greeted the Jewish leaders of the church in Jerusalem upon their hearing of these surprising developments. Their initial indignation turned to rejoicing when they realized that God had given the gift of repentance "even to the Gentiles" (Acts 11:18).

At the same time, the struggle over the status of Gentile converts was far from over. More conservative Jewish Christians continued to insist that in order to be saved the Gentiles must receive the rite of circumcision and keep the Law of Moses (Acts 15:5). The sharp debate over this question gave rise to the first council of the Christian church. All this is to say that although Old Testament Scriptures are clear that in eschatological times God would bring salvation to all peoples (Gen 22:18; Ps 22:27; Isa 49:6; Dan 7:14), the Jewish believers were completely unprepared for such a thing to actually happen. The story of these events leading to (and following) the first council of the Christian church illustrates the way in which the eschatological actions of God took his people by surprise.

As Paul's letters attest, for years after the Jerusalem council there continued to be those who insisted that Gentiles must keep the Mosaic Law in order to gain true inclusion into the family of God. This was the problem in Galatia, where believers were transferring their confidence from faith in Christ to good works. In his letter to the churches there, Paul aggressively argues that this type of development turns the Christian gospel on its head. Paul teaches that justification comes not by doing the works of the Law—for no one, Jew or Gentile, can be justified this way—but by believing in Christ (Gal 2:15–16).

The apostle then employs his eschatological outlook to explain the gospel in more detail. It was foretold that God would justify the Gentiles (Gen 12:3; 18:18; 22:18). Since Abraham was justified by faith, this is the way the Gentiles are justified as well (Gal 3:6–9). But in order to share in the full blessing of eschatological salvation, all human beings must place their faith specifically in Christ, who became a curse so that all could be freed from the curse of the Law (3:13). The result of this chain of ideas is the conclusion that, through faith in Christ, the Gentiles can receive the blessing of Abraham and the "promise of the Spirit" (3:14).

Fee points out the noteworthiness of Paul's association of the Holy Spirit with the blessing of Abraham, since such a connection is not made in Genesis. Here in Galatians Paul refers to both the blessing of Abraham and the gift of the Spirit with the word "promise." This indicates that for Paul they are both part of the same nexus of eschatological events in which believers are participating in the present age. Thus, the blessing of Abraham and the gift of the Holy Spirit are connected as components of this great and comprehensive move of God. But they can be joined more closely than that. Fee argues that for Paul the gift of the Spirit is *a part of* the blessing of Abraham. That is, the blessing of Abraham is defined in terms of justification *and* the reception of the Holy Spirit. "The blessing of Abraham, therefore, is not simply 'justification by faith.' Rather, it refers to the eschatological life now available to Jew and Gentile alike, effected through the death of Christ, but realized through the dynamic ministry of the Spirit—and all of this by faith" (811).

The Pauline tradition follows the apostle in associating the elements of promise and the inclusion of the Gentiles with the Holy Spirit. In Eph 1:13 the author relates that, according to God's plan, the Ephesians who believed the gospel had been "marked with the seal of the promised Holy Spirit." By describing the Spirit in this way the author is linking the present experience of the Spirit with prophecies recorded in days past. He also associates present experience with future blessings when he refers to the Spirit as a seal and guarantee toward complete redemption (1:14). He makes these two kinds of connection in the context of addressing the Ephesians as Gentile Christians who came to believe the gospel after the Jews. He emphasizes the full inclusion of the Gentile believers into God's eschatological blessings by informing them that they had been sealed with the promised Holy Spirit. The statement assumes that it is the same Holy Spirit by whom the Jewish believers had also been filled. This point is confirmed by the shift in language from "you" to "we," as the author—pseudonymously writing as Paul, a Jew—adds that the Holy Spirit is "the pledge of *our* inheritance toward redemption." Thus, the writer to the Ephesians makes it plain that first, the same Holy Spirit has been given to all believers, and second, the blessing of redemption includes all who believe the gospel and accept the grace of God—whether Jew or Gentile. As Fee remarks, "This is eschatological language. The Spirit as the 'fulfilled promise' confirms that God's eschatological salvation has now come. Jew and Gentile alike have obtained the inheritance, which they also patiently await" (812).

In conclusion, we see two distinct promises running together in the thought of Paul and his school. First, God has promised that the Gentiles will be included in the eschatological plan of salvation. Second, the Gentiles will be recipients of the eschatological outpouring of the Holy Spirit. For Paul there could be no salvation that is not accompanied by the gift of the Spirit. He reaches the conclusion that within the scope of eschatological blessings there is, in the end, no difference between Jew and Gentile.

The Spirit and the Church

THE ESCHATOLOGICAL COMMUNITY

As Paul understands it, the church is characterized by both unity and diversity. His emphasis on unity reflects a primary quality of the church—people united in their faith in Christ, and in the eschatological salvation of God. Just as primary a quality is the diversity of unique individual people and the many ways in which the Holy Spirit manifests himself in the everyday function of the church. Typically Paul emphasizes the unity of the church when he is arguing that racial and social background is of no ultimate consequence in the body of Christ. On the other hand, he can just as easily emphasize the diversity of the members of the body when he wants to discuss the individual uniqueness and the wide variety of manifestations of the Spirit in the proper function of the church. In this section I will discuss the unity of the body of Christ, and in the next section the diversity of spiritual gifts.

C. K. Barrett sums up Paul's ecclesiology by defining the church as the body of Christ composed of justified, reconciled people who are living by the Holy Spirit (1953: 146). It makes no difference to Paul whether these people come from a Jewish or a Gentile background. He states, "For in the one Spirit we were all baptized into one body—Jews or Greeks, slaves or free—and we were all made to drink of one Spirit" (1 Cor 12:13). The source of unity in the entire twelfth chapter of 1 Corinthians is the Holy Spirit. It is the one Spirit who activates each kind of gift (v. 11). It is in the one Spirit that each Christian is baptized into the same body. Paul makes it clear that diversity in the church is good and even necessary, but such diversity does not overshadow the unity of the body. The unity of the body of Christ, when approached as it is in 1 Corinthians 12, is a matter of source. Even though the church appears to be a gathering of multifarious people ministering in diverse ways, their identity as God's people and their ongoing Christian practices issue from one origin—the Holy Spirit.

In contrast, the unity described in Ephesians 4 is unity of purpose. God gives gifts to the church so that, ultimately, "all of us come to the unity of the faith and the knowledge of the Son of God, to maturity, to the measure of the full stature of Christ" (4:13). Here spiritual maturity is defined in terms of unity in faith and knowledge of the Son of God. Furthermore, such unity is called "the unity of the Spirit" (4:3), indicating this kind of spiritual maturity is pneumatically driven. That is, the Holy Spirit guides the church toward the goal of unity. Unfortunately, the goal of unity in faith and knowledge of God—whatever that means in detail—does not appear to have been reached. In other words, there remains disunity in the church. This is a sign that humanity's liberation from forces that disintegrate human community is still in process. The church's eventual victory over these forces will come about through the direct agency of the Spirit, who is the greater force of unity.

The Holy Spirit can also be identified as the source of the fellowship that is a part of the proper function of the church. This idea is expressed in 2 Cor 13:13, where Paul desires that "the fellowship of the Holy Spirit" be with all the Corinthian believers. However, it is not entirely clear what Paul means by this phrase. Some have interpreted this phrase as an objective genitive—the fellowship that the Holy Spirit creates. On this view what Paul has in mind is a deeper participation on the part of the Corinthians in the fellowship of which the Spirit is the author. Others have interpreted the phrase as a subjective genitive—the fellowship given by the Holy Spirit. In this case Paul is seen to be encouraging unity which only the Spirit can provide. However, a choice between the two interpretations may not be necessary. Ralph Martin reminds us that "Paul may not have been as precise as we would wish him to be" (117). Martin then draws on Eduard Schweizer's argument that in the end the two interpretations merge once we have a sense that the "fellowship of the church" created by the Spirit (subjective genitive) comes about only through "the common share in the Holy Spirit" (objective genitive) in which all believers participate. Martin concludes, "So the exegetical dilemma is largely an unreal one, and Paul's thought may well encompass both grammatical constructions" (117).

How is it that people come to be a part of the one body of Christ? According to 1 Cor 12:13, it is through being baptized in the one Spirit. Interpreters disagree on whether in this verse Paul is teaching that we are initiated into the body of Christ by water-baptism which includes Spirit-baptism (George Beasley-Murray), or that it is by an act of the Holy Spirit antecedent to baptism (George Ladd). Answering this disagreement is not necessary for our present discussion. Furthermore, it is not clear which part of the process of initiation Paul associates with the reception of the Spirit. Dunn argues effectively that it happens during the overall conversion-initiation process—a process that includes the hearing of the gospel, the believing of the kerygma, baptism in water, and possibly other events. Believers receive the Spirit either during one of these events, or possibly through the entire process (Dunn: 1970a).

What is important for our immediate purposes is that entry into the membership of the church is an eschatological event, and that it necessarily includes the indwelling of the Holy Spirit. Both Beasley-Murray and Ladd highlight the eschatological dimension of the church and incorporation into it. Ladd writes, "The eschatological character of the church is seen in the fact that the church is created by the Holy Spirit. . . . It is the coming of the eschatological Spirit in history that created the church. The church is therefore the product of the powers of the Age to Come" (1993: 587). For Ladd, the Holy Spirit creates the church and is thus the primary ecclesiological idea.[1]

Beasley-Murray, interpreting 1 Cor 12:13, emphasizes that incorporation into the church is an eschatological event. For in the reception of the Spirit the believer participates in the outpouring of the Spirit which was foretold by Joel. Beasley-Murray restates the thought of the verse to be, "We were *immersed* in one Spirit . . . and were *saturated* in His outpouring" (170).

Beasley-Murray also stresses that incorporation into the body of Christ is not an individual affair, and that the necessary reception of the Spirit is not a private event. This is true for Paul even while the apostle lays a great deal of weight, especially in 1 Corinthians 12, on individual manifestations of the Spirit. "The believer is baptized 'to one Body'; not so as to *form* the Body but to *participate* in it, to be added to it. The Body exists before the believer is baptized; through grace he is incorporated into it by the Spirit" (170). Such an emphasis on the corporate rather than the

---

[1] Marie Isaacs turns this around and asserts that for Paul the existence of the church is evidence of the presence of the Holy Spirit. The presence of the Holy Spirit, in turn, is a sign of the imminent consummation of God's eschatological purposes. The consummation may lie in the future, but the Spirit's presence is the first fruits of that consummation (87). Thus, whether we start with the presence of the Spirit and argue for the existence of the church, or we start with the experience of belonging to the church and argue for the presence of the Spirit, the conclusion is the same: The church is the eschatological community formed by the presence of the Holy Spirit.

individual side of Spirit-endowment is in keeping with an eschatological outlook on the event of incorporation into the body. For the primary quality of eschatological events is corporate, or even, in many cases, universal. Any individual participation in such events is secondary and derivative.

As the community created by the Spirit, the church is an eschatological entity for Paul. It is the body of Christ, into which no one may be incorporated without the eschatological Spirit. The church's primary sense of identity comes from its association with Christ, and its primary functional basis is the presence of the eschatological Spirit. What this means—as we shall see next—is that the church is a charismatic fellowship.

The Spiritual Gifts

In Paul's writings the spiritual gifts are fundamentally a corporate reality. They represent the church in action. That is, *charismata* are manifestations of the Holy Spirit, operating within the community which he has created. Understood in this way, *charismata* are an *essential* and *systemic* element of the church *qua* church.

Paul assumes that the church is more than a mere social gathering. Indeed, it is the community drawn together, enlivened and empowered by the Holy Spirit. Therefore, in order for the church to be the church, it must be a community founded on the presence of the Spirit. Although each individual believer is indwelt by the Holy Spirit, the effect of that indwelling is an immediate sense of oneness with God and with other believers. In other words, the indwelling of the Spirit connects each believer to the Christian community. As the believer takes part in community life, the Spirit works through that individual to serve others and demonstrate divine love. This demonstration is an *essential* part of the life of the church. Without it the church is not the church.

Not only are the *charismata* essential to the church, they are also *systemic* within the organism that is the church. Every believer, regardless of his or her background, position, or level of maturity in the faith, is indwelt by the same Spirit. The Spirit will work through every believer in the way he chooses (1 Cor 12:11). Therefore, the functioning Christian body is thoroughly permeated by the Spirit operating through believers. And this is nothing other than the exercise of the spiritual gifts. For Paul the church is thoroughly and necessarily a charismatic community.

Let us define 'spiritual gifts' in more detail. Rudolf Bultmann and James Dunn each bring out an aspect of *charisma* that is particularly helpful. First, Bultmann strongly emphasizes that for Paul the idea of a *charisma* is that of an enablement by God to do something of which a person is not otherwise capable. It can refer to a specific enablement or to the overall enablement to live a godly life, but in either case the point is that the Spirit is enabling someone to live or act in a way which is not ordinarily possible (153–54). Bultmann emphasizes that *charismata* involve the extra-ordinary power of the Holy Spirit.

The issue is not *how* spectacular a charismatic event is, but rather *that* it is charismatic—that it is made possible by the Holy Spirit. There is no sign that Paul viewed certain gifts as more 'charismatic' than others. His list of gifts in Rom 12:6–8 contains a mixture of the miraculous (prophecy) and the apparently mundane (ministry, teaching, exhortation, giving, leading and compassion). Likewise, his message to the Corinthians—who were obsessed with the miraculous—stresses that the real issue in the exercise of *charismata* is not spectacle but edification and love. Therefore, even though some spiritual gifts may not appear to be anything special, insofar as all *charismata* are empowered by the Spirit of God and involve actions not ordinarily possible, they are all miraculous.

Dunn would agree with Bultmann that the exercise of *charismata* is completely dependent on divine empowerment. Strictly speaking, although charismatic events happen in and through human beings, they are divine acts (1975: 254). This means that *charisma* "is not to be confused with human talent and natural ability; nowhere does *charisma* have the sense of a human capacity heightened, developed or transformed" (255).

However, Dunn moves beyond Bultmann in an important respect—identifying the divine power in *charismata* as being of a certain species: grace. As Dunn understands it, the idea of *charisma* derives from the more fundamental idea of χάρις, or grace. Dunn describes *charisma* as "a particular manifestation of grace within the context of the community of faith" (207), as "a particular expression of *charis* . . ." (253), and as "the inevitable outworking of *charis*" (254).

At this point we may return to Bultmann and take note of his statement that "grace is God's eschatological deed" (1951, I: 289). Just as grace is not a divine state but rather a divine deed (Bultmann), so *charismata* as expressions of that grace are also divine deeds (Dunn). Inasmuch as grace is eschatological, the charismatic expressions of that grace are eschatological events. For they reveal in a concrete and visible way that God has accepted believers into his family and is actively caring for them through his Spirit operating in their brothers and sisters. God's redemptive triumph is at work in the Christian community in the form of Spirit-empowered ministry.

The type of charismatic community in which every member is a functioning Spirit-bearer is what Joel foretold when he envisioned the Spirit operating through sons, daughters, old men, young men, and even male and female slaves (Joel 2:28). Thus, spiritual gifts fit into the larger picture of the new age with its new covenant of grace and its community of justified people, unified in the Holy Spirit and in their common faith in Jesus Christ.

The presence of *charismata* operating through the members of the church indicates the unique relation between the permanent and the occasional which marks the outpouring of the eschatological Spirit. That is, Paul understands the Holy Spirit to be poured out on all believers, indwelling and permanently resting on each one. At the same time, the influence of the Spirit is not static or uniform. Although the Spirit *rests on* believers, he is not *at rest*. There are occasions when the Spirit specially empowers a believer for a specific task or situation.

Both notions—permanent indwelling and occasional empowerment—are consistent with an Old Testament understanding of the Spirit. The Spirit permanently rested on only a few representatives of Israel—mostly judges, prophets and kings. And the stories of people being overpowered by the Spirit at particular times are legendary. But very few people experienced the Spirit in both of these ways. The main difference—the eschatological difference—is that now every believer can experience the Spirit as both a permanent endowment and a source of power for particular occasions (*charisma*). In other words, it is not new for the Spirit to rest on, and act through, certain people, but it is new for these things to happen to and through *all* God's people.

The picture we get of the charismatic community from Paul's writings is one of mutual edification and love, in which Spirit-empowered, charitable deeds are regularly displayed in a virtually endless variety of forms. When Christians are exercising the power of new life by actively building up others they have a charismatic community. It does not seem to matter to Paul how much miraculous activity is going on in a particular church (although he appears to assume that it is going on in all Christian churches), as long as believers are loving each other with the kind of *agapē* that is possible only by the power of the Holy Spirit. For according to Paul's understanding of spiritual gifts, the operative feature is the power of the Spirit enabling one to love and serve others in ways which are otherwise not possible. Although the apostle apparently saw recurring patterns of Spirit-activity such as prophecy, teaching, healing, and the like, he was more interested in the end result of edification than in the particular forms in which the Spirit may choose to manifest himself. Thus, on one hand, the Spirit is unpredictable in that he may be seen in a wide variety of operations. On the other hand, the Spirit is very predictable in that he always works toward love, edification and the unity of the body of Christ.

THE SPIRIT AND THE COMMUNITY OF LOVE

The Christian church is both a pneumatic community and an eschatological community, and both of these characteristics—pneumatic and eschatological—are essential to Christian *agapē*. That is, the Christian community is a community of love *because* it is pneumatic and eschatological. As the eschatological community of God, the church has been endowed with the promised Holy Spirit. This is in fulfillment of prophetic promises, especially from Jeremiah, Ezekiel and Joel, that in the next age God would bestow his Spirit upon all his people. The result of this pneumatic endowment is that God's people would be empowered to obey his Law. Consistent with Jesus' teachings as reported in the Synoptic Gospels, Paul understands the Law to be epitomized in the love commandment (Rom 13:8–10). Thus, the result of pneumatic endowment is *agapē*. Summarizing, as the eschatological community the church is the pneumatic community, and as the pneumatic community the church is the community of *agapē*.

The importance of the indwelling Spirit for true *agapē* is illustrated in the great chapter on love, 1 Corinthians 13. It is significant that this chapter falls squarely within a prolonged discussion of the spiritual gifts in chapters 12 and 14. The message, which Paul makes quite clear, is that the presence of the Spirit can be recognized in the loving, mutual edification of believers. Christians are to pursue both love and the spiritual gifts (14:1), for the two are inseparable and intertwined. On one hand, love is the purpose behind all the gifts (12:4–10). On the other hand, love itself is a charisma—an expression of divine grace that is only possible by the empowerment of the Holy Spirit. Therefore, Christians cannot strive exclusively for the gifts nor exclusively for love, because striving for one implies striving for the other.

Let us take a closer look at the eschatological dimensions of Paul's views on Christian love. Victor Furnish points out that the importance of Paul's eschatological orientation for his ethic is exhibited well in Romans 12–13. The exhortations of these chapters (12:3—13:10) are framed by an introduction (12:1–2) and conclusion (13:11–14), both of which emphasize the eschatological existence of the recipients (1968: 216). Paul exhorts the Roman believers not to be conformed to this age but instead to be transformed by the renewal of their minds (12:2). This language implies first that there is another age besides "this age," and second that the transformation into the state of being that corresponds to the next age is already underway.

In the conclusion (13:11–14) to this section Paul uses the metaphorical theme of night and day to describe the turning of the ages. He writes, ". . . the night is far gone, and the day is near. Let us then lay aside the works of darkness and put on the armor of light; let us live honorably as in the day . . ." (13:12–13). The state of the current age is that it is neither night nor day. The old age "is far gone," and the next age "is near." To continue with Paul's metaphor, the present age is the dawn, during which the first streaks of sunlight illuminate the waking countryside. At this hour one can behave according to the passing darkness of night, or according to the coming light of day. In other words, the previous age is gone; the eschatological age is already here in its proleptic form. The new age has broken in, although we now experience only the dawn, meaning that the dynamics of the eschatological age are altering present life, even though they have not completely transformed it. Those who are following the call to live according to the day must naturally behave consistently with the inbreaking dynamics of the new age. This means putting aside various forms of selfishness and debauchery, and embarking on a life of loving others. This is the message of the passage that is framed by the eschatological language of 12:1–2 and 13:11–14.

When Paul talks about living "as in the day" while it is still dawn, he is not advocating moral improvements under the aegis of the old age. For Paul's ethical norm is not grounded in the potentiality of this age but in that of the age to come (Keck: 86). Such eschatological potentiality comes in the form of the gift of the Holy Spirit. The Spirit is "the power of the New Age, present in the midst of the old; it is the power for moral action in the domain of the new creation, of which it is the pledge" (87).

Neither can we interpret Paul's ethic to lay out a lifestyle designed for some interim before the future comes. Rather, his exhortations are rooted in the future as it is already manifesting itself in the present (Furnish: 216). The sunlight that changes night into dawn is the same sunlight that changes dawn into day. The difference between dawn and day is not distinct sources of light, but varying degrees of intensity of the same light. In other words, *agapē* is not a temporary calling fitted for the interlude between the last age and the next. Rather, it is a way of life that is possible now by the power of the eschatological Spirit, and will continue in the age to come. Many things will pass away, but love is not one of them (1 Cor 13:8–13).

The paradox of the already-but-not-yet ethical situation of believers is reflected in the Pauline position that Christian love is at the same time both spontaneous and deliberate. That is, Christian love follows from an inner impulse, but at the same time it is a stance toward others that requires the utmost intentionality and effort out of every believer.

It is the inner impulse to love others that constitutes the spontaneity of Christian charity. The prophet Jeremiah anticipated a state in which God's people would have the Law written on their hearts, and Ezekiel foresaw the gift of a heart of flesh replacing the heart of stone that had marked God's people for so long. Paul no doubt understands these changes to have taken place, and they are the result of the promised Spirit of God indwelling believers. When one becomes a Christian he experiences the leading of the Spirit to love other people (along with God and all of creation). Thus, his new desire to reach out in love comes from within, as he is transformed by the indwelling Holy Spirit.

At the same time, Paul's letters plainly show that Christians who are indwelt by the Spirit still need to receive teaching and exhortation on ethical matters. For as long as the present age lasts, followers of Christ must add willful obedience to the spontaneous leading of the Holy Spirit—a deliberate response to the Spirit that is often exceedingly difficult to accomplish. As Furnish explains, the goal of Paul's imperatives is to summon believers to "that kind of *deliberate response* to God's claim without which faith forfeits its distinctive character as obedience" (1968: 227). Furnish quotes Robert Tannehill: "The believer is not simply dragged along by the Spirit as if he had no choice. The believer is actively enlisted in the struggle. He is *exhorted* to not let sin reign in his body, and this exhortation is a serious matter, for by sinning the believer can fall back into the old slavery to sin" (227 n47).[2] Therefore, the Law is written on believers' hearts, and they do have a heart of flesh, for these changes have already occurred. At the same time, believers have not been completely transformed; they must still strive to live according to the impulses of the new life. The relationship between the indicative and the imperative in Paul's writings

---

[2] I have referred to Furnish to support my assertion that Christian love is both spontaneous and deliberate according to Paul. It should be noted that on p. 227, Furnish is explicitly making the point that Christian love is *not* spontaneous. His point, however, is that even though Christians live according to the new age, or "the day," they still stand in need of ethical teaching and exhortation (the combination of indicatives and imperatives). What Furnish means is that Christian love is not *completely* spontaneous, as Paul's exhortations indicate. I am in agreement with Furnish's point, although I prefer to say that even though Christian love is not completely spontaneous, it still retains an element of spontaneity because of the indwelling Spirit.

reflects the reality of the need for both types of communication to communities of Christian believers living in the tension between the already and the not yet.

The Spirit and the Individual Believer

The eschatological action of God is so vast that one is hard-pressed to take it all in. It is complex, involving many cooperating elements. It is comprehensive, involving God and the entire scope of creation. Each person who becomes a believer is swept up into the flow of eschatological events and the community-oriented pneumatic activities we saw in the previous section.

The work of the Spirit within the individual believer is marked by the eschatological tension we saw in the previous chapter. This tension takes on specific characteristics, depending on the specific issue at hand. In this section I will illustrate this with discussions of the Spirit's role in new life, in indwelling the believer, in turning the believer to live according to the Spirit, and in the resurrection of the believer.

The Spirit and New Life

The theme of dying and rising with Christ, so important in water-baptism, reflects the Pauline idea of the regeneration of the believer in new life. There are two distinct ways in which Paul can speak of life—as life in the physical sense and as the life belonging to God and Christ, which believers enjoy by God's grace. This latter type of life can be further divided into two separate but continuous segments—the divine life which believers can enjoy now through regeneration and the future life of the resurrection. The type of life in which we are interested in this section is the second—the regenerated state of Christian believers.[3] The questions at hand are what Paul means by the notion of being given new life in Christ in the present age, and what the Holy Spirit has to do with such life.

We must first understand that the divine life that accounts for both regeneration and resurrection is the same life flowing from the one divine source (cf. Rom 8:9–11). That is, resurrection life is a continuation of the new vitality of regeneration. Resurrection is a distinct event from regeneration, but the two ideas represent the divine life being instilled in believ-

---

[3] I use the term 'regeneration' as a label for the phenomenon of new life which believers enjoy in connection with adopting a stance of faith in Christ. I use the term out of convenience, while being aware that it is a term which is used in later theology but not in Paul's letters.

ing humanity in two different modes. Thus, the theme of life constitutes a strong element of continuity between the eschatological life that believers now experience and that which they will experience at the resurrection of the dead.

The continuity between the present regenerated life and the future resurrection life of the believer shows up in the link between these ideas and the two main sources of life for Paul: the resurrected Christ and the Holy Spirit. "Through his resurrection Christ, the Last Adam, has become the author of a new life for humankind (Rom 5:12ff.; 1 Cor 15:20ff.)" (Link: 481). Christ lives within believers (Gal 2:20; Phil 1:21), and they live the life of Christ (2 Cor 4:10) (481). Through his resurrection Christ has defeated death, and the present regenerated life of believers is an initial foretaste of that victory which they will also enjoy at the day of the Lord.[4]

The link between new life and the Spirit is strong in the letters of Paul. The new life in Christ which believers enjoy is mediated to them through the Holy Spirit. In Rom 8, Paul argues that the Mosaic Law did not lead to eternal life; but the "new law of the Spirit" does (v. 2). The Spirit is referred to as "the Spirit of life" . . . or, rather, "the Spirit of life in Christ Jesus," signifying that the life we have is life in Christ Jesus that comes about through the Spirit. Signifying the close connection between life in Christ and the Spirit, Paul can also state that the last Adam became a life-giving Spirit (1 Cor 15:45). Paul's language can oscillate between "Spirit of God," "Spirit of Christ," and "Christ" when referring to the indwelling of the life-giving Spirit (Rom 8:9–11).[5]

New life in Christ through the Spirit is a signature feature of the new age. In 2 Cor 3:6ff. Paul contrasts the ministry of the old covenant, which he describes as a "ministry of death" (v. 7) because it is oriented toward the written Law, with the ministry of the new covenant, which is a "ministry of the Spirit" (v. 8) providing the life to its recipients which the old covenant could not deliver.

Therefore, in the present age there are some human beings who have received the gift of new life in Christ as mediated through the Holy Spirit.

---

[4] The tension between present and future is made clear in Col 3:3–4: ". . . for you have died, and your life is hidden with Christ in God. When Christ who is your life is revealed, then you also will be revealed with him in glory."

[5] See Fee, 544ff. (esp. 548) for the interpretation that Paul's rhetoric drives the terminological variations in these verses, so that Paul is not making the claim that both Christ and the Spirit indwell the believer "side by side," but that Christ indwells the believer by the Spirit.

The next question would naturally be what the contours of this new life are, since death still has a hold on all human beings other than Christ. That is, if Christians still die and will continue to do so until the day of the resurrection, what does it mean for them to gain new life in Christ? Here Paul is speaking of new life in a metaphorical way, referring to the phenomenon of the qualities of the future age penetrating the present. In Romans 8, one of Paul's key discussions of life in the Spirit, the foremost quality displayed by believers who live according to the Spirit is that they consistently live according to the requirements of the Law. Life in the Spirit means fulfillment of the Law. It also includes many other phenomena that are discussed in other sections of this chapter—spiritual gifts, assurance, loving others, and so on.

Summarizing, the eschatological life of the new age is a blessing associated with the gift of the Holy Spirit. That is, new life comes through the Spirit. Paul uses the metaphor of "new life" because the presence of the Spirit introduces potentialities that the believer did not have before. Most importantly, the Spirit enables one to live a life of righteousness, fulfilling the requirements and intention of the written Law. Put a bit differently, the indwelling Spirit sets the believer in a right relationship with God and gives her the ability to behave in accord with that relationship. Ultimately, the believer's new life in the Spirit will be made complete at the resurrection of the dead, when she will enter into a fully pneumatic existence and the potentialities of righteousness will no longer be limited by the weakness of "the flesh."

The Indwelling of the Spirit

Vos asserts that "the specific character of Paul's doctrine of the Spirit lies in the universal and equable distribution over the entire circle of believers, and within the life of every believer over the entire range, subconscious and conscious, religious and ethical, of this life" (58). This is illustrated nicely in the notion of the indwelling of the Spirit. For in Rom 8:9–11 Paul can speak of the Spirit indwelling Christians both individually and corporately. His language toggles back and forth, even within the same verse (v. 9). This suggests that in his mind there may not have been a fundamental difference between one and the other. The infusion of the Spirit permeates all dimensions of Christian existence, both individual and corporate. Both the believer and the church community can exhibit the same evidences of Spirit-endowment: freedom from the ways of the flesh, union with Christ, and a new life of righteousness.

In Rom 8:9 Paul tells his readers that they are in the Spirit if the Spirit of God dwells in them. These twin expressions of believers being in the Spirit and having the Spirit within them give a sense of how pervasive the presence of the Spirit is in the Christian life. The expressions speak in general and comprehensive terms. There is no aspect of the Christian's life that is without the Holy Spirit's presence and influence. Being indwelt by the Spirit also means being taken up "in the Spirit"—having one's entire being and life subsumed in a "spiritual" existence. This is not an existence that flees the world, but rather one that lives in the world in a new way. Paul describes the person who lives thusly as a slave "in the new life of the Spirit" (Rom 7:6). Whereas the old life was determined by the flesh, the new life is determined by the Holy Spirit. The Spirit is the norm and guide for all of life. Paul's terms for this state are life "in the Spirit" (ἐν πνεύματι), "according to the Spirit" (κατα πνεύμα) and "led by the Spirit" (πνεύματι ἀγεσθε).

The Spirit's leadership does not come from without, for the Spirit resides within the believer. The will that chooses to submit to the Spirit has the Spirit's assistance. All the same, the Spirit is to rule the Christian with the same authority that the Mosaic Law ruled God's people under the old covenant (Rom 8:9). It is likely that behind Paul's teachings about being indwelt by the Spirit and living by the law of the Spirit are the words of Jeremiah that under the new covenant God's people would have the Law put in their minds and written upon their hearts (Jer 31:33).

Beker argues that it is important to Paul that the Spirit indwell the embodied believer for two main reasons. First is the solidarity of the Christian with an unredeemed world. Beker draws attention to Paul's use of the expression "the mortal body" to indicate the historical existence of the believer "between the times." The Christian is no longer "the body of sin," but he does not as yet have his "spiritual body." In this present interim existence, the mortal body is subject to death, decay and weakness, but the Spirit still operates within it. "'The mortal body' now functions as the principle of continuity between the discontinuity of the ages . . ." (1980: 289). "The mortal body" (or "the Spirit in the body") forms a bridge between "the body of sin" in the era of sin and "the spiritual body" in the era of God's glory.

As 'mortal bodies,' believers can neither indulge in premature perfection nor languish in despair. Rather, they are reminded of the need for the final redemption of the whole mortal 'body' of creation, and thus they groan in the Spirit along with the groaning of the creation for the glory to come. The 'body' metaphor has a cosmic-universal connotation: 'the redemption of our bodies' (Rom 8:23) is not an individualistic matter but involves the redemption of the total body of the created order (Rom 8:19–21) (289).

Second is the ethical seriousness of the Christian in the world. "The 'mortal body' suggests not only the solidarity of believers with creation—because they and the created order are still subject to 'death'—but also the ethical seriousness of life in the Spirit, because believers are called to challenge the power of death in the world" (289). They are to demonstrate the new life that is God's design for the future of the created order. This new life is life in the Spirit.

Finally, the present indwelling of the Spirit is linked to the future resurrection of the body. Vos observes that in Rom 8:11, Paul speaks of the indwelling of the Spirit in direct connection with the future resurrection of believers. Along with other interpreters, Vos recognizes that the apostle is using the Spirit as a guarantee that the future resurrection will really take place. But for Vos there is more to Paul's claims than this. Paul is referring to the pneumatic activities surrounding the indwelling of the Spirit as a *process of preparation* with a view toward the eventual resurrection (164). Thus, the indwelling of the Spirit not only guarantees the future resurrection of the believer, it also provides a way in which the total transformation included in resurrection can begin to touch all aspects of present human existence. It is the partial presence of the future redeemed life.

Spirit and Flesh

The believer who is indwelt by the Holy Spirit has a long road in front of her. Paul continually admonishes his readers to live consistently with their new status vis-à-vis God. Often such admonishment takes the form of exhortations to live according to "the Spirit" and not "the flesh." The categories of flesh and Spirit are distinctive Pauline concepts that serve as a foil for contrasting the old life and the new.

To begin this subject let us take note of the ways in which Paul talks about flesh and spirit. Sometimes Paul speaks of life according to or in the flesh as a reference to historical/biological existence.[6] Other times he means a life according to old sinful habits[7] (Beker, 1980: 218n). Neither is consistent with the meaning attached to the prepositions he uses. That is, he equates "life *in* the flesh" in Rom 8:8, 9 with "life *according* to the flesh" in Rom 8:12, both being antithetical to life in/according to the

[6] Cf. Rom 1:3; 4:1; 9:3, 5, 8; 1 Cor 10:18; 2 Cor 10:3; Gal 2:20; Phil 1:22, 24.

[7] Cf. Rom 7:5, 18; 8:3, 8, 9, 12; 2 Cor 1:17; 10:2, 3; 11:18.

Spirit (287). But in general, language about living "according to the flesh" denotes existence that is opposed to new life in the Spirit. Life according to the flesh is life that is lived solely on a human level, to the exclusion of everything related to God (Ladd, 1993: 525).

Like the indwelling of the Spirit, the notion of life "according to the Spirit" is shorthand for a vast array of ideas about the Christian life. Inasmuch as the believer is living consistently with the leading of the Spirit, she is living according to the Spirit. This can include any number of dimensions of Christian existence.

Drawing from three important texts—Gal 5:16–26; Rom 8:1–17; 1 Corinthians 2–3—some general aspects of the contrast between life according to the flesh and life according to the Spirit take shape. Galatians 5:16–26 contains Paul's famous list of the fruit of the Spirit. The thrust of these verses is the antithesis between life according to the flesh and life according to the Spirit. In v. 17 he presents a simplistic picture of human existence as a battlefield between the desires of the flesh and the opposing desires of the Spirit. Next he points out (v. 18) that if the Galatian believers are "led" by the Spirit, which he assumes they are, then they need not be dominated by the desires of the flesh; rather, "the Spirit takes the lead, overwhelms, and thus defeats evil" (Betz: 281).

The antithetical desires of the flesh and the Spirit manifest themselves in opposite attitudes and actions. Paul lists the "works of the flesh" as "fornication, impurity, licentiousness, idolatry, sorcery, strife, jealousy, anger, quarrels, dissentions, factions, envy, drunkenness, carousing, and things like these" (5:19–21). This, in turn, is followed by a list of the "fruit of the Spirit"—"love, joy, peace, patience, kindness, generosity, faithfulness, gentleness, and self-control" (5:22–23).

Verses 19–23 constitute a catalogue of vices and virtues, which were commonly used in discussions of morality in Paul's day. As such, Gal 5:19–23 is relatively unremarkable, especially since all the items except love were featured in Greek philosophy (281–82). What is significant for our purposes is the way in which the catalogue is framed—as illustrating the opposition between the ways of the flesh and the ways of the Spirit. Betz points out that the catalogue presented in Gal 5:19–23 describes "phenomena or manifestations of the powers of evil ('the works of the flesh') and of the Spirit ('the fruit of the Spirit')" (282). With regard to the fruit of the Spirit, these phenomena are not qualities of personal behavior which one can "elect, cultivate, and appropriate as part of his good character," as are virtues in Greek philosophy. Nor are they "good deeds" in the sense of Jewish ethics, where lawful behavior is based on a statutory code. Rather, they are "benefits" which are given together with the Spirit (286).

It is also noteworthy that the list of virtues, so to speak, is not called "the works of the Spirit" to balance "the works of the flesh" in v. 19. The change to "fruit" is deliberate, carrying two implications. One is that for Paul the virtues of the Christian life are manifestations or outgrowths of the Holy Spirit who has been given to believers. Betz writes, "In other words, when the Galatians received the Spirit, they were also given the foundation out of which the 'fruit' was supposed to grow" (286). Eduard Schweizer adds, "Works are the things we do, the things we achieve on our own, whereas fruit grows by itself" (85). The other implication is that the "fruit" of the Spirit, being singular unlike the plural "works" of the flesh, is conceived as a unity. This means that the Spirit will manifest himself in all these ways, not just a few.

Our second passage is Rom 8:1–17. Fee observes that in Rom 8:5–6 there are two sets of balanced clauses in an AB/AB pattern (518). "For those who live according to the flesh set their minds on the things of the flesh, but those who live according to the Spirit set their minds on the things of the Spirit. To set the mind on the flesh is death, but to set the mind on the Spirit is life and peace." Next Paul elaborates on what it means to set the mind on the things of the flesh. It means hostility to God, rebellion against his Law and the inability to please him (vv. 7–8). Later in the passage Paul reiterates that to live according to the flesh is to die (v. 13). Thus, the picture we gain of life according to the flesh from Rom 8 is that it entails an attitude of hostility to God and actions that constitute disobedience to the statutes of God. The unrighteousness of living according to the flesh results in a broken relationship with God and ultimate death.

Life according to the Spirit, on the other hand, results in life and peace (v. 6). It is the Spirit dwelling within that is the principle of eschatological life (v. 10). The same Spirit is the guarantee that God will raise believers just as he raised Christ (v. 11).

In vv. 14–17 the theme of adoption dominates the discussion. Here adoption is linked to following the Spirit—"For all who are led by the Spirit are children of God" (v. 14). In other words, living according to the Spirit implies adoption into God's family, which in turn implies sharing in both the suffering and future glorification of Christ (v. 17).

The association between Spirit and life is fairly simple, but the application of this truth is not. For living according to the Spirit is not automatic; it takes effort. Hence, Paul points out the obligation the Roman believers have to live not according to the flesh but according to the Spirit. For the eschatological life of the present age is conditional: ". . . if you live according to the flesh, you will die; but if by the Spirit you put to death the deeds of the body, you will live" (v. 13). In other words, living the new life is something the believer does, but it is only possible *by the Spirit.* The sharp contrast between flesh and Spirit in this passage is intended to show Paul's readers the seriousness of the choice they are making when they walk either the path of the flesh or of the Spirit. The exhortational undercurrent relating to this choice is what drives Paul to widen the gap between the two ways of life (cf. Dunn, 1988: 441–42).

This point brings us to our third passage, 1 Corinthians 2–3, in which Paul takes the Corinthians to task for thinking and acting as people of the flesh and not people who have in fact received the Holy Spirit. In these chapters Paul is concerned with divine wisdom and the Corinthian church. He is addressing a congregation that places a high value on wisdom, but he does not tell them what they want to hear. Instead of praising the Corinthians for possessing great wisdom, Paul exhorts them to willingly become what the world would consider fools so they can obtain real wisdom (3:18).[8] For Paul, following Isa 29:14, sets up his argument with a juxtaposition between two types of wisdom—the world's wisdom which God opposes and destroys, and God's wisdom as it appears in the message of the cross, which the world views as foolishness (Furnish, 1993: 65). Paul holds that his preaching does convey wisdom, but it is of the latter type.

Although the Corinthians desire to know the wisdom of God, Paul informs them that they obviously do not, for a prerequisite for the human acceptance of divine wisdom is divine help in the form of the Holy Spirit. The divine wisdom of the message of the cross is only accepted by those who also receive the enabling power of the Spirit. Even though the Corinthians have received the Spirit, their behavior is contrary to the ways of the Spirit. Their congregation is marred by divisions and quarreling—sure signs that to the extent that these problems exist the Corinthians are living according to the flesh and not according to the Spirit. Paul perceives that they are not living in harmony with the Spirit, and he addresses them

---

[8] The Spirit-given ability to understand divine wisdom which is the topic of 2:6—3:23 is distinct from the spiritual gift of the utterance of wisdom mentioned in 12:8 in that the former is a gift given to all Christians enabling them to understand the truth of the gospel message, whereas the latter is Spirit-inspired speech proceeding from certain individuals which brings God's wisdom to bear in particular situations.

not as spiritual people but as people of the flesh who are not able to accept the deep truths of the divine mysteries.

In this passage there appear to be two prerequisites to accepting divine truth. One is the receipt of the Spirit of God. The other is living according to the Spirit and not according to the flesh. Clearly the Corinthian believers had received the gift of the Spirit, for Paul declares that they are God's temple with the Spirit of God dwelling within them (3:16). However, because of their tendencies to fall into "fleshly" attitudes and activities, Paul is still forced to speak to them "as people of the flesh, as infants in Christ" (3:1), and not as mature followers of Christ. Thus, in order to understand divine truths one must not only receive the Spirit but also live in harmony with the leadings of the Spirit (3:18–19).

The problem with the Corinthian believers is not that they do not have the Spirit, for they plainly do. Instead, the problem is that they think and behave as if they did not. It is these patterns of "fleshly" thought and behavior that put Paul in the position of needing to address the Corinthians as though they were babes in Christ. To put the matter in other terms, it is the fact that the Corinthians are thinking and acting as if they were still "people of the flesh" that Paul addresses them as babes in Christ. In reality they are "people of the Spirit"—the actual temple of the Spirit (3:16)—but Paul cannot address them as such until they act consistently with their true nature.

Drawing conclusions from these three passages, the first impression we get is that living according to the Spirit is diametrically opposed to living according to the flesh. The former consists of righteous attitudes and behaviors, the latter unrighteous. The former leads to life and peace, the latter to death. The former is possible only with the assistance of the Holy Spirit, the latter is the default lifestyle of all fallen human beings.

Second, although the indwelling Holy Spirit is constantly leading Christians to live righteously, this is no guarantee that they will do so. In Rom 8:5–6, Paul juxtaposes life according to the flesh and life according to the Spirit as two radically different lifestyles. When speaking about those living according to the flesh he means those outside of Christ who are conducting a thoroughly unrighteous life. However, in v. 12 he says that believers have an obligation to live according to the Spirit, which implies that they have a choice about the matter. Furthermore, in 1 Corinthians 2–3 Paul addresses his readers as believers who have been behaving according to the flesh. The apostle knows that even though the eschatological Spirit has given believers the ability to overcome sin, they will not always live according to the Spirit. Unfortunately, they will all too often live contrary to the Spirit—or, in Paul's way of speaking, "according to the flesh." Although flesh and Spirit represent two contradictory impulses—opposing desires which can be cleanly separated and contrasted—in reality things tend to be "messy" in the tension-filled life of the already-but-not-yet.

The contrast between the flesh and the Spirit corresponds to the contrast between the non-eschatological and the eschatological in Paul's thought. The two states of being are radically opposed, yet they overlap in the present age. Fee writes, "The 'flesh' perceives things from the old age point of view, where value and significance lie in power, influence, wealth, and wisdom (cf. 1 Cor 1:26–31). But in Christ, all of that has passed away; behold, the new has come, the time of the Spirit, in which there has been a total, radical restructuring of value and significance" (821). In speaking of life according to the flesh, Paul is describing a kind of life that belongs to the old age that is passing away. On the other hand, life according to the Spirit is eschatological life, which is lived in submission to the leading of the Spirit. It is the life of the dawning divine kingdom, which God has inaugurated by sending Christ and the Holy Spirit (Rom 8:3–4). Life according to the Spirit is marked by love, joy, peace, and so on (Gal 5:22), but paradoxically—and reflecting the eschatological tension of the present age—these traits show up in the midst of suffering and affliction.

The expression "according to the Spirit" is for Paul a concise way of referring to eschatological life in all of its facets. It is his shorthand for the new lifestyle that replaces the old. The fact that he has labeled this new life as being "according to the Spirit" indicates the centrality that the presence of the Holy Spirit holds for his understanding of eschatological life.

The Spirit and the Resurrection-Life of the Believer

When Paul opposes walking according to the Spirit to walking according to the flesh, he understands the admixture of these two ways of life to exist only in the present age. We have been discussing the present age in terms of eschatological tension. That is, by sending his Son and his Spirit, God has inaugurated his eschatological plan for the redemption of his people. However, as the word "tension" indicates, the current age is characterized by a combination of both the liberation of the new age and the bondage of the old age. This coterminous state is expected to last until the return of Christ and the resurrection of the dead, when all of Christ's followers join him in his glorification. At the consummation all the enemies of Christ and of humanity will be finally destroyed.

Paul links resurrection of the dead to both Christ and the Holy Spirit. First, the general resurrection *of* the dead is the completion of Christ's resurrection *from* the dead. This means that the Christ-event is not the center of history, for the Christ-event points to an even greater event: the resurrection of all the dead and the final triumph of God over his last enemy, death. This is indicated by the fact that when Paul talks about Christ's resurrection he often does so in connection with the general resurrection. It is the general resurrection of the dead that gives full meaning to Christ's resurrection (Beker, 1990: 32).

Christians struggling in the ambiguities of the present look forward in hope to the time when they will join their Lord in glory. That state will be one in which the tension produced by the inconsistencies of the present will give way to a new existence of complete and unhindered devotion to the Father and the Son through the Spirit. Resurrection existence will truly be life "according to the Spirit."

When Paul talks about the resurrection-state in 1 Cor 15:35ff., he invokes the expression, the 'spiritual body'. The question is what he means by such a term. He contrasts the two types of human body—the physical (ψυχικόν) and the spiritual (πνευματικόν). Modern readers should take note that in using the word "spiritual" in this context, Paul does not intend to make a statement about the immateriality of the resurrection body as opposed to the materiality of the physical body. He means to take in much more than issues relating to bones, muscles and tissues. When Paul speaks of the body in this way he has in mind the entire human person, physical and metaphysical, so to speak. Thus, it is the entire human being who is dishonored and weak in his or her present existence, and it is the entire human being who will be glorified and powerful in the resurrection. What Paul is contrasting is two types of existence. Therefore, when he speaks of the reception of a spiritual body, he takes in the complete transformation of the person. Human existence in a "spiritual body" is perfected human existence and is nothing other than the state in which the Spirit and the believer are in complete harmony, which in turn results in the believer's absolute dedication to Christ. As Dunn asserts, Paul's antithesis between a mortal body and a spiritual body does not reflect a dualism between matter and spirit. Rather, it indicates that the eschatological tension which believers experience now will disappear at the resurrection of the dead, for the unrighteous dimensions of their existence will be finally and completely overcome (1988: 445).[9]

---

[9] Dunn discusses the relation between life in a mortal body and life according to the flesh.

Not only does Paul understand the Spirit to constitute the power of resurrection-existence, he also implies that the Spirit is the agent of the resurrection. The main text regarding this issue is Rom 8:11—"If the Spirit of him who raised Jesus from the dead dwells in you, he who raised Christ from the dead will give life to your mortal bodies also through his Spirit that dwells in you." Fee correctly points out that this verse does not directly assert that the Spirit is the agent of resurrection, either Christ's or ours. Rather, resurrection is expressed here and elsewhere by Paul as being God's activity. Thus, he concludes that "the Spirit is not the *agent* of our resurrection, but its *guarantor*" (808).

In making this claim, Fee takes up a minority position regarding the relation between the Spirit and resurrection. Whereas Fee attributes resurrection strictly to the Father, most New Testament scholars see Paul as implying the Spirit's agency in resurrection, even if not directly asserting it.[10] For instance, Dunn takes the position that in Rom 8:11 Paul is clearly teaching that it is God who raised Christ and will raise believers from the dead.[11] However, God does so through the Holy Spirit (cf. Paul's words that God "will give life to your mortal bodies also *through his Spirit* that dwells in you").[12] For Dunn, the key to the issue is a pattern Paul exhibits in other passages (1 Cor 15:45; 2 Cor 3:6; Rom 8:2) of attributing the life-giving work of God to the Spirit (1988: 432). Dunn does not mention the nearest reference, Rom 8:10, where Paul says that "the Spirit is life . . ." Thus, assuming that the Spirit is a source of life for Paul—or, more precisely, the agent through whom God gives life—the indirect link between the Spirit and resurrection in Rom 8:11 is strengthened to the point that Paul's cryptic words in that verse warrant the conclusion that the

---

He claims that ". . . for Paul human bodiliness forms an unbroken continuum, of which the person's physicality is an integral part ('mortal body'; 'dead body'). It is his weakness as a mere mortal, the appetites and desires of his animal nature, which provide sin with its leverage and domain ('body of sin'). It is precisely here, of course, that human 'bodiliness' merges into the more pejorative concept of 'fleshliness' ('in flesh'; 'according to flesh'); humankind not merely with its appetites and desires but in dependence on their fulfillment, not only mortal but corruptible . . ." (1988: 445).

[10]   It should be noted that the issue of whether God raises the dead through the Spirit is not one about which Paul was explicitly interested. It is an issue that has become important in the minds of later thinkers, and many of those have looked to Paul for insight into the matter.

[11]   Paul makes the same point in 1 Cor 6:14 ("And God raised the Lord and will also raise us by his power.") and 1 Cor 15:15 (". . . we testified of God that he raised Christ . . .").

[12]   1 Cor 6:14 brings up the question of whether the "power" through whom God raised the Lord can refer to the Holy Spirit.

Spirit is the immediate agent through whom God raises Christ and his followers. In this vein, Vos paraphrases Rom 8:11 as saying, "If the Spirit of God who raised Jesus dwells in you, then God will make the indwelling Spirit accomplish for you what He accomplished for Jesus in the latter's resurrection" (1952: 164).

In summary, there are two ways in which Paul relates the Spirit to resurrection. First, the Spirit is the immediate agent of the resurrection. Second, the Spirit is the element, or the atmosphere, in which the resurrection-life is lived (1952: 163). In these two ways the resurrection of the dead is a profoundly pneumatic event.[13]

The Spirit's Relation to the Father and the Son

The Spirit and the Father

For Paul, the Holy Spirit never acts on his own. All his action is conducted in concert with that of the Father and the Son.[14] Let us first discuss Paul's view of the relationship between the Spirit and the Father. Paul understands the Spirit as having been sent by God (Gal 4:4–6). In addition, several times Paul asserts that God "gives" us his Spirit (1 Thess 4:8; 2 Cor 1:22; 5:5; Gal 3:5; Rom 5:5). Fee attributes this understanding to Paul's Old Testament roots, in which God "fills with" the Spirit (Exod 31:3) and pours out his Spirit (Joel 2:28), and the Spirit is referred to as the "Spirit of God" (835). Complementing his origin—being sent by the Father—the Spirit's work is ultimately oriented toward the glorification of the Father. For reasons like these, Christiaan Beker argues that Paul's theology is fundamentally theocentric (1980: xiv). Likewise, noting the

---

[13] When discussing Paul's views on the resurrection, another issue presents itself: Who does Paul believe will be raised? Does the resurrection include only believers, or all human beings? Although I do not intend to pursue the complex issue of Paul's general position regarding the resurrection, it is worth pointing out that Vos stakes out a position on the matter on pneumatological grounds. He asks how the pneumatic experience of resurrection could fall within the sphere of the unbeliever. If the ones who are raised are those "of Christ" or "asleep in Christ," then how could this apply to the unbeliever? Finally, if unbelievers do not have the Spirit, then how could they be the recipients of that part of the Spirit's quickening power that is productive of the resurrection? And how could they be expected to live the type of pneumatic life that is to follow the transformation of resurrection (1952: 216)? Vos interprets Paul's remarks in various passages, chiefly 1 Corinthians 15, to mean that the resurrection is a fundamentally pneumatic event. On this basis he concludes that it is most likely that Paul thought of resurrection as only applying to believers (1952: chapter 6).

[14] This theme later becomes quite familiar in the thought of the Cappadocian fathers.

structure of Paul's understanding of the relationship between the Father and the Spirit, as well as the fact that Paul speaks of the "Spirit of God" more often than he speaks of the "Spirit of Christ," Fee claims that Paul thinks of the Spirit *primarily* in terms of the Spirit's relationship to God the Father (835). Beker and Fee stand in contrast to a great many scholars who see Paul's understanding of the Spirit to be essentially christocentric.

The Spirit and the Son

Turning to the relationship between the Spirit and the Son, we must begin by considering that in two well-known verses Paul appears to equate them. First, in 2 Cor 3:17 he writes, "Now the Lord is the Spirit, and where the Spirit of the Lord is there is freedom." This is a saying notorious for apparently presenting a confusion in Paul's mind between Christ and the Holy Spirit. However, what is at work here is a literary device by which Paul refers to an Old Testament text and adapts it for his own purposes (Fee: 311). Thus, in 2 Cor 3:16 when Paul writes that "when one turns to the Lord, the veil is removed," he is alluding to Exod 34:34 which describes Moses as removing his veil upon entering the tabernacle to converse with the Lord, but replacing the veil upon returning to proclaim God's instructions to the Israelites. Paul adapts this imagery and asserts that a veil lies over the minds of the Jews, but it is removed when they turn to the Lord, indicating that there is a barrier separating them from the Lord that is removed when they turn to him. Who is this Lord? In v. 17a Paul identifies the Lord to whom the Jews—and the Corinthians—turn as the Holy Spirit. Paul is not, as is often claimed, identifying Christ with the Spirit.[15] His use of the word κύριος in this case should not be taken as an automatic reference to Christ. Rather, as he is given to do, Paul is using a familiar term in a unique formulation and attaching a meaning to it that is completely driven by the context of the verse.[16] The argument surrounding 2 Cor 3:17 is concerned with a contrast between the old ministry of the Law and the new and far more glorious ministry of the Spirit. As Fee correctly observes, "This is, after all, a pneumatological passage, not a christological one" (311, n91). Thus, what Paul means by stating that "the Lord is the Spirit" is that the Lord to whom the Corinthians turned at their conver-

[15] In 312 n91, Fee cites two well-known cases in which this is done: I. Herrmann, *Kyrios und Pneuma*, "who bases his entire case on his misreading of this text," and N. Hamilton, *The Holy Spirit and Eschatology in Paul*: 4–8.

[16] The importance of context for determining the meaning of v. 17 is argued forcefully by Furnish, 1984: 235.

sion is the God of the new covenant whom they have met in and through the Spirit (Furnish, 1984: 236). In other words, rather than making an identification between Christ the Lord and the Spirit, Paul is making an identification between Yahweh, the God of the new covenant, and the Spirit. At the same time, in order to prevent an absolute identification of the Spirit with Yahweh, Paul turns around in v. 17b and uses the construction "the Spirit of the Lord" in order to make it plain that "the Spirit is, as always, the Spirit *of the Lord*" (Fee: 312).

Therefore, when the dust settles and the air clears, 2 Cor 3:17 does not offer any new information about the relationship between the Spirit and Christ. Indeed, the verse has little if anything to say about Christ at all.

The second verse that appears to speak interchangeably of Christ and the Spirit is 1 Cor 15:45, where Paul says that Christ became a "life-giving Spirit." The fact that elsewhere Paul knows of only one life-giving Spirit (Rom 8:2, 11; 2 Cor 3:6; 4:16; 5:5) immediately casts doubt on the hypothesis that here he is naming Christ as another life-giving Spirit. This hypothesis falls apart when, once again, the context of the verse in question leads to a quite different interpretation. In the passage including v. 45, Paul is showing the superiority of Christ, the second Adam, over the first Adam by making two sets of contrast between them. First, Adam is merely ψυχή, whereas Christ is πνεῦμα. The former corresponds to the type of "natural" body that Adam bequeathed to all human beings—one living but subject to death and decay. The latter corresponds to the resurrected, incorruptible, πνευματικόν body that Paul is taking great pains to explain in the fifteenth chapter of First Corinthians. Second, Adam is "living," but Christ is "life-giving." That is, whereas Adam was animated by having life breathed into him (Gen 2:7), Christ *gives* life by bestowing it on others. This attributes to Christ a life-giving function related to that attributed to God in Gen 2:7. Since 1 Corinthians 15 is concerned with the resurrection of the dead our first inclination is to wonder if Christ's life-giving function is as an agent of the resurrection of believers. However, it is pushing the text too hard to suppose that Paul assigns the work of resurrection to Christ himself. In fact, as I argued in the section on the Spirit and resurrection, Paul's language about resurrection indicates that he understands the raising of Christ and all the dead to be done by God acting through the Holy Spirit. Thus, a proper conclusion would seem to be the modest proposal argued by Fee that what Paul has in mind in 1 Cor 15:45 is that Christ's resurrection is the ground of the resurrection of other human beings (265). Paul argues throughout 1 Corinthians 15 that the resurrection of believers is tied directly to the resurrection of Christ, the first fruits of the resurrection.[17]

Whether Paul means any direct connection between Christ and the Holy Spirit cannot be confidently inferred from his description of Christ as a "life-giving spirit." He is simply not talking about the Holy Spirit in this verse. Nonetheless, a case could be made that the way in which Christ gives life to his followers is by bestowing the Holy Spirit on them, much as he does in John 20:22 when he breathes the Spirit on his disciples. In other words, believers receive new life from Christ, who graciously gives it through the Holy Spirit. In this way both Christ and the Spirit appear as "life-givers," or alternately, as joint "life-giver."

Summing up our analysis of 1 Cor 15:45 and 2 Cor 3:17, although both verses have been interpreted as positing a direct identification between the Spirit and Christ, neither verse is doing such a thing. When the context of these two verses is taken fully into account, it becomes apparent that in 2 Cor 3:17 what Paul means by ku,rioj is not Christ but the God of the new covenant, and that in 1 Cor 15:45 what Paul means by pneu/ma is not the Holy Spirit but the superiority of Christ over Adam. *In other words, whereas 2 Cor 3:17 is a pneumatological but not a christological statement, 1 Cor 15:45 is a christological but not a pneumatological statement.* Contrary to common opinion, neither verse tells us much about the relationship between Christ and the Spirit. Most importantly, neither verse supports the position that Paul identifies the Spirit and Christ so closely that he can speak about them interchangeably.

Of course, this is not to say that Paul does not posit an extremely close relationship between the Spirit and Christ. It is only to say that when theologians turn immediately to the phrases "the Lord is the Spirit" in 2 Cor 3:17 and "life-giving Spirit" in 1 Cor 15:45 for such information, they are barking up the wrong textual trees.[18] Still, the reference to the Spirit in 2 Cor 3:17b as the "Spirit of the Lord" does hint at an important element in Paul's conception of the work of the Holy Spirit.

---

[17] Paul makes a similar identification between the resurrection of Christ and that of believers in Rom 6:4–10 and 1 Cor 6:14.

[18] Cf. Hendrikus Berkhof, who in *The Doctrine of the Holy Spirit* immediately cites 1 Cor 15:45 at the beginning of his argument that for Paul the dominant motif in the relationship between Christ and the Spirit is that of Christ as sender of the Spirit (18). Later Berkhof claims that when Paul says that "the Lord is the Spirit" in 2 Cor 3:17a, he is speaking of the relationship between Christ and the Spirit because "the word 'Lord' in verses 17 and 18 always means Christ" (25). He then adds, "[Christ] himself is the Spirit" (25)—a comment which concisely expresses the backbone of his pneumatology.

Paul's construction "Spirit of Christ" indicates the extent to which he considers the work of one to be bound up with the work of the other. Fee writes, "The Spirit of God is also the Spirit of Christ (Gal 4:6; Rom 8:9; Phil 1:19), who carries on the work of Christ following his resurrection and subsequent assumption of the place of authority at God's right hand" (837). To have the Spirit is to have the mind of Christ (1 Cor 2:12) and to unite us with Christ as joint heirs of the blessings of God (Rom 8:14–17). Paul considers the Spirit to be the mode in which Christ is present to the church in the present age. This means that Christ cannot be experienced except through the Spirit. By the same token, the Spirit cannot be experienced apart from Christ (cf. Dunn, 1986: 703). James Dunn adds that Paul gives the more formless and impersonal power of the Old Testament a sharper definition and personality, for the Spirit has taken on the shape and character of Christ (703). In this way, to experience the Spirit is to experience Christ. In addition, Paul conceives of the Spirit as the agent of the transformation of believers into a state of holiness. However, holiness is defined in terms of the Son of God. Paul conceives of the existence of all believers to have a common yet specific teleology—transformation into the image of Christ (Rom 8:29; 2 Cor 3:18). This transformation will find its final expression when all believers join their Lord in resurrection and full harmony with the Spirit. On that day followers of Christ will also join him in glorifying the Father, and in turn sharing in the glory of God.

Conclusion

In this chapter we have seen that in all major issues regarding the work of the Spirit in the present age, Pauline pneumatology is eschatological pneumatology. Approaching things from a different angle, we may likewise observe that the Holy Spirit is a vitally important element in Paul's understanding of the flow of eschatological redemption. Just as Paul's claims about the Spirit typically carry eschatological overtones, his claims about the new age often involve the work of the Spirit. This quality of his pneumatology shows that the vast working of eschatological events is the context in which Paul reflects on the activity of the Holy Spirit and his relation to the Father and the Son.

Paul does not write about the Spirit's role in creation, in the life of Israel under the old covenant, or in the incarnation and ministry of Jesus. Rather, his concern is with ongoing events within his churches. Consistent with these immediate concerns, he often speaks in more general terms about God's action in the redemption of all his people. The latter subject has a vast scope indeed, reaching all the way to the eventual renewal of all of creation. Involved in this work are figures ranging from the most obscure member of the body of Christ to God himself. Not only is redemption a vast process involving participants from the least to the greatest, it also reaches from one end of history to the other, and beyond. Paul's focus is on the phenomena of the present age and those in the age to come, but the resurrection of the dead and the renewal of all things will amount to the completion of God's original act of creation. To anticipate an argument that will reappear late in this work, the difference in scope between Pauline pneumatology and later Protestant pneumatology is striking. The scope of Protestant institutional pneumatology tends to be limited to Christ's work in the church in the present age. In Protestant experiential pneumatology, the work of the Spirit is centered in the individual believer. Paul would lead us to place both of these emphases within a much greater context, thereby altering our perception of the Spirit's work in both the church and the individual.

The dynamics of this overall context give Pauline pneumatology its characteristic eschatological tension. For Paul, the new age has been inaugurated but not yet consummated. All aspects of the eschatological plan of redemption are stamped by this tension, and his pneumatological reflections are no exception. This is illustrated no better than in two of the metaphors we discussed in Chapter Two. The idea of first fruits indicates that the gift of the Spirit is a part of the eschatological harvest, but also that the rest of the harvest is yet to come. The language of down payment presents a picture of a partial sum given in advance of the full payment. The currency is the same, reflecting the continuity between dynamics of this age and the age to come. What is different is the amount, reflecting discontinuity.

Eschatological tension determines the character of Pauline pneumatology in all its main aspects, as we have seen in the loci treated in this chapter—the new covenant, the Law, the inclusion of the Gentiles, the eschatological community, the spiritual gifts, the community of love, new life in the Spirit, the indwelling of the Spirit, Spirit and flesh, and the resurrection-life.

In these aspects of Pauline pneumatology, the admixture of eschatological optimism with hard-nosed realism continually reappears. Paul's life was profoundly altered by his existential realization that the age of salvation had miraculously come in a form which he did not expect. When he entered the messianic community, his experiences were often painful. However, this did not drive him to water down his assessment of the magnitude of the changes that had taken place in the coming of Christ and the Holy Spirit. In the coming chapters as we turn to the pneumatology of Jürgen Moltmann, we will see some ways in which he follows Paul along these lines, and other ways in which he seems a little less certain of the eschatological standing of the present age. In general, in Moltmann's theology as well as Paul's, the Holy Spirit plays a crucial role in the turning of the ages, as well as the connection between this age and the age to come.

4

Main Themes in the Theology of Jürgen Moltmann

WE have seen that eschatological awareness profoundly marks Pauline theology. For him the Holy Spirit is the eschatological Spirit—the first fruits of complete redemption. Jürgen Moltmann shares these basic positions, although in a contemporary and modified form. In the next five chapters we will examine Moltmann's theological views with particular interest in the ways his eschatological sensibilities inform his concept of the person and work of the Holy Spirit. In order to set the stage for this inquiry, we will first take a brief look at the defining events of Moltmann's life and the development of his thought in the sequence of his major books.

Turning Points in the Life of Jürgen Moltmann

Jürgen Moltmann was born in Hamburg, Germany in 1926. He was raised in a family that placed a high value on learning. However, religion, in specific Christianity, was not prized so highly. Moltmann relates that the interests of his youth were not theology, but instead the study of physics and mathematics. He explains that Max Planck and Albert Einstein were the heroes of his youth (*HIC*: 13).

Moltmann would never reach his goal of teaching these subjects in the university, for the events of World War II turned his life in a completely different direction. When he was sixteen his school class was drafted to serve in the antiaircraft batteries in Hamburg. In July of 1943 the city was destroyed by incendiary bombs dropped by Allied forces as a part of 'Operation Gomorrah.' The city was consumed by fire. During the attack a friend standing next to him was torn away in an explosion, but Moltmann was left untouched. Although he had never pursued a relationship with God, the night of the bombing he cried out to the heavens, asking where God was and why he was alive and not dead like his friends. He discloses that he has been struggling with these questions ever since (Hall: 30). After that horrifying night in Hamburg he no longer found physics and mathematics as captivating. The Hamburg firestorm was the first main turning point in Moltmann's life.

In 1944 Moltmann was drafted into the German army as a reluctant soldier of the Third Reich. He was poorly trained but was sent to the front anyway. One night in February of 1945 he became confused in the darkness and stumbled into a trench of British infantry. He immediately surrendered and was taken prisoner. He spent the next three years in prisoner-of-war camps in Belgium, Scotland and England. His experiences in these camps became the second turning point of his young life. While there he found—or, as he says, was *found by*—God.

Moltmann did not experience a sudden conversion. Rather, he felt all his former mainstays dissolve and something new arises in their place. He describes it as the experience of the dark night of the soul. He was deeply drawn to the Psalms which gave him the words for his own suffering. "They opened my eyes to the God who is with those 'that are of a broken heart'" (*EG*: 8). He also established a special connection with the crucified Christ. Out of the experience of God's fellowship with him, a man who would otherwise have no hope in the world, there grew a new hope based completely on what God is able to do and has promised to do for humanity and all of creation. "It was those experiences that induced me to give up my dream of mathematics and physics, Einstein and Planck, and study theology. This made me the first 'black sheep' in my 'enlightened' Hamburg family" (9).

Out of these prison camp experiences came the backbone of Moltmann's characteristic dialectic between suffering and hope. His suffering reached beyond the personal agony of losing his freedom. He was also devastated by the realization of what had happened in the Nazi death camps. The knowledge of the genocide his country had inflicted on the Jews filled him with shame for his people. He felt the necessity to face up to it all, but the reading materials he had brought with him into war—the poems of Goethe and the works of Nietzsche—did not offer the help he needed. He saw other men collapse inwardly, giving up all hope and succumbing to illness and death because of it. He almost fell to these maladies himself. What prevented his own collapse was the rebirth to a new life. It represented much more than a return to his old life, for "the old" referred to Germany, the Fatherland which was Moltmann's home, but which collapsed from its own mistakes and had committed unpardonable sins in Auschwitz and the other death camps. Instead, he was driven to a life which brought hope for something that transcended Germany, science and existentialism. His new hope was reinforced by his suffering, in that the depth of his suffering called for a hope just as deep. And it was founded on the Christian gospel, which filled out the content of that hope.

Just as Moltmann's theology is marked by a dialectic of suffering and hope, it is also marked by an ecumenical inclusiveness. This also grows out of his experiences in the prison camps. In 1947 in an English camp Moltmann began theological studies with a group of Protestants, some of whom were learned enough to function as lecturers. He looks back on those months as a wonderful time of discovery and cooperation among Christians of all kinds.

Thus, there were fundamental experiences for Moltmann during his years as a youth and a young man. The Hamburg firestorm opened up the question of God for him, and in the camps he found his answer. The combination of suffering and hope took on the Christian form of God's presence in suffering and God as the power of hope (cf. Bauckham: 1). Also in the camps he experienced the fellowship of Christians from a multitude of traditions, as they searched together for the God who could address their personal and collective agonies. It was as a changed man that Moltmann was repatriated to Germany in April of 1948.

Upon returning to Germany, Moltmann began his formal theological training at Göttingen in 1948. He was getting a theological education, but he was not connected to any particular church. The Protestant state churches which had either kept silent or rejoiced with the Hitler regime did not appeal to him. He appreciated the clear Yes and No of the Confessing Church, so he joined the groups which succeeded the Confessing Church in the post-war period. Moltmann reports that these groups were very Barthian, wanting to find answers in Scripture and christology. There has been an ongoing conversation with Barth in Moltmann's theological development ever since.

In 1952 Moltmann finished his studies at Göttingen and took a position pastoring a church in the rural farming community of Bremen-Wasserhorst. He also married his wife Elizabeth Wendel that same year. When he completed his professorial thesis in 1957, he accepted a teaching post at the Kirchliche Hochschule in Wuppertal, which had been founded by the Confessing Church. However, he has spent the majority of his theological career at Tübingen, where he was professor of systematic theology from 1967 to 1994.

In his early years as a theologian, Moltmann was so awed by Barth's massive *Church Dogmatics* that he did not believe there was anything more to be said about theology. From Barth Moltmann took themes like the recovery of the significance of the Trinity for Christian theology, a focus on christology, the embrace of eschatology, and the authority of Scripture. Of course, Moltmann came to develop all these themes in his own distinctive way.

It was the work of Arnold Van Ruler which awakened Moltmann to new possibilities for theology. Van Ruler's writings led him to eschatology and to the possibility of dealing imaginatively with dogmatics (*EG*: 11). From Bonhoeffer and Ernst Wolf he developed a concern for social ethics and the church's involvement in society (Bauckham: 2). Hegel and Iwand contributed to Moltmann's dialectical understanding of the relationship between the cross and the resurrection. And from von Rad and Käsemann he gained a deep respect for biblical studies (2).

In 1960 Moltmann discovered Ernst Bloch's *Das Prinzip Hoffnung*, which he read on holiday in Switzerland. He was so captivated by Bloch's philosophy of hope that he "ceased to see the beauty of the mountains" (*HIC*: 15). Moltmann, who was exploring the idea of hope, wondered how it was that Christian theology had left this important theme behind. His *Theology of Hope* is his attempt to rediscover it with Bloch's help. It was Bloch who gave Moltmann the full ability to find his way beyond Barth. Lyle Dabney observes, "Moltmann took up Bloch's ontology of 'being which is not yet' to both escape from the dead end of Barth's vertical contradiction between time and eternity and to express the horizontal eschatological horizon of present and future" (Dabney, 1993: 93). At the same time, Moltmann was critical of Bloch for failing to see that the future becomes a possibility not because of human potentialities but because of the logic of the Christ-event. By emphasizing the theme of divine promise, Moltmann differentiates himself from both Barth and Bloch (94). Moltmann's *Theologie der Hoffnung* hit the theological scene in 1964 with such force that it catapulted Moltmann into international notoriety.

Moltmann also cites the influence of a handful of Jewish theologians with regard to his eschatology. All theologians had to deal with the global catastrophe that was the First World War. No longer was it possible to talk about the utopian goals of historical progress as the Hegelians had done. Instead, theologians turned to Kierkegaard and identified eschatology with the eternal moment which towered above history. Christian theologians like Barth, Althaus and Bultmann saw the eternal present as redemption in the midst of this unredeemed world. In contrast, Jewish theologians including Franz Rosenzweig, Gershom Scholem, Walter Benjamin, Jacob Taubes and Karl Löwith, see in the eternal moment the possibility for a different future than what is due to develop with the status quo. For them, God's messianic future can be glimpsed in the moment of hope (*CoG*: 45).

Another connection with the Jewish community came on the heels of the Second World War. After the end of the War when the truth emerged about Auschwitz, Bergen-Belsen and the other concentration camps, Moltmann suffered through a "dark night of the soul" as he dealt with the horror and the guilt of knowing what his country had done to the Jews. The theological positions developed in *The Crucified God* are in part an attempt to work his way through this morass. He sees this work as a "Christian theology after Auschwitz," mirroring "Jewish theology after Auschwitz." On the cross God enters into the godforsakenness of human existence. "Even Auschwitz is taken up into the grief of the Father, the surrender of the Son and the power of the Spirit" (*CG*: 278).

The Moltmannian Corpus

The writings of Jürgen Moltmann can be divided into three groups. The first group is his earliest publications from his dissertation in 1952 to the early 1960s. These are concerned primarily with the history of Reformed theology in Germany. The second group includes his works from the late 1950s to the late 1970s, including studies of Bonhoeffer, Barth and Bloch, and reaching a high point in his first three major books, *Theology of Hope*, *The Crucified God* and *The Church in the Power of the Spirit*. Each book of this well-known trio examines all of theology from one particular perspective. The third group consists of Moltmann's "contributions to systematic theology" (Dabney, 1993: 81–82). Whereas in his first three books Moltmann approached all of theology from a single viewpoint, in his subsequent books he is striving for the more modest goal of offering his insights for the advancement of the discussion in a particular field of theology. To illustrate the difference, *Theology of Hope* is Moltmann's attempt to see what happens when we consider eschatology to be the absolute core of Christian theology, so that eschatology sets the agenda for Christian theology. *The Coming of God*, on the other hand, is a more systematic treatment of the field of eschatology, taking into account many of the questions that have developed in the field throughout the tradition.

The First Three Books

Moltmann's first three major works are in a certain way extreme. They try to see all of theology from a particular vantage point—hope (*Theology of Hope*), suffering and the cross (*The Crucified God*), the Holy Spirit (*The*

Church in the Power of the Spirit). In these initial offerings, the goal for Moltmann was "the renewal of the church for men and women, society and our common life in the world" (*CPS*: xiii). Moltmann aimed at renewal, which required more radical steps. In his later systematic works, he was more concerned to make contributions to specific fields in systematic theology. This is a more circumscribed objective and does not call for one to attempt an outlook for all of theology.

THEOLOGY OF HOPE (THEOLOGIE DER HOFFNUNG, 1964)

In *Theology of Hope* two fundamental realizations of Moltmann take effect. One is that the Christian faith is essentially eschatological. The other is that Christian eschatology can be articulated in terms of hope for a promised future.

Moltmann observes that eschatology has traditionally been understood as "the doctrine of the last things," which includes the return of Christ in glory, the judgment of the world, the consummation of the kingdom of God, the resurrection of the dead and the new creation of all things. "But the relegating of these events to the 'last day' robbed them of their directive, uplifting and critical significance for all the days which are spent here, this side of the end, in history" (*TH*: 15). Thus, eschatology lost much of its relevance for the rest of systematic theology. It did not fulfill its potential of serving as a basis for mobilizing and revolutionizing within history. With the institutionalization and social hegemony that Christianity developed in Western history, eschatology did not need to be revolutionary, and so it was not. But in Moltmann's hands, Christianity and eschatology take on a different form. "From first to last, and not merely in the epilogue, Christianity is eschatology, is hope, forward looking and forward moving, and therefore also revolutionizing and transforming the present" (16). The rest of *Theology of Hope* is largely a fleshing out of this claim.

Moltmann was able to make such a powerful reorientation of theology using the conceptual tools which Bloch's work gave to him. Moltmann first read Bloch's *The Principle of Hope* with astonishment, for it articulated many of the very principles with which Moltmann was working, and it tied them together in a coherent, thematic treatment. Moltmann, already convinced that eschatology needed further development in systematic theology, was now able to approach the subject from the standpoint of hope. His first and lasting impression of Christian theology after reading Bloch was: "Why has Christian theology paid no attention to the subject of hope?" Catalyzed by Bloch's philosophy of hope, the *theology* of hope was born.

Although it was Bloch who opened up the territory of hope for Moltmann, the latter states that he had no intention of being a follower of, or playing heir to, the Marxist philosopher. Moltmann explains, "What I was thinking of was a parallel theological treatment of the philosophy of hope on the basis of the Christian faith's own presuppositions and perspectives" (*EG*: 11).

What Moltmann was also thinking of was a way to get beyond the existentialism of the post-World War II era. In *Theology of Hope* he criticized modern theology for reducing faith to internal self-identity glimpsed in the immediacy of the moment and reducing love to interaction between individuals beyond the political and economic conditions of society (Meeks in *EH*: xii). Rather than the eternal moment and the individual human being, Moltmann's new paradigm for theology was hope, which gave his theology a decidedly historical and social orientation.

Meeks points out that early on Moltmann understood the church to be called to an "ethic of hope," which Moltmann and others later came to call "political theology." "The sphere of new obedience for the Christian is politics, that is, the comprehensive situation of power relationships among human beings and between human beings and nature" (*EH*: xiii). The most notable practitioners of the ethic of hope were Christians in Third World countries who began espousing various liberation theologies. Moltmann attributes this reception of his work to the combination of eschatological redemption and historical liberation in a single perspective (*TH*: 11).

THE CRUCIFIED GOD (DER GEKREUZIGTE GOTT, 1972)

The social ferment of the 1960s took hold of Moltmann. Most of that decade represented for him a time of "movements of hope and experiences of rebirth and renewal" (*EG*: 12). Specifically, the movements that excited him included the opening of Vatican II which featured a new ecumenical theology, the humanist wave of European Marxism and the Christian-Marxist dialogues. Moltmann perceives that in 1968 many of these movements reached their zenith. In Prague under Alexander Dubcek there appeared "socialism with a human face"; in Rome Vatican II concluded; in Medillin the Latin American episcopal conference featured a strong theme of liberation of the people; in Upsalla the General Assembly of the World Council of Churches took as its motto "behold I make all things new"; in the USA the civil rights movement reached its peak; in Paris there were the May student revolts; and in West Germany there was a peace policy towards other states and a policy of internal reform (13).

However, 1968 also saw the beginning of the breakdown of these movements of hope. Warsaw pact troops marched into Czechoslovakia and "robbed socialism of its 'human face'"; John F. Kennedy and Martin Luther King were murdered; the Vietnam War was escalating; the student protest movement brought brutality on both sides; and a conservative evangelical movement was formed in opposition to the ecumenical activism that followed the council in Upsalla (13). Moltmann perceived that these reactions and disappointments did not signal the end of hope, but rather served to make hope wise. Hence, he set out to develop a political theology out of the theology of hope with the help of Johann-Baptist Metz. However, the dominant experience of that time for Moltmann was one of forsakenness and desolation, and this led him in the direction of working out a theology of the cross instead. *The Crucified God* was the result.

Like *Theology of Hope*, *The Crucified God* is an attempt to discuss Christian theology as a whole from a single viewpoint—in this case, the cross. Moltmann does this by making two fundamental claims. One is that the cross is the *foundation* for all of theology. That is, the Christian God is a suffering God. He has suffered for us, and he suffers with us. The second claim is that the cross is the *criterion* of all of theology. "It is the suffering of God in Christ, rejected and killed in the absence of God, which qualifies Christian faith as faith, and as something different from the projection of man's desire" (*CG*: 37). A Christianity which loses its identity in the cross becomes a chameleon religion, becoming indistinguishable from the surrounding culture.

Although *Theology of Hope* and *The Crucified God* share the same general methodology of approaching all of theology from one vantage point, they are very different works. The second book complements the first in several ways. First, *Theology of Hope* argues for a vision of history that is eschatologically open to a universal future. *The Crucified God* deepens this picture by giving the eschatological message of Christianity a more specific identity and criterion—the cross of Christ. Not only eschatology but all of theology must be marked by the cross, or it is not Christian theology.

Second, the two books complement each other just as resurrection complements the cross. *Theology of Hope* focuses on the resurrection of the crucified Christ, whereas *The Crucified God* focuses on the crucifixion of the risen Christ. Both are christological in character, but they highlight a different aspect of the dialectic of cross and resurrection. The resurrection gives us hope, and the cross gives our discipleship its particular form.

Third, there is a dialectic between past and future that reflects the relationship between the two books. *Theology of Hope* focuses on the promised future and our hope in God's faithfulness to bring that future about. *The Crucified God* highlights the past event of the suffering of Christ on the cross. It is because of what happened long ago that we have any hope for the future.

As well as these complementary and dialectical relationships that mark Moltmann's theological work, there is another characteristic feature that appears in *The Crucified God*. It is approaching a phenomenon by asking not only what it means for humanity, but also what it means for God. Thus, in his *theologia crucis* Moltmann follows the traditional query of what the cross means for the church, for theology and for discipleship. But he went on to ask what the cross means for the triune God. Answering this question led Moltmann to reject the philosophical axiom of divine *apatheia*.[1] A. J. Conyers aptly states that "a theology of the cross brings a completely indigestible element into the idea of an apathetic God" (110). If the cross is a trinitarian event, then God suffers deeply in the cross-event. The Father feels the pain of rejecting his Son, and the Son's agonizes in his godforsakenness.[2]

Moltmann sees such suffering not as a weakness in God, but as a strength. For if God is incapable of suffering in this way, then he is also

---

[1] Moltmann does not categorically reject the axiom of *apatheia*. Instead, he points out that Christian *apatheia* "only really says that God is not subjected to suffering in the same way as transient, created beings. . . . It does not exclude the deduction that in another respect God certainly can and does suffer. If God were incapable of suffering in every respect he would be incapable of love. . . . God does not suffer out of deficiency of being, like created beings. To this extent he is 'apathetic'. But he suffers from the love that is the superabundance and overflowing of his being. In so far he is 'pathetic'" (*TK*: 23).

[2] Although Moltmann speaks of a break in the relationship between the Father and the Son, it seems to be elastic not brittle. Even at its weakest point during the abandonment of the Son by the Father on the cross, the relationship remains intact. This is due to three factors. First, the Holy Spirit functioned as the bond of unity between the Father and the Son. Second, the trinitarian perichoresis could not be broken. Third, the Father and the Son had a unified will. The Father required the Son to suffer, and the Son willingly and intentionally obeyed. For these reasons, although Moltmann speaks of a separation between the Father and the Son on the cross, he does not hold to a complete severance of the relationship. The relationship between Father and Son must remain intact because even at Golgotha it continued to function in and through the Holy Spirit, because divine perichoresis is permanent and constitutively relational, and because their united will assumes a continuing relationship.

incapable of loving human beings in all their weaknesses, ambiguities and destructive behavior. Thus, for Moltmann, God is not to be worshipped because he is apathetic, but because his love is pathetic—characterized by pathos for his creatures.

THE CHURCH IN THE POWER OF THE SPIRIT
(KIRCHE IN DER KRAFT DES GEISTES, 1975)

Moltmann's aim in this, his third book, was to argue for church reform. "By reform I mean the transformation of the church from a religious institution that looks after people into a congregational or community church in the midst of the people, through the people and with the people. This means moving away from an impenetrable, large-scale organization to an accessible small-scale community" (*CPS*: xiii). In other words, reform means that the church takes on more of a congregational character than a monolithic, centralized one.[3] Concretely for members of the congregations, it also means breaking away from passive church membership to active participation in the life of the community.

In carrying out his call for ecclesiastical reform, Moltmann's theological foil was to see the church from the angle of pneumatology. His reasons for taking this tack are understandable. One is that he sees the Holy Spirit as the impetus for fellowship in the community and the breath of life which draws us into the struggle on behalf of life.

Another reason is his criticism of the Western theological tradition, which has tended to neglect pneumatology. "After the West committed itself to the *filioque* in the Nicene Creed by separating itself from the Eastern church in 1054, and after the persecution of the so-called Enthusiasts by both the Protestant and the Catholic churches at the time of the Reformation, the experience and theology of the Spirit of God ceased to play much of a part in our churches (xv)." Moltmann began to work toward the rectification of this shortcoming with *The Church in the Power of the Spirit*.

A third reason Moltmann took the angle of pneumatology is that he was well aware that, true to the tradition from which he comes, the Third Person of the Trinity was all but absent from his preceding theological positions. When he wrote *Theology of Hope* Moltmann was not particularly interested in the doctrine of the Trinity, much less the theology of the Holy Spirit. He claimed to have addressed the problem in *The Crucified God*, but the theology of that book is more binitarian than trinitarian. The

---

[3] He has in mind here especially the institutional church in Germany.

Father's role in the event of the cross is that he delivers Jesus up to death. The Son gives himself up voluntarily and suffers a godforsaken death on the cross. The Spirit's role is as follows: "What proceeds from this event between Father and Son is the Spirit which justifies the godless, fills the forsaken with love and even brings the dead alive . . ." (*CG*: 244). This remark reveals the extent to which Moltmann's account of the cross in *The Crucified God* is a description of an event of intense relational pain between the Father and the Son, without the Spirit really being a part of that dynamic. Rather than being a key figure in the event of the cross, the Spirit proceeds from the cross, meaning that he emerges from that event between the Father and the Son as the power through which other godforsaken people can obtain life and relationship with God. This shows the functional binitarianism of Moltmann's thought in *The Crucified God*. The irony is that Moltmann criticizes Barth's *theologia crucis* for failing to be sufficiently trinitarian (*CG*: 203), but then he commits the same error in a different form. For this reason, he saw *The Church in the Power of the Spirit* as a way to correct this shortcoming and round out his presentation of the Trinity.

Unfortunately, Moltmann did not succeed in presenting a strong offering in pneumatology with *The Church in the Power of the Spirit*. Although he claims that the main idea of the book is "the experience of the divine Spirit, the giver of life" (xiii), this work is far from an attempt to see all of theology from the vantage point of pneumatology. Rather, it is fundamentally a contribution to the field of ecclesiology with the relationships between the church and the Spirit coming only in the last third of the book. If Moltmann was attempting to see all of theology and in particular ecclesiology from the vantage point of the gift of the Spirit, he failed to carry it off. (Perhaps it is not ironic that Moltmann turned to contributions to systematic theology after this book.) Moltmann himself admits, "But in spite of keeping that unifying theme before me [the doctrine of the church and the sacraments in the perspective of the Holy Spirit], I did not succeed in gathering everything together into a single focus as wholly as I had in the two previous books, because this doctrine of the church had to cover too many different themes" (xiv). This is a revealing comment, because it sheds light on two points. First, *The Church in the Power of the Spirit* was never really meant to be an attempt to see all of theology from the vantage point of pneumatology, but rather an attempt to see ecclesiology from the standpoint of pneumatology. Second, the doctrine of the church entirely took over this project, so that if one reads *The Church in the Power of the Spirit* with the goal in mind of deepening one's understanding of pneumatology, there is not that much to glean from these pages. The end result of Moltmann's labors is a pneumatological work reminiscent of Barth's fourth volume of the *Church Dogmatics*, wherein he explicates the statement in the third article of the Creed— "I believe in the Holy Spirit . . ."—by engaging in a lengthy discussion of ecclesiology, not pneumatology.

Thus, Moltmann is to be commended for recognizing the Western tradition's weakness regarding the theology of the Holy Spirit, but his attempts to overcome the problem are not effective. What makes Moltmann special to students of pneumatology is that he did not quit here. He continued to turn more and more attention to the Third Article, until with *The Spirit of Life* in 1991 he succeeded in making a major contribution to the field.

The Church in the Power of the Spirit was the last book Moltmann attempted to write from one single viewpoint. One can see that the method was already beginning to fail him, so that he was wise to abandon it. Besides the methodological difficulty, there was another reason Moltmann made the transition to his "contributions to systematic theology." It was his changing relationship with liberation theologies.

In 1977 Moltmann attended a conference in Mexico City with liberationist, feminist and black theologians. There he came to the realization that he did not really belong to any of these groups, since he was not oppressed, not black and not a woman. He still worked to support these movements, but he now understood that he could not be a member of any of them. Upon coming to grips with this reality, Moltmann entered into a period of "self-critical disengagement" and began writing his contributions to systematic theology. These contributions no longer attempted to view all of theology from Moltmann's own standpoint. Rather, they self-consciously became parts of the whole which is the wider community of theological conversation. Thus, Moltmann's contributions to systematic theology are not dogmatic treatises; they are suggestions intended not to conclude conversations but to open them up (*TK*: vii).

Moltmann wants his contributions to systematic theology to be offerings in an ecumenical conversation. This involves recognizing one's own limitations of perspective and letting one's voice be one among many. He sets ecumenical thinking over against "particularist thinking," which is schismatic and satisfied merely to justify its own premises and conclusions with absolute claims. Ecumenism thinks not over against other viewpoints, but along with them in ongoing conversation (xiv).

"Contributions to Systematic Theology"

As he laid out his intended volumes in systematic theology, Moltmann originally planned to write five books—volumes on trinitarian theology, creation, christology, eschatology and theological method. There was a surprise entry into this series—Moltmann's book on pneumatology, *The Spirit of Life*—which was written after the volume on christology and before the volume on eschatology.

THE TRINITY AND THE KINGDOM (TRINITÄT UND REICH GOTTES, 1980)

The fundamental question in this book is: "What is the relation of the trinitarian history of God, the Father, the Son and the Spirit, which the New Testament relates, to God's sovereignty?" (*TK*: viii). Moltmann sees two main ways to answer this question. Barth and Rahner answered in favor of the sovereignty of the One God, and they were then only able to talk about the Trinity in terms that bordered on modalism. Moltmann answers in favor of the Trinity, specifically a social doctrine of the Trinity, "according to which God is a community of Father, Son and Spirit, whose unity is constituted by mutual indwelling and reciprocal interpenetration" (viii). The social model for the Trinity leads Moltmann away from the autocracy of a single ruler and toward the democratic community of free people, away from the lordship of the man over the woman and toward their equal mutuality, and away from an ecclesiastical hierarchy and toward a fellowship church (viii).

In this work Moltmann develops his version of the social doctrine of the Trinity, in which God is one who is "rich in relationships." Moltmann's trinitarian model is marked by *perichoresis* and fellowship among the three divine Persons. Furthermore, the social doctrine of the Trinity gives Moltmann a way to draw the christocentrism familiar from Protestant and dialectical theology into the wider trinitarian framework of the social doctrine of the Trinity. Western christology is complemented by "giving the appropriate independence both to the person and efficacy of the Father in the creation of being, and to the person and efficacy of the Spirit in the living energy of life" (*SL*: x).

GOD IN CREATION (GOTT IN DER SCHÖPFUNG, 1985)

The central idea of *God in Creation* is the construction of an ecological doctrine of creation. Moltmann was interested in taking up this project for three main reasons. First, criticism of his early eschatological work had pegged him as one who is hostile toward nature and the body. He wanted to show that this is not true. Second, if eschatology is the future that God has prepared for the whole world, then it is proper to develop an eschatology of nature. Thus, whereas *Theology of Hope* targeted the eschatological future of human beings, *God in Creation* integrates the eschatological future of humanity with that of nature. As Moltmann explains, this project means integrating the eschatological symbol of the kingdom of God with that of the new creation of all things (*GC*: xi).

Third, Moltmann was concerned to take back from science a defining concept of nature. Whereas science conceives of nature as a godless object of exploration, theology conceives of nature as created by God and infused with divine presence. Such an understanding of nature calls for reverence for life instead of technical exploitation of it (xi).

Thus, the picture of nature coming out of *God in Creation* is of a world created by God and sustained by him—a world indwelt by God (this is a pneumatological theme for Moltmann)—and a world groaning in anticipation of the new creation of all things.

THE WAY OF JESUS CHRIST (DER WEG JESU CHRISTI, 1989)

The subtitle of this book is "Christology in Messianic Dimensions." Moltmann wants all his theology to be messianic, for messianic expectation is the basic matrix within which Jewish hope has always developed. Christianity, as an explicitly messianic religion, grows out of Jewish messianic hope. By stressing the messianic character of theology, Moltmann intends to maintain "the enduring link with Judaism, which nothing can ever destroy . . ." (*WJC*: xiii).

The messianic dimensions of christology also carry a strong theme of hope and future. Moltmann reveals that he toyed with several other titles for this book: "Christ—The Hope of the World"; "Christ—The Coming One"; "Christ on the Way"; and "Christ in Becoming." These titles reflect Moltmann's interest in defining christology in dynamic terms, stressing the "forward movement of God's history with the world," rather than in static terms, stressing the two natures of Christ. He believes that a dynamic christology is of more value today for people who need to know that Christ will be an advocate in the midst of their conflicts, than a static christology would be (xiii). The title "The Way of Jesus Christ" puts emphasis on Moltmann's "christology of the way (*christologia viae*), which points beyond itself and draws people towards the future of Christ, so that they remain on Christ's path, and move forward along that path" (xiv).

SPIRIT OF LIFE (DER GEIST DES LEBENS, 1991)

Moltmann explains that there are both objective grounds and external reasons for the particular development of pneumatological views set forth in *The Spirit of Life*. The objective grounds are to be found in the logic of trinitarian thinking—specifically, Moltmann's social doctrine of the Trinity, in which the Spirit is understood to have a certain level of "relative independence" in activating "the living energies of life" (*SL*: x). His starting point in this regard is that "the efficacy of Christ is not without the efficacy of the Spirit, which is its goal; but that the efficacy of the Spirit is nevertheless distinguishable from the efficacy of Christ, and is not congruent with that or absorbed by it" (xi). The efficacy of the Spirit is universal and "ministers to life and resists its destruction" (xi).

The external occasion for this book is to be found in "the experience of affirmed and loved life." This is far from being a universal experience, since human beings continually inflict harm on nature and on each other. Under such conditions it is easy to become conditioned to accept violence and death. Standing in the face of violence and death is the affirmation of life, both one's own and that of others. On the social level this means taking a stand against violence and injustice. Moltmann asserts that it is in the affirmation of life that we experience the Holy Spirit (xii).

Thus, *The Spirit of Life* develops a pneumatology that is holistic. It certainly includes phenomena that Christians consider to be "holy," such as justification and sanctification, but it integrates these phenomena into the larger picture of liberated, affirmed and celebrated life. Whereas 'on the way' is a central metaphor for Moltmann's christology, it is the notion of 'life' which carries the weight in his pneumatology.

One will recall that one of Barth's last comments before his death was to lament that he had not adequately integrated the doctrine of the Holy Spirit into his theology. Moltmann is one student of Barth who has taken up this call for a new pneumatological paradigm (Wood: 50). This paradigm can be characterized as trinitarian, historical (in the sense of linking the Spirit's work from creation all the way through to consummation), and holistic.

The Spirit of Life is Moltmann's main contribution to the field of pneumatology. Using 'life' as its controlling metaphor, its contributions chiefly regard the relationship between the Holy Spirit and creation, and between the Holy Spirit and individual believers. That is, the Spirit's work involves giving life to all creatures and eventually renewing all of creation. As for followers of Christ, the Spirit gives them not only life but "new life," which opens up new possibilities for them in terms of personal growth and in terms of the strength to affirm the life of other people and creatures around them.

THE COMING OF GOD (DAS KOMMEN GOTTES, 1995)

The Coming of God is Moltmann's most recent book in his series of "contributions to systematic theology." It is a thorough treatment of Christian eschatology. Moltmann organizes eschatology in four concentric circles. First is personal eschatology, which deals with death, immortality and resurrection. Second is historical eschatology, which includes millenarianism and the kingdom of God. Third is cosmic eschatology, examining the future of creation and the end of time and space. Last is eternal or divine eschatology, which is the ultimate state of the glorification of God. Moltmann observes that in traditional medieval, Protestant and modern eschatologies—ever since Augustine—there is such concentration on the individual human soul that the salvation of the body, of human society and of the cosmos were all pushed aside. He concludes, "But if the Christian hope is reduced to the salvation of the soul in a heaven beyond death, it loses its power to renew life and change the world, and its flame is quenched . . ." (*CoG*: xv). Indeed, it would not be surprising to discover that when eschatology has been reduced to the hope of the human soul it also has become largely irrelevant to the rest of theology.

Moltmann expresses that the eschatology in *The Coming of God* is entirely in line with that of *Theology of Hope*, written thirty years prior. In this later book Moltmann explores the concrete content of hope in the four different horizons just mentioned. In 1965 Moltmann was trying to establish that "Christianity is wholly and entirely eschatology, not just an appendix" (Barth); in 1995 he was concerned with the content of that forward-looking vista (xii).

For Moltmann, Christian eschatology is not about the end of things; it is about beginnings—more specifically, "the new beginning in the end" (*HIC*: 20). The resurrection of Christ marked the beginning of the resurrection of the dead and the new creation of all things. By the same token, the new creation of all things will be the beginning of the eternal glorification of God. Thus, for Christianity the end is the beginning. For this reason Moltmann did not choose to entitle this book "The Last Things" or "The End of All Things," but rather *The Coming of God*, for the notion of the coming of God points to the hope of Christianity that God is coming to make all things new (*CoG*: xi).

FORTHCOMING: THEOLOGICAL METHOD

The final "contribution to systematic theology" is expected to be a work on theological method. This will be welcome material for students of Moltmann, for so far he has had little to say about the method by which he believes theology should be done. Still, there are some hints one could glean from his works to date, which I will cover in the next section.

Distinctive Aspects of Moltmann's Theology

Having traced the development of Moltmann's theology through a brief description of his major works, we will next take a more thematic look at the distinctive features of his thought. The remainder of this chapter will deal with seven areas in which he has developed significant and characteristic ideas. The topics of eschatology and pneumatology will not appear in this list, as they are the focus of the next four chapters.

Theological Method

"A TREMENDOUS ADVENTURE"

Moltmann's theological method is marked by three distinctive features. One is that for Moltmann theology is a great quest. He writes, "Right down to the present day, theology has continued to be for me a tremendous adventure, a journey of discovery into a, for me, unknown country, a voyage without the certainty of a return, a path into the unknown with many surprises and not without disappointment. If I have a theological virtue at all, then it is one that has never hitherto been recognized as such: curiosity" (*CoG*: xiii–xiv). Thus, when Moltmann does theology it is a journey of exploration and experimentation, not a defense of ecclesiastical dogmas. "So I write without any built-in safeguards, recklessly as some people think. . . . Some people think that I say too much theologically, and more about God than we can know. I feel profoundly humble in the face of the mystery that we cannot know, so I say everything I think I know" (xiv). That is, method takes a back seat to creativity for Moltmann. One gets the impression that he would rather be criticized for being too bold and missing the mark than for being too timid and not contributing to the advance of ideas.

AN ECUMENICAL APPROACH

Another feature of Moltmann's theological method is that he believes theology should always be done in an environment of ecumenical discussion and cooperation. Theology for Moltmann is intensely *dialogical* and openly *public*. He stresses that he is not out to provide definitive answers and close down conversations, but rather to put forth suggestions and open conversations. This open and inclusive attitude is reflected in many of Moltmann's theological proposals, like his universalist doctrine of redemption, his emphasis on the openness of God for relationship, and his passion for fellowship which reaches out to all types of people.

The openness of Moltmann's theology reflects his experiences in the war camps and his years of enthusiastic participation in ecumenical dialogue (evangelical Christians, Marxists, Jews, Catholics, Eastern Orthodox and liberation theologians). Conyers remarks that Moltmann has never founded a school of followers, but he draws dialogue partners to himself "as a magnet draws iron filings" (xi).

Moltmann has always operated with a global concept of the gospel, accepting the input of all fellow believers. One could suspect that this openness translates into a Christianity that will accept all views equally, but this is not so of Moltmann. He insists on a strong sense of Christian identity that is christologically shaped. The church is to be defined by hope in Christ's resurrection and judged by its willingness to follow Christ in suffering. Hope is the mark of the church (*Theology of Hope*), and the cross is the criterion of its thought and action (*The Crucified God*).

RELEVANCE AND IDENTITY

A third feature of Moltmann's approach to theology is that he sets a twofold criterion for successful theology. It must be relevant to society, and it must also maintain a strong Christian identity. Failing to meet both of these requirements has resulted in a twofold crisis in theology. Some theologies are in a crisis of relevance, wherein the church slips out of contact with the problems of the present day. These typically conservative theologies operate by the maxim, "Change yourself and then your circumstances will change." Unfortunately, says Moltmann, circumstances do not oblige. Discrimination and other such problems are institutionalized in society to the extent that individual people have little impact on them (*CG*: 23). Generalizing a great deal, Moltmann states that those who take such an individualized approach often join the evangelical movement. Evangelicals have tended to be strong on personal, interior transformation but weak on social involvement (*EH*: 5).

Theologies of a more liberal stripe—Moltmann identifies existentialist theology, hermeneutical, ontological, cultural, social, indigenous, political, the theologies of secularization, of revolution, and of liberation (*CG*: 10)—tend to slip into a crisis of identity, wherein the church strives to be relevant but often loses its self-identity as a *Christian* church. The approach of these theologies is typically, "Change the circumstances and people will change with them." Unfortunately, people do not oblige. Marital breakdowns, drug abuse, suicide and other such problems continue on unabated (*CG*: 23). Those who commit this error usually have a political identity that is stronger than their Christian identity (*EH*: 5).

Moltmann calls these "chameleon theologies." "But Christian theology should not adapt itself in order to hide; it is required rather to reveal what is specifically its own in the changing times. Christian theology should rather be an 'anti-chameleon theology,' and that means displaying colors which contrast with its environment" (3).

Moltmann calls the twofold crisis in theology that is represented by the problems of conservative and liberal churches "the identity-involvement dilemma." It is not a modern problem, for it can be traced back to the very beginnings of Christian theology (1). The solution is a "mediating theology" that combines relevance with identity. Such a theology will advocate the change of both individuals and social structures at the same time.

Moltmann finds the source of both identity and relevance in the person of Christ. The cross separates Christianity from modern ideologies of power as well as from other religions. "And Christian theology finds its relevance in the *kingdom of the crucified one* in that it suffers with those who bear 'the sufferings of this present time' (Rom 8:18), and makes the cry of the oppressed its own cry, and fills it with hope of liberation and redemption" (4).

Thus, in the end there is no "identity-involvement dilemma" for Christianity, because identity with the crucified and risen Christ is a distinctive identity that non-Christians do not share, but it is also an identity that brings Christians into solidarity with the poor, the miserable and the oppressed (4). For Moltmann, being disciples of Jesus Christ means that the church will by nature have a strong identity that does not dissolve into the surrounding culture, and also be involved in altering the culture to bring it more in line with the will of God. The key is identification with Christ. It is this identification that separates socially involved "anti-chameleon" Christianity from socially involved "chameleon" Christianity. However, Moltmann assumes that identification with Christ will always mean solidarity with the poor. It is possible that such assumptions can lead to "chameleon" theologies, for the criterion for Christian social action becomes a particular political agenda, rather than Christ, who transcends all political agendas. Ironically, it appears that Moltmann occasionally falls into this very trap.

SCRIPTURE AND EXPERIENCE

The balancing act that Moltmann describes in terms of relevance and identity is reflected in his use of Scripture and experience as authorities for theology. He is committed to the preservation of a distinctive identity for the Christian church, and consistent with this concern, he holds Scripture in high regard. He clearly believes that God has revealed truth to humanity in and through Scripture. It is only on the basis of a doctrine of revelation that Moltmann could make the claims he does about the world's eschatological future.

At the same time, much of Moltmann's theological agenda is defined by his own experience. For instance, his interest in ecumenical dialogue is no doubt deeply connected to his experience of ecumenical fellowship in the prisoner-of-war camps. Furthermore, he also draws on experiences that are important to other people in today's world. His passion for liberation on behalf of the poor, women and other oppressed groups is driven primarily by experiences that they have, but that he cannot share, no matter how much he empathizes with them. Moltmann continues to champion the cause of the oppressed out of an effort to make the Christian gospel relevant to his society. The effort to be relevant leads one straight to experience, for it is only by understanding what interests and concerns people have that the church can effectively speak to them.

Maintaining a balance between identity and relevance causes Moltmann's use of Scripture and experience as sources and authorities for the Christian faith to be somewhat complex and easily misinterpreted. Moltmann's readers alternately view him as an old-fashioned liberal who begins theology from experience, or as an "the evangelicals' ally"[4] who relies on a high view of Scripture to address current issues. In reality, Moltmann is not so much either of these, as he is a little bit of both. His method varies somewhat with the issue at hand, and this lends a certain element of instability to his development of positions. What is fairly consistent is that he begins with the scriptural witness regarding the issue at hand. He relies on Scripture to lay out the territory and the basic parameters of the subject. Within these parameters, he then exercises a great deal of freedom in rendering an interpretation of Scripture that draws on the texts but then

---

[4] Cf. Roger Olson, "Is Moltmann the Evangelicals' Ally?" 32. Olson's article assumes that many evangelicals view Moltmann as sympathetic to their general cause.

often ends up conforming to a theological, moral or political agenda.[5] Sometimes his conclusions are consistent with a historical-critical exegesis of the relevant biblical texts. However, at other times he strays into conclusions that are defined more by theological speculation and/or political and social rhetoric than by the scriptural witness.

Therefore, Moltmann does not quite stand within the evangelical community, nor completely within the community of Protestant liberalism, although he shares concerns with both camps. Is he confused or is he creative? It is up to the reader to decide. One can appreciate Moltmann because of his power as a visionary, while not necessarily hailing him as a consistently rigorous thinker. This way, one can glean from his writings a fresh view of theological issues, all the while being aware that there are occasionally difficulties in the details. For some readers, however, the inconsistencies in his thought are too great to bear, and they reject it. The danger for these critics is that they fail to learn from Moltmann, whose mind is nothing if not fertile. Moltmann is aware of these criticisms, and of the dangers of his particular method, but he considers it worth the risk if he can participate in the "tremendous adventure" of theology.

Trinitarian Theology

While Scripture is a key authority for Moltmann, he also relies heavily on tradition. Along with the Eastern tradition, Moltmann believes trinitarian theology to be the crown of Christian theology (*SL*: xi). Therefore, he places great emphasis on maintaining a strong trinitarian identity in all of his theology.

According to Moltmann, there are three main models for trinitarian thinking in the Western church. One is that of God as Supreme Substance. This is the approach taken in most natural theology. Natural theology consistently stumbles over the problem of getting from the unity of God to the Christian doctrine of the Trinity, and it is deficient for this reason.

The second main model is of God as Absolute Subject. This conception grows out of the modern assumption that the human subject is the center of reality. The point of reference for knowing all reality is the human subject. It was with Fichte and Hegel that Western thought went from the absolute human subject to God as the absolute divine subject.

Like the model of God as Supreme Substance, the model of God as Absolute Subject tends to produce trinitarian theologies that tend toward

[5] Along these lines, I will have more specific comments on the role of experience in his formulation of pneumatological positions in chapter 7.

modalism. The two models share the same general starting point: a philosophical notion of divine unity as it has been developed in the West since Augustine (*TK*: 18). Thus, when Barth uses the model of God as Absolute Subject, he ends up taking the position that Father, Son and Holy Spirit are three divine modes of being. Moltmann rejects such an approach for constituting a thinly veiled modalistic monarchianism.[6]

The approach Moltmann advocates takes a different starting point from Western philosophy. He believes that the best way to construct a trinitarian theology that remains faithful to the biblical witness is to begin with the history of Jesus the Son as it is conveyed in Scripture. Thus, it is from christology and the biblical account that Moltmann develops his doctrine of the Trinity. More specifically, he states that he begins with the history of the Son and shows that this is also the history of the Trinity. He perceives that this is the way the New Testament presents its incipient trinitarian leanings. "The history of Christ is already related in trinitarian terms in the New Testament itself. . . . *The New Testament talks about God by proclaiming in narrative the relationships of the Father, the Son and the Spirit, which are relationships of fellowship and are open to the world*" (64). What this approach means is that Moltmann begins not from the monotheistic notion of the one God, but from the relationships described in Scripture between Father, Son and Spirit.

Although Moltmann most often builds trinitarian positions from the foundation of christology, this is not his only method. In *History and the Triune God* he explains that "the Christian doctrine of the Trinity proceeds from the concrete and particular history of the Father, Son and Spirit attested in the Bible and leads to the universal revelation of its unity and Godhead" (*HTG*: 82).[7]

---

[6] It is important to note that Moltmann does not completely reject the ideas of God as Absolute Substance or as Absolute Subject. He writes, "We go a step further when we say that the unity of the triune God does not *just* (*nicht nur*) consist in the one, homogeneous, divine substance nor *just* (*nicht nur*) in the identical divine subject but *above all* (*vor allem*) in the unique fellowship, communion, of the three persons" (*HTG*: 59; italics mine). That is, the best approach to the doctrine of the Trinity comes through a social model, but this does not mean completely rejecting the other two models. At the same time, Moltmann does not hold back criticism of Barth and Rahner for teaching that the one God exists in three different modes of being, since this leads to the loss of concrete agents in salvation history. For instance, the passion story does not portray one mode of being crying out to another mode of being. Thus, the Father is not a divine Fatherhood, and the Son is not a divine Sonship. "What distinguishes the Father from a Fatherhood is the same as what distinguishes a concrete being from a mode of being" (85).

[7] Moltmann illustrates this principle with these remarks about the history of the Spirit and the Son: "So those who begin from this salvation history begin not only from the his-

Whether he proceeds from the history of the Son or the history of all three divine Persons, the point is that Moltmann rejects proceeding from one-ness to three-ness in favor of proceeding from three-ness to one-ness. The biblical witness calls for this latter strategy (82). Although such an approach can tend toward tritheism, Moltmann considers it worth the risk if it means working with a trinitarian paradigm that first retains faithfulness to Scripture, and second delivers a model that emphasizes relationality and mutuality.

"Social Trinity"

Moltmann's trinitarian model is his well-known doctrine of the "social Trinity." The idea of a social Trinity relies heavily on John of Damascus' notion of *perichoresis*. "The doctrine of the perichoresis links together in a brilliant way the threeness and the unity, without reducing the threeness to the unity, or dissolving the unity in the threeness" (*TK*: 175). In *perichoresis*, the unity of the divine Persons is formed by the circulation of the divine life that they fulfill in their relations to each other. The perichoretic unity of the Trinity is defined in terms of love.

In the idea of *perichoresis* Moltmann finds a solution to all of the main problems in trinitarian theology. First, it prevents trinitarian theology from beginning from a concept of the unified divine Substance. Neither can the perichoretic Trinity be conceived in terms of one divine Subject, for the character of the trinitarian life consists much more of fellowship and community among the three Persons. Second, *perichoresis* also prevents subordination, which is a problem in many formulations of pneumatology. The circulation of the divine life assumes three equal members who "live and are manifested in one another and through one another" (176). Finally, *perichoresis* prevents trinitarian constructions from leaning toward either tritheism or modalism, for it creates a balanced picture of the one God consisting of three interrelated, mutually indwelling Persons (*HTG*: 86).[8]

Moltmann takes this approach because he defines the concept of person by relationship. 'Person' has no meaning apart from interrelation with

---

tory of Christ but also from the history of the Spirit which is bound up with the history of Christ. They perceive the eschatological horizon of this salvation history which is denoted by the symbol 'Kingdom of God' and which consists in the glorification of the Father" (*HTG*: 83).

[8] The divine *perichoresis* is not merely a symmetrical network of divine relations, for each Person of the Trinity is unique and indwells the others in a personal way. The three persons of the Trinity are unique, not only in their relations to one another—as the tradition has always held—but also in their respective personalities (*HTG*: 88).

other persons. Thus, the unity of God begins with the oneness of relationship within the social Trinity. The source of the unity of the Godhead is not primarily a matter of substance or subjecthood, but of communion between the three persons.

He also believes that the best way to give a satisfactory account of the Christ-event is with a social model for the Trinity in which there are distinctions among the three divine persons requiring deep and mutually giving relationships. However, there was another element that Moltmann needed besides an account of the cross in order to have all that is necessary to construct a social doctrine of the Trinity. It was an activity of the Spirit in which he stands as subject over against the Son and the Father. This activity was the Spirit's work of glorifying the Son and the Father. This work makes it clear that all three divine persons are subjects in relation to each other.

Finally, Moltmann utilizes the idea of the social Trinity as a model with which he can make claims about human social relationships. Moltmann understands the Scriptures to be a witness to the mutual interdependent and self-giving relationships among the three divine Persons. But beyond this, the Trinity is portrayed in Scripture as being open and inviting, not only within itself, but also beyond itself. This is reflected in Jesus' prayer: "That they may all be one, as you, Father, are in me and I in you, that they may also be one is us" (John 17:21) (60). It is such an atmosphere of open and mutually self-giving relationship that becomes for Moltmann the quintessential model for all relationships, especially those in the sphere of human communities. He makes this move despite the fact that in the Trinity we find a much deeper communion than the word "community" can possibly convey (LaCugna: 757). For Moltmann, the goal of all human relationship is this divine model of *perichoresis*, and whether or not we will ever reach the goal, he wants to use the divine life to show us the beauty of interdependence, mutuality, openness and love.

Theology Proper

Between the primordial Trinity before time and the eschatological glorifying and unifying of God with all things lies the history of God's dealings with the world. "By opening himself for this history and entering into it in his seeking love through the sending of Christ and the Spirit, God also experiences this history of the world in its breadth and depth" (*CPS*: 62). Thus, it is necessary to dispense with traditional philosophical axioms about the nature of God. For instance, God can change, inasmuch as he is free to open himself to the changeable history of his creation. God is capable of suffering, inasmuch as he is free to suffer over the contradiction of humanity and the self-destruction of his creation. God is vulnerable, inasmuch as he can open himself up to the pain of the cross. And God is not perfect, "if this means that he did not in the craving of his love want his creation to be necessary to his perfection" (62).

The idea of creation is inherent in the idea of God from the outset, because creation is "a fruit of God's longing for 'his Other' and for that Other's free response to divine love" (*TK:* 106). Creation flows from the very essence of God as a God of outreaching love (106). Thus, it is essential to God's nature that he create and love his creation. Nevertheless, this does not mean that God has no freedom in the matter, for he is not being constrained by any other being. Just as it is axiomatic for God to love, it is axiomatic for God to love freely (107).

The picture Moltmann wants to paint is of a God who intentionally and out of love opens himself to experience the ups and downs of his creation. Because he is open in this way, God undergoes internal changes in and through his interaction with creation. For instance, through his love for the Son who experiences the sin of the world, God experiences something new: pain. Through the Son's death on the cross, God experiences abandonment in the form of this death and this rejection. "We must add that this is a new experience for God, for which he has laid himself open and prepared himself from eternity in his seeking love" (62–63).

The same applies to God's involvement in the history of the Spirit. "God does not desire glory without his glorification through man and creation in the Spirit. . . . God does not desire to be united with himself without the uniting of all things with him" (63). In the uniting of God and all things with God at the consummation, God experiences salvation. In sum, the history of the Son and the Spirit brings about for God "an experience, something 'new'" (62). This claim must follow from Moltmann's axioms that God is immanent in creation and is essentially a relational being. Therefore, if God is truly immanent in creation and truly open to relationship with it, then in the process of his interaction with creatures he must be affected and in some ways changed by what they go through and what he goes through with them. This includes not only the joy of creation's glorification, but also the pain of creation's suffering.

Christology

AN ESCHATOLOGICAL CHRISTOLOGY

According to Moltmann, there are two main ways in which God enters into the life of humanity. One is the *shekinah* presence of God in the Holy Spirit (discussed later). The other is the incarnation of the Son. "In the incarnation of the Son the triune God enters into the limited, finite situation. Not only does he enter into this state of being man; he accepts and adopts it himself, making it part of his own, eternal life . . ." (*TK*: 118). This deep interaction with the world is something that is internal to God's nature. Moltmann goes so far as to claim that even if there was not the necessity constituted by sin, the Son would have become incarnate anyway. Moltmann considers the incarnation to be a function of God's self-giving love over and above the necessity of dealing with sin.

There have been two popular approaches to christology. In the early centuries of church history Jesus was understood to be the incarnation of the one, eternal, original, true and immutable divine Being. This understanding of the Second Person of the Trinity represents a constriction of the broader teaching of the New Testament. Lost in the process were Old Testament promises regarding the Messiah, the earthly ministry and proclamation of Jesus, and the parousia of the exalted Christ. "The christology of the ancient church is vertical, not horizontal: it focuses on the eternity of God, not on the history of the future of God's kingdom" (*WJC*: 69–70).

In contrast, the modern approach to christology has been anthropological, taking as its subject the life and historical personality of the man Jesus. Whereas the ancient church focused on Christ as the divine human being, modern anthropological christology focuses on the God-consciousness of the man Jesus. The boundaries of this type of christology are also too narrow as compared to that of the New Testament. "Although its subject is the historical Jesus, no particular importance is ascribed to the Old Testament's history of promise; for as the perfect and true human being, Jesus could not well have been merely 'a Jew'" (70). In addition, in modern christology the existence of Jesus typically ends at his death, and the raising of Christ from the dead is reinterpreted in figurative terms. But in this case, Christ's death can have no special salvific meaning. The result is that many of the central themes of christology evaporate (70).

Moltmann describes his own approach to christology as "christology in the eschatological history of God." By "eschatological" Moltmann means "the coming redemption of the world, which is to be found in the universal messianic kingdom of peace, and in the perfecting of creation to be the kingdom of glory" (70). By "eschatological history" he means "the history which is aligned towards this future through God's calling and election, his promise and his covenant, and which is experienced and effected in the context of that future" (70). Eschatological history is "history under the promise of life," which is set in opposition to the history of death. It is God's history with Jesus, and Jesus' history with God, which amounts to the trinitarian history of God's dealings with the world (71).

The resurrection of Christ demands the development of an eschatological christology. The resurrection has set in motion an eschatologically determined process of history, the goal of which is the annihilation of death and the victory of resurrection-life and righteousness in which God receives in all things his due and the creature thereby finds its salvation (163). Thus, Paul's words in 1 Corinthians 15 do not reflect a relapse into an outmoded apocalyptic mythology; rather, they reflect the type of process Moltmann has described here.

THE DIALECTIC OF CROSS AND RESURRECTION

The resurrection of Christ is a key to the construction of an eschatological christology, but resurrection is only one side of a dialectic that is fundamental to Moltmann's christology: the dialectic of cross and resurrection. Moltmann is adamant that the dialectic of these two events must be retained. Otherwise the resurrection can be subsumed under the cross so that it must derive all its meaning from the cross; or alternatively the cross can be subsumed under the resurrection as a kind of preliminary (*TH*: 200). For Moltmann, both events draw meaning from each other, but they also have a meaning of their own. This means that christology must have both sides: crucifixion and resurrection, suffering and glorification. Christology suffers unless both dimensions are present.[9]

Creation

Moltmann lays out a three-stage concept of divine creation. First is God's original act of creation, which for Moltmann is creation *ex nihilo* with an orientation toward the eschatological future when God will take up creation as his dwelling place. The beginning implies the end.

---

[9] In the same way, theology of the cross is the reverse side of theology of hope. Theology of the cross concentrates on *the crucifixion of the risen Christ*, whereas theology of hope concentrates on *the resurrection of the crucified Christ*.

Second is ongoing creation. This continuous process flows out of original creation and points forward to the new creation of all things. Along this vein, Moltmann claims that it is possible to see in the preservation and evolution of species, symbols for the future of creation in its completion and perfection. On the other hand, the adaptation of species typically takes place in order to preserve a species from extinction by protecting it from predators or by developing new killing skills for itself. This would hardly be a foreshadowing of the new creation.[10] For this reason, it is best to resist linking evolutionary processes with the ongoing movement of God in creation.

The third stage is the new creation of all things, and it is necessary because of the ambiguity in evolution and the world's present processes. God is driving creation toward a goal, but it is not the goal of higher evolution. Rather, it is the goal of the eschatological new creation of all things. Because it is eschatological and redemptive, the new creation of all things is not a movement that flows out of the past. Rather, it is a movement that runs counter to the past. Redemption is something that evolution could never achieve (WJC: 303).

A TRINITARIAN DOCTRINE OF CREATION.

Moltmann's complaint with traditional theology is that it has too often paid attention only to the first aspect of this trinitarian process, placing God the Father over against creation in a monotheistic way. Others have attempted to construct christocentric doctrines of creation. Moltmann hopes to do two things in relation to the tradition. One is to explain creation in trinitarian terms, over against monotheistic formulations. Moltmann's understanding is that God the Father creates heaven and earth through the Son in the Spirit. Christ mediates creation, and the Holy Spirit represents God's presence in creation.

His other objective is to highlight the relation between the Spirit and creation, thereby filling in the third aspect of the trinitarian creation process. Moltmann emphasizes the presence of God in nature, and he understands this presence in terms of the Holy Spirit. That is, "the Creator,

---

[10] Moltmann acknowledges the ambiguity of evolution when criticizing Teilhard de Chardin's link between Christ and evolution: "But in his firm faith in progress Teilhard does seem to have overlooked the ambiguity of evolution itself, and therefore to have paid no attention to evolution's victims. Evolution always means *selection*. . . . In this way higher and increasingly complex life systems, which can react to changed environments, undoubtedly develop. But in the same process millions of living things fall by the wayside and disappear into evolution's rubbish bin" (WJC: 294).

through his Spirit, *dwells in* his creation as a whole, and in every individual created being, by virtue of his Spirit holding them together and keeping them in life" (*GC*: xiv). "The experience of the Spirit is the experience of the *shekinah*, the indwelling of God . . ." (96). Therefore, what is true of the *shekinah* presence of God in his people Israel is also true of the *shekinah* presence of God in creation: God enters into the struggles, the victories and the sufferings of his entire creation by virtue of his presence in it (97).

AN ECOLOGICAL DOCTRINE OF CREATION

Moltmann regularly brings up ecological matters when talking about creation. He is deeply concerned with the ecological crisis of our time. Human beings are destroying fragile ecosystems and wiping species off the face of the earth. In addition, the specter of nuclear weapons threatens all life on the planet.[11] The current ecological crisis is not due merely to the technological exploitation of nature, nor to the sciences themselves. Rather it is due to fundamental human striving for power and domination. In this case it is the quest for power and domination over nature, with science and technology providing the means and tools with which to accomplish these goals. Christians are not guiltless in this regard, for the scriptural command to "take dominion" over the earth (Gen 1:28) has often been interpreted in terms of conquering and dominating nature (21).

Coupled with the human quest for power and domination is the habit of viewing God's creation as *nature*, from which God is distant and unrelated. Moltmann argues that many problems in the relation between humanity and the world can be resolved by changing our view of it from nature to *God's creation*. To view creation as nature is to approach it with the desire to dominate it. To view nature as creation is to approach it with the desire to participate in it (32).

Hand in hand with viewing the world as God's creation is appreciating the immanence of God in his creation. Despite the fact that the Christian tradition has usually stressed the transcendence of God over creation and his distance from it, Moltmann holds that God is both transcen-

---

[11] Moltmann's doomsday rhetoric must be tempered by his other claims that God would never allow the world to be destroyed. "How should the Creator-out-of-nothing be diverted from his intention and his love through any devastations in what he has created? Anyone who expects 'the end of the world,' is denying the world's Creator, whatever may prompt his apocalyptic anxiety. Faith in God the Creator cannot be reconciled with the apocalyptic expectation of a total *annihilatio mundi*" (*GC*: 93). Rather than expect the end of the world, Christians are called to expect the eschatological transformation of the world. "The expectation of 'the end of the world' is a vulgar error" (93).

dent beyond the world and immanent in it. He picks up the lost theme of divine immanence and develops it pneumatologically. The Holy Spirit is God immanent in creation to such an extent that Moltmann claims that God dwells within it. God creates the world, thereby being distinguished from it, but he also enters into the world by his indwelling Spirit (*GC*: 15). If we can learn to appreciate the presence of God in the world, it should lead to increased sensitivity toward creation.

A SABBATH DOCTRINE OF CREATION

In the Christian tradition creation is usually thought of as being six days of divine work. The seventh day is typically neglected. Moltmann focuses special attention on the sabbath, holding that the sabbath was not a day of rest following six days of work. Rather, "the whole work of creation was performed *for the sake of the sabbath*. The sabbath is 'the feast of creation,' as Franz Rosenzweig says" (277). This sabbath feast marks the completion or consummation of creation. It is the final cause for the making of creation (277–8). Creation in the beginning points forward to ongoing creation, and they both point forward to the new creation of all things, during which God will fulfill the purpose of creation and dwell within it. A sabbath doctrine of creation means that creation looks forward to that time when God is at rest and creation is at rest within him.

Ecclesiology

Richard Bauckham observes that Moltmann alternatively describes his ecclesiology as 'relational ecclesiology' or as 'messianic ecclesiology.' The two terms highlight complementary aspects of Moltmann's ecclesiology.

MESSIANIC ECCLESIOLOGY

"'Messianic ecclesiology' is shorthand for 'a christologically founded and eschatologically directed doctrine of the church' (*CPS*: 13), or, more precisely, for an ecclesiology rooted in Moltmann's eschatological Christology" (122–23). That is, the church is founded upon Christ, but Christ points beyond himself to the reconciliation of the entire cosmos to God. Christology is inherently eschatological. Similarly, the church as the community founded upon Christ is the anticipation of the coming kingdom of God.

The eschatological character of the church deepens Moltmann's ecclesiology. He assumes that the church will have to combine Christian identity and social relevance in order to be successful. Beyond this, the church must also understand itself within the context of God's history in the world. That means the church must understand itself in three dimensions: before God, before people and before the future. "For the church is an open church. It is open for God, open for men and open for the future of both God and men" (2).

The church's specific place in the history of God's dealings with the world is between the remembrance of Christ's history and the hope of his kingdom. "Its remembrance of Jesus, his mission, his self-giving and his resurrection is past made present and can be termed 'remembrance in the mode of hope'. Its hope of his parousia is future made present and can be termed 'hope in the mode of remembrance.' If the eschatological orientation is lost, then remembrance decays into a powerless historical recollection of a founder at the beginning of things" (75).

RELATIONAL ECCLESIOLOGY

'Relational ecclesiology' is a term which signals that the church, like everything else that exists in a living history—including the triune God—exists in relationships with others (125). Therefore, the church does not exist in and for itself. Its essence is relational community wherein the members give of themselves to each other, and the community gives of itself to the world. As the eschatological community, the church's message will consist of hope. But the church is also the community under the cross. Therefore, its message will also consist of empathic solidarity with fellow believers and all people who suffer in the world's present systems.

The cross is a source of ecclesial unity for Moltmann. The unity of the church consists in the one Lord Jesus Christ, and more specifically in his death on the cross. That is, the church in all its fragmentation and disagreements is united in being the church under the cross. This theme comes out of Moltmann's activity in ecumenical dialogue. He notes that ecumenical dialogue about the meaning of the cross has brought about a deeper appreciation of the passion of God and the "liberating strength that comes from discipleship with the Crucified One." He adds, "But this fruitful dialogue *about* the cross of Christ would remain abstract and merely theoretical if it did not at the same time lead to a dialogue *under* the cross of Christ" (*PL*: 83–84). The difference signified by the shift from *about* to *under* represents the key to real ecumenical progress. It is the difference between talking about unification and actually taking steps toward unification.[12]

---

[12] Because the Eucharist takes place under the cross, Moltmann finds no reason to exclude other Christians from eucharistic fellowship. Moltmann welcomes to the communion table anyone who hears and responds to the invitation of the Crucified One (*PL*: 87).

Being "under the cross" means more than church unification, though. It also means that the church will feature fellowship in the midst of persecution and tribulation. Finally, it means that the church suffers in the hope of God's final salvation from all forms of injustice and death (85).

In the prison camps of World War II, Moltmann himself experienced this unity of Christians of all kinds under the cross. "Behind barbed wire fences traditional doctrinal differences of the divided churches no longer had any special relevance" (88). He observes that the same kind of ecumenical fellowship is experienced today wherever the church is facing severe hardship and persecution. The common trend is: "From the depth of shared suffering and shared prayer a new fellowship comes into existence" (89).

Political Theology

Moltmann's theology has always been strongly oriented toward political action. On one hand, he is credited for being one of the major catalysts of liberation theologies. On the other hand, he is criticized for defining salvation and the kingdom of God in terms of political activism and liberation. In this section we will look at his political theology and briefly assess this and related objections.

Moltmann is critical of most modern theology for allowing its form to be determined by industrial society. Modern industrial society is oriented around the satisfaction of needs. "Men associate themselves with each other necessarily only as the bearers of needs, as producers and consumers" (*TH*: 308). Inasmuch as religion is a felt need, the modern person embarks on a search to acquire what satisfies him or her. This goes on in atmosphere of freedom of choice.

What has become of the church in this atmosphere? It has lost the status of *cultus publicus* that it enjoyed for so many centuries. It has been relegated to the status of *cultus privatus*, a new and foreign role for the church. Moltmann argues that various revivalistic and pietistic movements have furthered this process. "There prevailed within [Christianity] a pious individualism, which for its own part was romanticist in form and withdrew itself from the material entanglements of society" (310). Thus, the strength of pietistic forms of Christianity is their emphasis on personal interaction with God. However, this has also led to their greatest weakness—the privatization of the Christian faith. Pietism has profoundly influenced evangelicalism, which has also inherited the tendency toward privatization. According to Moltmann's analysis, what evangelicalism needs is to retain its pietistic roots and strengths but add to them social consciousness. Most evangelicals desire to experience God, and they seek to do so through private experiences in church and home devotions. What they need is to become aware that God can be experienced in social activism as well.

Before I continue with Moltmann's analysis of Christianity and political action, I must make an observation. He is right that pietistic and revivalistic movements have tended to highlight personal faith. However, it is not true that this has failed to translate into social action. The evangelical revivals in England and America resulted in significant improvement in the treatment of prisoners, public education for the poor, the abolition of the slave trade, and so on. It is only in the middle decades of this century that American evangelicalism was withdrawn from social and political involvement. This trend was reversed in the 1970s and 1980s with the birth of the Christian Right. Today, evangelicalism, at least in America, is active politically and socially. Because this activity tends to take place in the context of conservative political agendas, it will not match Moltmann's vision for Christian social and political involvement.

Regarding non-evangelical churches, many of them have struggled against the privatization of religion, making social action constitutive of their identity. Unfortunately, Moltmann observes, these liberal churches too often lose their distinctive *Christian* identity. The solution for both conservative and liberal churches is to be found in the combination of eschatological hope and identification with the cross of Christ.

Having a strong eschatology helps the church associate itself with something other than existing social and political structures. For its eyes will be drawn to the coming kingdom of God, in which all creatures will be liberated from oppression, sin and death. Because it transcends all present realities, the coming kingdom of God cannot be equated with capitalism, socialism, or any other current structure. And because it represents a future society of unlimited cooperation, the kingdom of God provides a model for society and calls us to approximate it even under present conditions.

The cross of Christ functions as the single most defining aspect of Christian theology. It cuts across humanity's natural tendency toward domination and oppression, showing that Christ himself, "taking the form of a slave . . . humbled himself and became obedient to the point of death—even death on a cross" (Phil 2:7–8). The church can do no better than to assume the form of a slave, seeking not to dominate but to serve. Specifically for Moltmann, the first ones the church should serve are the outcasts and the oppressed. For it is these people who experience the isolation and helplessness of the cross. Moltmann's theology of the cross has always brought with it a political praxis of solidarity with the poor and the powerless.

Moltmann writes, "The crucified God is in fact a stateless and classless God. But that does not mean that he is an unpolitical God. He is the God of the poor, the oppressed and the humiliated" (*CG*: 329). This string of sentences reveals one of the difficulties with Moltmann's political theology. If God is classless, how can he be the God of the lower classes? Such rhetoric is not unusual in the writings of Moltmann. In *The Experiment Hope* he states, "The hope about which [the Bible] speaks is valid for the hopeless and not for the optimists. It is valid for the poor and not for the rich. It is valid for the downtrodden and the insulted . . . it is valid for the oppressed . . ." (*EH*: 46). In *The Way of Jesus Christ* he states, "In a divided world destroyed by enmity, the one gospel has two faces, according to the group to which it turns. Jesus proclaims to the poor the kingdom of God without any conditions, and calls them blessed because the kingdom is already theirs. But the gospel of the kingdom meets the rich with *the call to conversion* (Mk 1:15 par.)" (*WJC*: 102). This is an especially problematic claim, for it implies that conversion to salvation is only necessary for the rich and powerful. The poor and powerless have no conditions on their salvation; they are called "blessed" because they are redeemed, apparently by virtue of their poverty.

Utterances like these have drawn harsh criticism for Moltmann. Fortunately, such statements do not represent the balance of Moltmann's thought. On the next page in *The Way of Jesus Christ* he goes on to say that those who responded to the Sermon on the Mount included the poor, those who are hungry for justice and righteousness, people who are persecuted for the sake of righteousness, the sad and the gentle. All of these people were in the process of converting (103). If this is true, then the poor need conversion just like everyone else. Moltmann does not make a distinction between poor and rich in terms of the need for conversion on a consistent basis, so it is best to attribute the extreme comments above to rhetoric gone out of control. The use of extreme rhetoric is, in fact, one of Moltmann's weakest tendencies. However, the problem may go beyond the use of rhetoric. Donald Claybrook notes that Moltmann defines poverty as deprivation in *any* area, spiritual or otherwise. However, when theory becomes practice, Moltmann seems to limit the poor to those who are physically or materially oppressed (234).

Claybrook is correct in his observation. Moltmann's theology is aligned toward the 'outcast,' which he identifies as the poor, the uneducated, the helpless, the unwanted. He locates these people in lower socio-economic strata. However, when we begin to search for outcasts in higher levels of society, they are not difficult to find. There have always been outcasts in the most wealthy and powerful families in the world. They may not be outcasts of society in general, but they can be outcasts within their own families, outcasts of inattentive parents, and so on. Even in the highest levels of society there are always people who are living with the pain of rejection, neglect, abuse and lack of love. Let us recall the insistent concentration on *relationship* in Moltmann's theology. Perichoretic relationship is the foundation of his trinitarian theology, and for him the Trinity is the primary model for human society. This being the case, it is curious that politics and economics—not relationship—define oppression and liberation.

Moltmann's writings are ambiguous and not entirely consistent. At times he appears to define salvation in political terms and speak one-sidedly in favor of the oppressed, while at other times he speaks in a more balanced and temperate tone. This inconsistency is the reason Moltmann cannot entirely escape from the criticism that his political theology constitutes a fundamental alteration of the historical Christian gospel. One can possibly explain Moltmann's periodic rhetorical excesses with the idea that by transforming society at its lowest level we can ultimately save all its levels. This is what he understands Jesus to have done (*EH*: 115). In this view, the lower classes are not the only ones the church goes to, but they are the first ones.

In one of his more balanced statements, Moltmann distinguishes his own praxis-oriented theology from typical liberation theologies. He writes, "The chains which liberation has to strike off differ in every situation. But the freedom that is sought can only be a single and a common freedom. It is the freedom for fellowship with God, man and nature. The open concept of liberation is thus more comprehensive than the limited concept of political liberation or the fixed concept of revolution" (*CPS*: 17). Here he is criticizing most class-oriented liberation theologies from having too narrow a focus. Moltmann wants to take in issues of class, but social liberation is only one type of emancipation. Because oppression can take many forms, poverty being only one of them, liberation must also take many forms. The common denominator among all forms of oppression is that they hinder "freedom for fellowship with God, humanity and nature." Likewise, all forms of liberation provide that freedom for fellowship. Here is the needed emphasis on relationship that will set social oppression in its proper context. Here is the type of message that can correct both conservative and liberal churches. For both types of church need to see the comprehensive nature of oppression and liberation rather than continuing to favor the type with which they particularly associate.

Conclusion

Jürgen Moltmann is a unique figure in twentieth-century theology. His experiences have marked him in profound ways. The firestorm in Hamburg caused him to reach out to God and gave him an appreciation for life. His years behind barbed wire following the War introduced him to Christian fellowship in which differences of nationality, rank and religious background fell away in a search for God, who could meet the defeated and shamed soldiers of the Third Reich in the midst of their pain. Moltmann himself teetered on the brink of destruction, but he found a reason to hope again in the person of Jesus Christ. These themes—life, suffering, ecumenism and hope—have marked Moltmann's theology throughout his life.

Moltmann has also been influenced by key thinkers. Reading Bloch's philosophy of hope gave him the conceptual framework in which he could develop his own theology of hope. Karl Barth provided a theological foundation emphasizing christology, trinitarian theology, dialectical thinking and scriptural authority. Moltmann owes a great deal to Barth in these areas. However, much of Moltmann's development as a theologian has involved a process of moving beyond Barth—beyond his time-eternity dialectic, his tendency toward christomonism, and other themes. In particular, as Moltmann has concentrated more on developing a full account of the work of the Holy Spirit, he has had to move beyond Barth's relative neglect and subordination of the Third Person.

As we turn to Moltmann's pneumatology in the coming chapters, we will see many of the themes mentioned in this chapter coming to expression in the work of the Spirit. Moltmann's pneumatology is a thoroughly trinitarian one, shaped by the Cappadocian concept of the Trinity. The Spirit is God present in the world, suffering with it and comforting it with the salve of hope. The Spirit is certainly active in the church, but Moltmann works to correct any assumption that the Spirit is confined to the church, let alone to a select few within the church. For Moltmann, the Holy Spirit is the universal presence of God. The Spirit is constantly leading the church outside of itself in ecological and social action on behalf of the kingdom of God.

5

Moltmann's Eschatology

General Eschatological Concepts

As we prepare to focus directly on the eschatological aspects of Moltmann's pneumatology, we must take a closer look at Moltmann's eschatology. That is the task of this chapter. In the first part of the chapter we will investigate the general eschatological concepts that emerge throughout the sweep of his work. The second part will focus on the four spheres of eschatology that Moltmann develops in *The Coming of God*—personal, historical, cosmic and divine. In the coming chapters on his understanding of the Holy Spirit, I will organize the pneumatological analysis around the first three of those spheres.

Eschatological Options

In surveying the lay of the land in the study of the last things, Moltmann identifies three types of eschatology from which he differentiates himself. They are historicized eschatology, transcendental eschatology, and apocalypticism.

Historicized Eschatology

Historicized eschatology involves the reduction of eschatological phenomena into temporal processes and historical events. This has happened in three ways. First, in the "prophetic theology" of the seventeenth century, the Bible was read as a record of inerrant divine prophecies about the future history of the world. Second, Albert Schweitzer's consistent eschatology claimed that history does not have the apocalyptic end that is expected by the mistaken eschatology of Jesus. Instead, Schweitzer looked for history to continue and run its never-ending course. In contrast to Schweitzer, Moltmann looks to the parousia and an end of the present era. Third, Oscar Cullmann's attempt to mediate between the "not yet" of consistent eschatology and the "already" of existentialist eschatology rested on a linear concept of time. Christ was the midpoint of history; with him a new division of time began as it marches on toward its completion. The problem with Cullmann's thesis according to Moltmann is that Christ does not come "in time"; he comes to transform time (6–13).

TRANSCENDENTAL ESCHATOLOGY

The general form of transcendental eschatology is based on the epiphany of the eternal logos. Moltmann considers this to be a leftover from ancient Greek philosophy. Twentieth-century examples of transcendental eschatology include Karl Barth, for whom eschatology is the unhistorical, supra-historical or 'proto-historical' (*TH*: 40). It is basic to Barth's thought to work out eschatological positions within the dialectic of time and eternity. The eschaton is the boundary between time and eternity. Being eternal, it deals as much with the beginning as it does with the end (50). Rudolf Bultmann took transcendental eschatology in an existential direction, considering eschatology to be the contact of eternity with each present moment in time. Finally, Paul Althaus saw "every wave of the sea of time break as it were on the strand of eternity." These three theologians are examples of Christian thinkers who have elevated the place of eschatology, but in transcendentalist, non-historical terms.

Regarding transcendental eschatology, Moltmann states, "It was precisely the transcendentalist view of eschatology that prevented the breakthrough of eschatological dimensions in dogmatics" (40). The breakthrough Moltmann has in mind is the revival of futuristic, hope-based eschatologies that mirror the thought-forms of the early church. The early Christians operated on the basis of promise, not the epiphany of the eternal logos.

By switching from an epiphany religion to religion based on promise, "Moltmann tilts the axis of classical transcendence from a vertical orientation that directs faith toward a supernatural, superintending deity, to a horizontal orientation that directs faith toward the future—a future anticipated as the coming of God" (Conyers: 6). In doing this Moltmann finds himself in agreement with Barth that Christianity is altogether eschatological, but in disagreement with Barth's notion that eschatology is an unveiling of what is already accomplished in Christ. For Moltmann, eschatology must be historical and history must be eschatological (6).

APOCALYPTIC

Regarding apocalyptic, Moltmann flatly states, "Christian eschatology is not Christianized apocalyptic" (*TH*: 193). This is because the resurrection of Christ shows the future of the crucified Christ for the world. It does not show, as apocalyptic would, the course of history, the secrets of the world of heaven, or the outcome of the future world. Although the early church borrowed from apocalyptic thought, it did not completely adopt the Jewish apocalyptic worldview. Christian eschatology goes beyond late Jewish apocalyptic when it declares: (a) that the resurrection has already begun, (b) that God raised Christ not as one faithful to the Law but as one crucified, and (c) that participation in the future resurrection is not based on obedience to the Law (193). The use of apocalyptic imagery and ideas is one source among several upon which the primitive church drew (193).

In contrast to the prophetic writings that influence New Testament thought, apocalyptic is much more deterministic. "The temporal sequence of the aeons is settled from the start and history gradually unfolds a plan of Yahweh's. In the prophets, however, there is no trace of the idea that the *eschata* have been firmly determined since the beginning of time" (*TH*: 133–34). In apocalyptic God's judgment is inevitable and determined, whereas in prophetic eschatology it can be recalled and averted in the event of widespread repentance.

Although Moltmann differentiates his prophetic-based eschatology from apocalyptic, Stephen Travis argues that in fact Moltmann is influenced by apocalyptic. "Whereas Pannenberg stresses the concept of universal history leading towards its goal in the age to come, Moltmann makes use of apocalyptic's radical discontinuity between the present and future ages" (Travis: 56–57). As we will see, the contradictions between present and future form the basis for Christian hope. Although Travis' observation is true of Moltmann's early theology, it is less accurate regarding Moltmann's later work. One of the effects of Moltmann's "turn to the third article" is that the lines between the present and the future have become softened. The Holy Spirit functions as the presence of the future, the power who brings resurrection-life into current reality.

Eschatology of Hope

Moltmann rejects the eschatological schemes just discussed in part because they do not adequately deal with hope. In *Theology of Hope*, Moltmann defines eschatology as the doctrine of the Christian hope. It encompasses both the object hoped for, and the hope inspired (*TH*: 16). He believes this is the structure of thought in the New Testament. What is more, with the help of Gerhard von Rad's scholarship, Moltmann traces the understanding that God is a promise-maker and promise-keeper back to the writings of the Old Testament. Israel began with a nomadic religion. A nomadic religion must be based on promise, for the nomad lives in continual migration. Thus, whereas the religions of agrarian cultures emphasized the recurring, cyclical nature of reality, the nomadic Hebrews understood God as the one who called their nation into being with a promise. Theirs was always a future-oriented culture. When the Israelites settled in the promised land and became agrarian themselves, they did not also transition into a cyclical agrarian religion. Instead, they purposely maintained their understanding of God as the One who makes promises and keeps them (*TH*: 96–97).

This conception of God informs the New Testament writings. God is still understood to be one who makes promises and fulfills them. In fact, the New Testament is saturated with the sense that many of God's promises regarding the eschaton were already being fulfilled. This sense of fulfillment gave the early Christians even greater reason to hope that the resurrection of Christ would indeed lead to the resurrection of all human beings—that the presence of the Holy Spirit meant that complete redemption would truly be theirs.

Hope

Moltmann's eschatology of hope relies on the philosophy of Ernst Bloch to bring New Testament eschatology into a form that can impact the life of present-day Christians. Living by hope means regarding the essence of reality to lie in the future. It is the coming state of affairs that must define our perception of the present. Our picture of the future activates our desire to create approximations of it. So we look to the consummation, and we wait, but our waiting is a state of purposeful activity.

Moltmann emphasizes that the hope Christians have for the future is a universal hope. It is a hope for all human communities, and for the entire community of creation. In keeping with this vision, he takes issue with those postmodern styles of theology which particularize the gospel to their own special interests. "Some people use the term 'postmodern' when they abandon their concern for the common future of humanity and withdraw into their own histories, calling everything arbitrary or 'multi-optional.' This decline of community is the coming anarchy and is the surest road to disaster" (*SoL*: 42).

What is the main category for eschatology? In *Theology of Hope*, it is hope. By the time he writes *The Coming of God*, his view has shifted slightly, so that eschatology is defined mainly by "the coming God."[1] That is, Moltmann seeks a concept of the future "which neither allows the history 'which continues to run its course' to swallow up every eschatology, nor permits the eternity that is always present to put an end to every history. The eschaton is neither the future of time nor timeless eternity. It is God's coming and his arrival" (*CoG*: 22). Thus, rather than history or eternity, the fundamental eschatological category for Moltmann is *Advent* (appearance, arrival) with the category *Novum* (the new thing) as the historical category which characterizes the eschatological event in history (6).

ADVENT

Because *futurum* develops out of the past and present, it cannot bring anything astonishingly new. Under this concept of time there is no category *novum*. But in Christian theology *adventus*, which is a Latin translation of the Greek *parousia*, emphasizes the coming and arrival of Christ in his glory. Parousia is not a "second coming" in the sense of being a second arrival of Christ. Rather, it is a new arrival—the definitive arrival—for it is accompanied by the glory of God. Furthermore, with the advent of Christ and God's glory, "future time ends and eternal time begins. Without a transformation of time like this, eschatology cannot be thought" (26).

NOVUM

The category *novum* reflects the expectation of the Hebrew prophets that God will "do a new thing." In this case the future does not merely reflect the tendencies and directions of the past but introduces something so new that it makes the old obsolete. "It is not simply the old in new form. It is also a new creation" (27). The new thing does not issue out of the old, but at the same time the new thing is not without analogy. If it were completely incomparable, there would be no way of saying anything about it at all. Furthermore, what is eschatologically new is a re-creation of the old, not an entirely new creation without relation to the old. Hence, Paul expects this perishable nature to put on the imperishable and this mortal nature to put on immortality (1 Cor 15:53) (29).

---

[1] Compare Rev 1:4: "Grace to you and peace from him who is and who was and who is to come . . . ."

For those critics who complain that Moltmann's eschatology can be reduced to human political achievements,[2] the category *novum* shows that this is not the case. As Moltmann emphasizes, the eschatological consummation is something that *cannot* come out of human achievements of any kind. It can only be brought in by a new and decisive act of God.

Contradiction

The concept of Christian hope is the trust that God will do a new thing. This train of thought implies a contrast between present conditions and future conditions when God appears. In Moltmann's eschatology, this contrast reaches the point of contradiction. The notion of contradiction is expressed in the theme underlying *Theology of Hope* and *The Crucified God*, that cross and resurrection stand in an antithetical relationship (cf. Bauckham: 9). Without pressing the point too far, we can say that present is to future as cross is to resurrection, or that present and cross correspond, and future and resurrection correspond. This means that the present will be characterized by suffering and the future by glorification. It also means that the wonders of the future cannot be expected to grow out of the present by some process of development. Rather, the future is so radically different—so contradictory—that it can only be brought about by a new and decisive act of God.

The category *novum* gives Moltmann's theology the room to allow for eschatological surprise. He argues that if the fulfillment of the promise is directly related to the faithfulness of God the promise-maker, then we can be free of the need to construct a *schema* that constricts fulfillment to a string of historic necessities. Rather, we can let God surprise us as he fulfills his promises in his own creative way (*TH*: 104). Past examples of eschatological surprise include the coming of a suffering Messiah and the Old Testament expectations of the "Day of the Lord" being split into *two* comings of the Messiah.

---

[2] See Randall E. Otto, *The God of Hope: The Trinitarian Vision of Jürgen Moltmann*. Bauckham charges that Otto's book is wildly distorted by rhetorical excess. Illustrating Bauckham's complaint, Otto's radical criticisms of Moltmann's work include the following. Moltmann's God is the idea of human community. His theology is based more on atheistic humanism and revisionistic Marxism than on biblical thought. Moltmann inverts the Creator-creature relationship, revealing his religious motivation to make human beings to be as God (11). If Bauckham means by "rhetorical excess" that Otto slips into expressions that overstate his criticisms, I do not believe that is the case. Otto does not engage in rhetorical excess so much as he demonstrates a radical suspicion of any themes in Moltmann's work that echo modern philosophy and historiography, Marxism, humanism and the like. One is left wondering whether there is anything safe to say theologically at all.

By highlighting contradiction, Moltmann draws attention to eschatological discontinuity. That is, he urges us to reflect on the consequences of the radical distinction between present and future conditions. At the same time, the present is not absolutely unlike the eschatological future. The present is not completely characterized by suffering. For the resurrection of Christ and the ministry of the Holy Spirit bring the dynamics of eschatological life into the present in a definite but incomplete form. Nevertheless, Moltmann's theology does tend to stress discontinuity over continuity—contradiction over correspondence. Contradiction lends to Moltmann's eschatology its apocalyptic flavor, with the category *novum* signifying a future that cannot grow out of the present but requires the agency of God to bring it about.

Moltmann's critics have taken him to task for simultaneously claiming that the future contradicts the present, and that it also exerts a powerful influence on the present. They have asked how the future can influence the present if it completely contradicts it. Moltmann has been accused of devaluing the world so much that the sense that the present and future can exert influence on each other fades (Dabney, 1993: 95–96). Dabney argues that Moltmann later remedied this problem, arguing for more continuity. The way he has done this is through pneumatology. The Spirit brings the dynamics of the future into the present. According to Dabney, this is one of the reasons Moltmann has turned to pneumatology (96).

Eschatology and Christ

Based on the ideas of *novum*, contradiction and hope, history takes on a certain structure for Moltmann. This structure is centered in the Christ-event. Moltmann speaks of the resurrection of Christ as a "maker of history." What he means is that theology can construct its own unique view of history on the basis of the reality of the resurrection. That is, if we start with the resurrection, our idea of what is possible in history and of what history is all about will radically change. In this way, the resurrection of Christ can be regarded as a "history-making event" (*TH*: 180). The resurrection gives all history a future and a hope. "Then the resurrection of Christ does not offer itself as an analogy to that which can be experienced any time and anywhere, but as an analogy to what is to come to all. The expectation of what is to come on the ground of the resurrection of Christ, must then turn all reality that can be experienced and all real experience into an experience that is provisional and a reality that does not yet contain within it what is held in prospect for it" (180). Thus, the Christian faith rejects the idea of a fundamental analogy to all historical events. Instead, Christianity works with *eschatological analogy* and anticipation of the future (180–81). The resurrection is a history-making event because it redefines history for us. For Moltmann, eschatology is messianic because it is based so much on the resurrection of Christ. Christ is messianic because his future becomes the universal future of creation.

The resurrection of Christ is hope's foundation, and the parousia is hope's horizon (*EG*: 33). Moltmann exclaims that conditions in the world are grave and that drastic change is needed in order to turn things around. "Without the expectation of Christ's second coming there is no Christian hope; for without it hope is not putting its trust in a radical alternative to this world's present condition" (33). Consistent with this axiom, it was a sign of Christianity's middle-class respectability when the expectation of the parousia lost its power. That is, people who are generally happy or apathetic about present conditions, who can do without the alternative future offered by the image of the returning Christ, find less compulsion to believe in it. This is one reason for Moltmann's dire rhetoric about the condition and future of life on earth.

By holding that the resurrection of Christ is hope's foundation and the parousia is its horizon, Moltmann implies that belief in both the resurrection of Christ and his parousia are vital elements of the Christian faith. "Christianity stands or falls with the reality of the raising of Jesus from the dead by God. In the New Testament there is no faith that does not start *a priori* with the resurrection of Jesus" (*TH*: 165). "A Christian faith that is not resurrection faith can therefore be called neither Christian nor faith" (166).

The central statements of the primitive Christian missionary proclamation are: (1) God has raised the crucified Jesus from the dead. (2) Of this we are witnesses. (3) In him is grounded the future of righteousness for sinners and the future of life for those subject to death (166). Thus, Christ's resurrection represents ultimate victory for God and his people. It is to be understood "as a conquest of god-forsakenness, as a conquest of judgment and of the curse, as a beginning of the fulfillment of the promised life, and thus as a conquest of all that is dead in death, as a negation of the negative (Hegel), as a negation of the negation of God" (*TH*: 211).

Likewise, Moltmann believes that the coherence of the Christian gospel requires a parousia of Christ. "The character of promise in the history of Jesus, the eschatological character of his cross and resurrection from the dead, the hopeful character of faith and the unique nature of the experiences of the Spirit, which point beyond themselves, would be incomprehensible without this future orientation towards Christ's parousia and would hence ultimately themselves be null and void" (*CPS*: 131).

The Four Spheres of Eschatology

We have seen that Moltmann's eschatology has distinctive themes. To think eschatologically is to look beyond the chaos and pain of present conditions to the coming new thing that God will do, beginning with the parousia of Christ and the resurrection of the dead. This is done in an attitude of trust and hope in God's faithfulness. These themes impact the way Moltmann works out eschatology in four concentric circles: eternal life (personal eschatology), the kingdom of God (historical eschatology), the new creation of all things (cosmic eschatology), and the glory of God (divine eschatology). In this section we will turn to these arenas of eschatological phenomena.

Eternal Life: Personal Eschatology

For Moltmann all of eschatology is inclusive. Personal eschatology—resurrection to eternal life—pertains first to the individual, but its inner dynamic carries the conquest of life over death to all of creation. Thus, personal eternal life is necessarily connected to cosmic renewal.

THE INTERMEDIATE STATE

Concerning the intermediate state, Moltmann begins by evaluating the position of Luther and some modern Catholic theologians. In answer to the question of what happens during "death's long night," Luther does not project the time and space of the living onto the continuing existence of the soul, as does the doctrine of purgatory. Instead, he teaches that at death the soul enters into God's time, which is the eternal present. "So how long is it from a person's death in time to the End-time raising of the dead? The answer is: just an instant! And if we ask: where are the dead 'now,' in terms of our time?—the answer has to be: they are already in the new world of the resurrection and God's eternal life" (*CoG*: 102).

Moltmann asserts that the deficiency of this idea about resurrection is that it does not begin with Christ and his fellowship with other human beings. Moltmann holds to an "eschatological proviso"—that although Christ has already been raised from the dead, the rest of us have not. Death still reigns over us who wait and hope for our resurrection. "So there is after all an 'intermediate time'—a time between Christ's resurrection and the general resurrection of the dead" (104). During that period, "the dead are dead and not yet risen, but they are already 'in Christ' and are with him on the way his future" (105). Moltmann thus holds that the dead are "with Christ," which means that they are not separated from God, nor are they sleeping, nor already risen. The question is what "with Christ" could mean.

The fact that the intermediate state covers a period of time implies that there is time for the dead—the time defined by fellowship with Christ. "So the dead also have time—not, certainly, the time of our present life, which leads to death, but none the less Christ's time, and that is the time of love, the accepting, the transfiguring, the rectifying love that leads to eternal life" (106).

RESURRECTION

In Western culture there are two basic images of hope in the face of death: the immortal soul and the resurrection of the dead. The majority of people have more faith in the immortality of the soul than in the resurrection of the body, but Moltmann does not hesitate to take the minority opinion.

For Moltmann the key difference between the immortality of the soul and the resurrection of the dead is that the former is an opinion, whereas the latter is a hope. "The first is a trust in something immortal in the human being, the second is a trust in the God who calls into being the things that are not, and makes the dead live" (65).

Furthermore, the immortality of the soul is a way to accept death and move beyond it. In contrast, the resurrection of the dead is the belief that death itself will be defeated. "The immortal soul may welcome death as a friend, because death releases it from the earthly body; but for the resurrection hope, death is 'the last enemy' (1 Cor 15:26) of the living God and the creations of his love" (65–66).

If death itself is defeated, it means that the whole person lives on. In other words, if death is an event that affects the whole person, then the defeat of death also affects the whole person. For this reason, Moltmann concludes that we cannot reduce the resurrection to a disembodied life after death. The resurrection, like death, is an event belonging to the whole of life. "I shall live *wholly* here, and die *wholly*, and rise *wholly* there" (67).

The theme of the defeat of death shows up strongly in the New Testament. Just as God brought Israel out of Egypt in the Old Testament, in the New Testament God is identified as the one who raised Christ from the dead (Rom 10:9). Christ's resurrection is an eschatological event that has significance for all people. "He is 'the leader of life' (Acts 3:15), 'the first to rise from the dead' (Acts 26:23), 'the first-born from the dead' (Col

1:18) . . . . The process of the resurrection of the dead has begun in him, is continued in 'the Spirit, the giver of life,' and will be completed in the raising of those who are his, and of all the dead" (69). Furthermore, Christ's resurrection is not a resuscitation to this or any other mortal life. Rather, it is entry into life that is eternal. It is life without the specter of death (69).

The notion of resurrection is thus an inclusive idea in Moltmann's interpretation. The resurrection of the dead implies the renewal of all creation. Moltmann draws on the expression "resurrection of the body" to show that even though the early church always reduced this expression to the *human* body, it can also refer to all living beings, for "the wording of the acknowledgement leaves it open for 'the resurrection of all the living'" (70). In other words, in a holistic concern for all created beings, Moltmann advocates going beyond the early church's proclamation of the resurrection of the human body and speaking of a resurrection of all living beings. He goes on to state, "Hope for the resurrection of the dead is therefore only the beginning of a hope for a cosmic new creation of all things and conditions. It is not exhausted by personal eschatology. On the contrary, every personal eschatology that begins with this hope is constrained to press forward in ever-widening circles to cosmic eschatology" (70).

Let us recall that in the Jewish tradition, resurrection is often oriented toward not only redemption but also judgment. Moltmann himself makes this point (67–68). Apparently, then, what Moltmann means is that non-human creatures will be resurrected but will not face judgment. Lacking moral culpability, they will simply be given the gift of never-ending life. However, Moltmann does not explain whether there is any difference between human and non-human beings in the sharing of the divine glory. He claims that all creatures will be glorified along with God, but does this mean the same thing for non-human beings as it does for humans? If so—if the reward of glorification is the same for all creatures—then it seems that humanity is being shortchanged for being the only segment of creation that has to undergo judgment. It may be that Moltmann justifies such inequality on the basis that humans have done so much to harm creation, but he does not say.

At any rate, the bottom line for Moltmann is that personal eschatology means life and glory for all creatures. Hence, it means resurrection: "Anyone who says 'resurrection of the dead' says 'God' (Barth). On the other hand, anyone who says 'God' and does not hope for the resurrection of the dead and a new creation from the righteousness of God, has not said 'God'. What other belief can be held by those who are 'dead' unless it is 'resurrection faith'?" (*CG*: 218).

The Kingdom of God: Historical Eschatology

The concept of the kingdom of God is always a central issue in explorations of eschatology. Moltmann is no exception to this rule. Our first question will be what he has in mind when he speaks of the kingdom of God. From there we will pursue questions of the relationship between the kingdom and hierarchy, the timing of the kingdom, how the rule of God takes effect, and how the concept of the rule of God ultimately functions in Moltmann's eschatology.

HISTORY AND THE KINGDOM OF GOD

In *The Coming of God*, Moltmann associates the kingdom of God with "historical eschatology," which overlaps with, but is differentiated from, personal eschatology or cosmic eschatology. He explains, "Historical eschatology is political eschatology, and more than that" (146). Moltmann wants to develop the notion of historical eschatology in two ways. One is that he wants to make sure we do not reduce historical eschatology to political eschatology. The other is that historical eschatology has implications for the wider horizon of cosmic eschatology. It impinges on the Last Judgment and ultimate justice, as well as on the new creation of all things.

Moltmann explains that *"the kingdom of God* is a more integral symbol of the eschatological hope than eternal life. Of course the different hopes complement one another and merge into each other; but the two also say something different" (131). The symbol 'eternal life' applies to "our experience of a life loved and a death suffered," whereas the symbol of 'the kingdom of God' applies to "our experiences of history and our sufferings in history" (132). That is, eternal life is an individual type of experience (although it overlaps with more universal type of experience), and the kingdom of God is a collective type of experience (although it overlaps with both individual and cosmic types of experience). The notion of the new creation of all things is the most comprehensive and integral of the three symbols (eternal life, kingdom of God, new creation).

Historical eschatology depends on personal eschatology and cosmic eschatology, just as they depend on it. This type of interrelation contrasts with modern ideas that human history is the quintessence of reality (Hegel). Moltmann rejects such a notion because its myopic focus on humanity averts its vision from nature. The result has been theologies that are forgetful or even hostile toward creation (132).

In this threefold scheme historical eschatology takes up a mediating position between personal eschatology and cosmic eschatology. It includes more than the individual human being, but it does not include the entire cosmos. It takes in the flow of social and political history.

Moltmann's notion of historical eschatology has its strengths and weaknesses. Its integration with personal and cosmic eschatology reminds us that the consummation of all things is just that—a consummation of *all* things, not just *human* things. On the other hand, it defines the kingdom of God in terms of social and political phenomena. However, is not the rule of God to be found in the arenas of personal eschatology and cosmic eschatology as well? Certainly it is—or should be—a primary consideration in personal eschatology. For the rule of God centers around the defeat of sin and death, two problems that are acutely painful experiences for every individual human being. It is also at home in the social and political realm, although many Christians have not defined it in as richly political terms as Moltmann does. For many Christians the kingdom of God is associated more with the church and the advance of the gospel for winning converts than with social and political action taken with the gospel as its impetus. In this case, Moltmann's political concept of the kingdom can be a welcome corrective.

Finally, is the kingdom of God a component of cosmic eschatology? Inasmuch as the rule of God is liberation *from* sin and death *to* life and harmony with God, cosmic eschatology should also be included under the symbol of the kingdom of God. If all of creation needs liberation from death and strife to life and peace, then it is in need of the liberating rule of God. Moltmann himself holds that death will be defeated for all creatures. It follows that the rule of God must extend to the renewal of all things and the universal gift of unending life. Therefore, it is not consistent within Moltmann's own eschatology to define the kingdom of God in terms of experiences within social and political history.

It is true that Moltmann never explicitly restricts the kingdom of God to the social-political arena. However, this does not avert the above criticism, because it remains a fact that the primary location that he identifies for the kingdom is human history. Such a location implicitly amounts to a reductionistic concept of the rule of God.

Therefore, on the one hand, Moltmann's way of breaking down eschatological hope into the three arenas of personal eschatology, historical eschatology and cosmic eschatology is very helpful and illuminating. It keeps us mindful that all three arenas are interdependent and need to be considered together whenever we talk about eschatological hope. It also paints eschatology on a wide canvas and allows us to do the subject more justice. When Moltmann adds the fourth arena—divine eschatology and the glory of God—he stretches the canvas even further, as we will see.

On the other hand, Moltmann has made a mistake in locating the kingdom of God in the social/political arena of eschatology. Whereas it is a fine heuristic device to have a symbol for each of the three arenas of eschatology, one also has to be sure to choose appropriate symbols. In this case, Moltmann has not succeeded.

THE TRINITARIAN KINGDOM

An essential element of Moltmann's understanding of the kingdom of God is that it is trinitarian in nature. God reigns, but not in a monarchical, hierarchical way where the Father rules through the Son in the Spirit. Instead, God rules as a divine community that is open to others entering into this fellowship.

Moltmann plays off of Joachim of Fiore's threefold taxonomy of the kingdom as three historical stages corresponding to Father, Son and Holy Spirit. Moltmann notes that since all three of these stages take place within history, and because Joachim also expected a kingdom beyond history, that Joachim really has a four-stage theory of the kingdom. Moltmann follows this general idea, but instead of positing three successive stages of the kingdom within history, Moltmann posits three coterminous and complementary aspects of the ongoing rule of God, followed by the fourth stage of the glorification of God.

The kingdom of the Father "consists of the creation of a world open to the future, and the preservation both of existence itself and of its openness for the future of the kingdom of glory" (*TK*: 209). The dimension of the future is important, for it identifies the goal of the creation of the world as the glorification of the triune God. Creation "in the beginning" implies a goal for it "in the end." The Father preserves the world through his patience because he holds out hope for it. In his patience God gives created beings time and freedom to pursue his future.

The kingdom of the Son "consists of the liberating lordship of the crucified one, and fellowship with the first-born of many brothers and sisters" (210). The Son liberates men and women from sin and death. He leads people to liberty by making them like himself in fellowship with him.

The kingdom of the Holy Spirit "is experienced in the gift conferred on the people liberated by the Son—the gift of the Holy Spirit's energies" (211). In the kingdom of the Spirit, people lay hold of the freedom for which the Son has made them free. They also experience the energies of the new creation in the form of a new community without privileges or subjugation, a community of the free. Yet the present kingdom of the Spirit is not yet the kingdom's consummation. It presupposes the kingdoms of the Father and the Son, and it points forward to the eschatological kingdom of glory (212).

The kingdoms of the Father, the Son and the Spirit all point forward to the kingdom of glory. Moltmann defines the kingdom of glory "as the consummation of the Father's creation, as the universal establishment of the Son's liberation, and as the fulfillment of the Spirit's indwelling" (212). Creation is the material promise of glory, the kingdom of the Son is the historical promise of glory, and the rule of the Spirit is the actual dawn of the kingdom of glory, albeit within the present conditions of history and death. "The trinitarian doctrine of the kingdom therefore sums up 'the works of the Trinity' (creation, liberation, glorification) and points them towards the home of the triune God. The kingdom of glory is the goal—enduring and uninterrupted—for all God's works and ways in history" (212).

THE KINGDOM AND HIERARCHY

A. J. Conyers has argued that Moltmann operates with a general suspicion of hierarchy, and that this affects his concept of the rule of God. Conyers begins with Moltmann's critique of monarchial monotheism. For Moltmann, it represents an endorsement of the status quo and an argument against change. This is because it has been the preferred model of the Western church since the Middle Ages, when the church exerted a monolithic rule over society and theologians like Aquinas thought of God's unity before considering his tri-unity. The notion of a divine monarchy can serve to justify earthly domination, because the dominant model of God renders him as standing over against creation as a transcendent monad, controlling and dominating its processes. In human society the hierarchy becomes an excuse for lording it over others and dominating them.

In contrast to this monarchial domination, Moltmann thinks of the rule of God in terms of openness and freedom. Because these ideals are eliminated in monarchial theism where God dominates creation, Moltmann sees eschatology as possible only within trinitarian theism, where God's relational nature opens him to not only move but also be moved by his creation. God involves himself in history by his own choice—a choice made out of his love for creation. For Moltmann, saying that God rules over his creation is not the only thing, and is perhaps not the most helpful thing, that can be said about God. It is most helpful to say that God is *in* his creation, living in open relationship with his creation (Conyers: 184).

Conyers argues that Moltmann is mistaken about his association of hierarchical thought with domination and suppression. He argues that, in fact, hierarchy can function along with eschatology and freedom. Not only can eschatology and hierarchy function together, an eschatological view of history and theology actually requires a hierarchy. Conyers' thesis is that "Christian theology requires not a choice between the superintending power of a Lord or the missionary hope of a Messiah but both: not hope without power, not power without hope, but both power and hope" (15).

THE TIMING OF THE KINGDOM

One issue that has divided theologians interested in eschatology is how they conceive of the timing of the kingdom of God. That is, is the kingdom a present reality (realized eschatology), a future reality (consistent eschatology), or a reality that functions in the "already" but awaits its fulfillment in the "not yet" (inaugurated eschatology). How does Moltmann view the timing of the kingdom? One can find three different answers to this question in Moltmann's writings.

In some passages his remarks reflect the position of inaugurated eschatology. Moltmann uses the term 'messianic' to mediate between history and the kingdom of God. That is, it reflects the eschatological tension between the already and the not yet. In the messianic life, hope becomes realistic and reality becomes hopeful. It is a life lived in anticipation, not in deferment. The difference is that in anticipation the thing hoped for has already impinged on the present state of things. "An anticipation is not yet a fulfillment. But it is already the presence of the future in the conditions of history. It is a fragment of the coming whole. It is a payment made in advance of complete fulfillment and part-possession of what is still to come" (*CPS*: 193). This language of "a fragment of the coming whole," "payment in advance," and "part possession" reflects the description of an inaugurated kingdom, where the kingdom is truly present now, but in an incomplete form.

In many other passages, Moltmann speaks the language of consistent eschatology, which holds that the kingdom is not yet here, but it is so close that it impacts present reality. For instance, Moltmann asks what it means to say that the kingdom of God was "present" or "at hand" in Jesus' ministry. He reflects on the translation of Luther, "*Das Himmelreich ist nähe herbeigekommen.*" He writes, "I shall adopt this translation, and say: it has come so close that the signs of the messianic era are already visible: the sick are healed, demons are driven out, the lame walk, the deaf hear, the poor have the gospel preached to them. It is so close that we can already pray to God as 'Abba,' dear Father. It is so close that the Torah has to be messianically interpreted through the Sermon on the Mount, and can find its fulfillment in the discipleship of Christ" (*WJC*: 97). We may notice that the signs and the effects of the kingdom are already present. However, the kingdom itself is not. In fact, Moltmann says that if the kingdom itself was present, then it would be visibly present. But it is not visibly present. "If the kingdom is not visibly present, but only invisibly, then it is in heaven, not yet on earth" (97). Therefore, the kingdom is not present, but it influences the present by its nearness.

In another passage Moltmann associates the kingdom of God with the eschatological consummation. The kingdom of God is "the ultimately liberating, all-redeeming and therefore eschatological kingship of God over his creation. It differs from providence because it makes an end of the history of violence, suffering and death and brings about a new creation of all things. It differs from the creation at the beginning through the fact that God himself, with his eternal life and glory, will dwell in this creation and be 'all in all'" (*CPS*: 99–100). When Moltmann talks about God entering into his glory, dwelling in creation, and being "all in all," he is referring to the eschaton.

The third way in which Moltmann speaks of the kingdom of God is by differentiating between the "rule of God" and the "kingdom of God." The former applies to the reign of God in the present. The latter means "the dimension and new order of all things according to God's precepts," which will come to pass in the future. The kingdom is the *coming* kingdom, anticipated by the first installments of God's rule. "We therefore have to understand the liberating activity of God as the *immanence* of the eschatological kingdom of God, and the coming kingdom as the *transcendence* of the present lordship of God . . . the present lordship of God determines *the messianic era* and the future kingdom of God is the definition of *eschatological eternity*. . . . God's *lordship* is the *presence* of his kingdom, and God's *kingdom* is the *future* of his lordship" (98).

Moltmann warns that it is a mistake to confuse the present rule of God with his future kingdom. "It would be one-sided to see the lordship of God only in his perfected kingdom, just as it is misleading to identify his kingdom with his actual, present rule" (*WJC*: 97). The problem is, how do we go about separating the rule of God and the kingdom of God? It is not possible to support such a distinction exegetically. The closest one can come is 1 Cor 15:24, where Paul speaks of Jesus handing over the kingdom to the Father. However, the word Paul uses is βασιλεία—Jesus hands over *the kingdom* to the Father. Furthermore, it does not appear that throughout his writings Moltmann consistently retains a clean separation between God's rule and his kingdom. His language about these matters can be quite fluid.

In the end, it is difficult to answer the question of Moltmann's timing of the kingdom. His position could end up being aligned with either consistent or inaugurated eschatology. Like consistent eschatology, Moltmann holds that the kingdom is a future reality. Like inaugurated eschatology, he also holds that God rules in the present, and that this rule will someday be consummated (in what Moltmann calls the "kingdom of God"). However, unlike inaugurated eschatology, Moltmann does not speak in terms of an inaugurated-and-someday-consummated kingdom.

THE RESTORATION OF ALL THINGS AND UNIVERSAL SALVATION

The question of universal redemption has always been important to the Christian community. Moltmann calls it "the most disputed question in Christian eschatology." Is there a dividing of believers and unbelievers, the former receiving heavenly bliss and the latter receiving the torments of hell? Or are all redeemed in the end? Moltmann sees behind this question a deeper inquiry into the person of God. "Does God, as their Creator, go with all his created beings into life, death and resurrection—or does God as judge stand over against those he has created, detached and uninvolved, to pardon or condemn?" (*CoG*: 236).

Noting that the discussion between Barth, Brunner and Ebeling a few decades ago over this question was argued mainly on the basis of the testimony of Scripture, Moltmann begins by looking to the words of the Bible. He concludes that Scripture attests to both universal salvation and a double outcome of judgment. Therefore, the decision about the issue cannot be decided purely on the ground of Scripture.

Because both sides of the issue have their strengths and weaknesses, the issue for Moltmann comes down to the relationship between divine and human decision. The doctrine of the double outcome of judgment places a great deal of stress on the mutuality of God's salvation and human faith. People are convinced that they can determine their destiny by choosing to believe or not believe. Moltmann sees this as a statement of tremendous self-confidence on the part of human beings who believe that their eternal destiny rests on their own volition and behavior. Such an attitude fits the modern age well, "in which human beings believe that they are the measure of all things, and the centre of the world, and that therefore everything depends on their decision" (245).

He also returns to Scripture, concluding that even though there are particularist and universalist statements in Scripture, one can incorporate the particularist statements into the universalist statements. Moltmann thus reads the whole of Scripture to teach that final judgment is preliminary to the new creation. Final judgment is penultimate; the new creation is ultimate.

This beings the case, Moltmann's interpretation of punishment is that it is not eternal as God is eternal but is *aionios*—a long time (Moltmann, 1993: 41). The final punishment of hell was endured by Christ on the cross. Moltmann follows Luther in holding that Christ "descended into hell" before he died, meaning that he suffered the anger and curse of God. He continues,

> The *Christian* doctrine about the restoration of all things denies neither damnation nor hell. On the contrary: it assumes that in his suffering and dying Christ suffered the true and total hell of God-forsakenness for the reconciliation of the world, and experienced for us the true and total damnation of sin. . . . *The true Christian foundation for the hope of universal salvation is the theology of the cross, and the realistic consequence of the theology of the cross can only be the restoration of all things* (CoG: 251, emphasis Moltmann's).

The universal restoration of all things links up with the idea of the kingdom of God in that Moltmann's doctrine of universal restoration has two sides: "*God's Judgment*, which puts things to rights, and *God's kingdom*, which awakens to new life" (255). Moltmann's idea of punishment resembles the Catholic doctrine of Purgatory. He believes that there will be an intermediate period during which all creatures will be transformed into a state of holiness sufficient that they will be appropriate for the presence of God. It appears that Moltmann believes this state to be the final judgment that precedes the kingdom of God.

Once again, the notion of the kingdom of God appears muddled in Moltmann's presentation. Are we to understand that the kingdom of God consists of this life-giving function and not also in judgment? If so, then what becomes of the subjugation of all of God's enemies, including sin and death, that marks the triumph of God? To define the kingdom of God as Moltmann does would be to take a significant departure from the teaching of the New Testament authors.

In the end, Moltmann's treatment of the kingdom of God is a mixture of the insightful and the problematic. On one hand, his integration of historical eschatology with personal, cosmic and divine eschatology is a good reminder of the scope of God's plan of redemption. On the other hand, we have reason to reject Moltmann's social-political concept of the kingdom of God, and we cannot discern his final position on the timing of the kingdom. For these reasons, the idea of the kingdom of God is the weak link in Moltmann's eschatological program.

New Heaven—New Earth: Cosmic Eschatology

Certainly, Christian eschatology must include the individual and human history. However, Moltmann states that there are several reasons why it must be widened out to include cosmic eschatology. First, such a move prevents Christian eschatology from becoming a gnostic doctrine of salvation teaching redemption *from* the world rather than *of* the world, and redemption *from* the body rather than *of* the body.

Second, eschatology must be integrated with the doctrine of creation. That is, if God created all things, then all things must be included in the divine plan of redemption. The goal of creation is to someday be the home of God, so that God can be "all in all" (1 Cor 15:28).

Third, Christian theology has lost so many battles with modern science that it has tended to withdraw from making claims about anything other than human existence. "But without cosmology, eschatology must inevitably turn into a gnostic myth of redemption, as modern existentialism shows" (*CoG*: 260). It is illusory to attempt to separate private human existence, which is the realm of religion, from natural existence, which is the realm of the sciences. Human existence is bodily existence, and human life is participation in nature. Thus, the fate of humanity is also the fate of nature, and vice versa (260).

In Moltmann's view the most fundamental question for cosmic eschatology is whether redemption should be understood in the light of creation, or creation in the light of redemption. If creation is primary, then grace is needed to counteract human sin, which has spoiled creation. Redemption becomes a doctrine of restoration to creation's pristine beginnings. On the other hand, if redemption is primary, then

> creation-in-the-beginning is the creation of a history of God's
> which will arrive at its goal only in 'the new creation of all things'
> and the universal indwelling of God in that creation. In the first
> case there is an eschatological hope for redemption only because of

sin and its destructive consequences. In the second case the hope
for the eschatological consummation of creation takes us beyond
the redemption from sin and its consequences (262).

It is the first case—redemption understood in the light of creation—that
has been predominant in the Western tradition. Moltmann agrees that
there is a restorative function to cosmic eschatology. Nonetheless, it remains true that in Christian theology "the end is much more than the beginning" (264). For the end involves a transition from temporal existence
to eternal existence. Moltmann explains, "In *personal* eschatology the consummation of temporal creation is the transition from what is temporal
into eternal life, in *historical* eschatology it is the transition from history
into the eternal kingdom, and in *cosmic* eschatology it is the transition
from temporal creation to the new creation of an eternal 'deified' world"
(265). Eschatological fulfillment involves much more than liberation *from*
the maladies that plague creation; it also means liberation *to* a new existence with God.

What, then, is the difference between creation in the beginning and
the renewed creation of eschatology? For Moltmann it is a matter of the
presence of God in his creation. In the beginning he "finished" creation
and began his sabbath rest on the seventh day (Gen 2:2). In other words,
in the beginning his presence entered into the time of those whom he created. This is the presence of eternity in time, which links beginning and
end, awakening both remembrance and hope.

The eschatological difference is analogous to the difference between
the presence of God in Israel before the Exodus and his presence with
his people in the cloud and pillar of fire during their wanderings in the
dessert. It is a matter of the concentration of the divine presence. God is
present in all of creation, but not in the way that he will be present in the
eschaton.

Moltmann correlates creation in the beginning with the symbol of
sabbath and eschatological new creation with the symbol of *shekinah*.
"Sabbath and Shekinah are related to each other as promise and fulfillment, beginning and completion" (266). Sabbath is time-related, showing
that creation began in time and looks forward to a future in which all its
hopes will be fulfilled. *Shekinah* is space-related, reflecting the concentration of the divine presence in particular places, people and events. The
eschatological new creation will put an end to uneven concentrations of
the divine presence, where God is present in some places more intensely
than he is in any other. Instead, the *shekinah*—the Holy Spirit, to be specific—will permeate all of creation in one overall concentration.

ETERNITY AND THE END OF TIME

The primary symbol Moltmann uses for creation is the temporally oriented idea of sabbath, and for the consummation it is the spatially oriented idea of *shekinah*. This does not mean that there is not a change in temporality in the consummation. It is the change from time to eternity.

Moltmann argues that if we keep in mind that eternity is more about the fullness of creative life than about the mere negation of temporality, then it becomes possible to conceive of an opening for time in eternity. The idea of the primordial moment and the eschatological moment are what he has in mind.

The *primordial moment* has two aspects. First is the creative resolve God demonstrated before he created the world. "'The beginning' in which God 'created' heaven and earth is to be found in this divine self-determination" (281). Second is God's primordial self-restriction. "God restricts his eternity so that in this primordial time he can give his creation time, and leave it time. God restricts his omniscience in order to give what he has created freedom. These primordial self-restrictions of God's precede his creation" (281–82).

The *eschatological moment* corresponds to the primordial moment connected with original creation. Moltmann argues that Paul is talking about the eschatological moment in 1 Cor 15:52—the dead will be raised and the living will be transformed "in the twinkling of an eye." Moltmann believes that this moment of transformation constitutes the moment when time ends for creation and eternity begins. The eschatological moment is the moment of transition between historical time and eternity (295).

Moltmann argues that for heaven and all who dwell within it there is aeonic time, which is a form of time but is distinct from transient time (282). Therefore, the eternity into which creation enters in the eschaton is the aeonic time of heaven. It is "the 'fulfilled time,' the aeonic time, the time filled with eternity, the eternal time" (295). In contrast to historical time, aeonic time is cyclical, rhythmic and unending. Corresponding to this, the main images for eternal life are dance and music. Although it is difficult to imagine such an eternal time, we must at least understand that it is not the same as an empty, silent eternity. On the contrary, Moltmann asks us to imagine it as "the time of eternal livingness" (295).

The reason Moltmann rejects the idea of a static eternity is that he views eschatological life as a life of possibilities. In its transformation, creation will transition into a state of unlimited possibilities, no longer fettered by sin and death. Because creation will be taken up into the life of God, it will experience as many of the potentialities of God as fits its maximum capabilities. The realization of those potentialities requires time of some sort—or at least an active eternal existence other than the "death-like silence" of static eternity.

THE PRESENCE OF GOD AND THE END OF SPACE

The key text for Moltmann's idea that space will come to an end is Rev 20:11: "Then I saw a great white throne and the one who sat on it; the earth and the heaven fled from his presence, and no place was found for them."

Once again, in order to explain the eschatological end of space, Moltmann compares the eschatological state of affairs to the primordial state of affairs just before original creation. He explains that when God restricted his omnipresence in order to make space for creation, a *primordial space* was brought into being. But since space by definition creates distance between objects, in the self-restriction of God there emerged distance between God and creation (297). What Moltmann means is that God withdraws himself so as to become a counterpart to creation. As counterpart, God is distinct from creation. A potential problem here is the use of spatial language to make these points. Moltmann could be claiming that if God withdraws his presence from the space of creation, is he no longer omnipresent. However, what he means is that part of God's self-restriction in the primordial moment was a restriction to spatiality. Whereas he had never been an object that takes up space and therefore can be separated from created objects by distance, in the primordial moment he entered into created space in this way. Such an idea is assumed by the doctrine of the *shekinah*, which expresses the idea that God is present in some places in a different way than he is present in others. At the same time, Moltmann has never given up on divine omnipresence. He believes that God is present in all things, people and places, but that God is present in a special way in some of those things, people and places.

Moltmann makes strong connections between the incarnation of Christ and the *shekinah* of the Holy Spirit. In fact, incarnation presupposes *shekinah*. The idea of the *shekinah* provides the crucial link between the infinite God and finite, earthly space. "Shekinah theology is temple theology. Shekinah means the act of God's descent, and its consequence in his indwelling" (302). The doctrine of the Shekinah contains two presuppositions. One is contraction in God. This must happen in order for God to enter into finite space and time. The other is self-differentiation in God. God becomes differentiated in that he is both in heaven and in the world. He is both in eternity and in time.

In rabbinic writings there are instances when the *shekinah* comes near and instances when the *shekinah* withdraws. For instance, the *shekinah* dwells in the Garden of Eden but withdraws after the Fall. In the history from Abraham to Moses there is a step-by-step descent of the *shekinah* upon Israel, running through the story of the Exodus, through the Ark of the Covenant to the temple of Zion. After the destruction of Solomon's temple in 587 BC the rabbinic tradition is split on whether the *shekinah* returned to heaven or went into captivity with God's people. In either of these two cases the *shekinah* is understood to be absent or in exile. "If the Shekinah returned to heaven after the destruction of God's city, then the time of history is without it, and has therefore been forsaken by God's presence. But if the Shekinah journeyed with the captive people into Babylonian exile, then it remains 'in the midst of the Israelites,' but as the exiled Shekinah, as a divine presence without a home" (304–5).

In either case it is hoped that the *shekinah* will return to Israel with the end-time revelation of God's glory (304). Actually, the ultimate destiny of the *shekinah* is that in the consummation God and his *shekinah* will become indistinguishably one (306). There will no longer be any kind of "distance" between creatures and God. The *shekinah* presence of God in Christ and in the Holy Spirit points forward to the time when God will indwell his entire creation with his glory. The Scriptures relate that God will dwell among his people in the New Jerusalem. This divine indwelling is *the cosmic Shekinah*. "What in history was experienced only among the people of God and in the temple, in Christ and in the Holy Spirit, and was expected of God's future, is there fulfilled: God's immediate presence interpenetrates everything" (317).

Glory: Divine Eschatology

The ultimate sphere of eschatology is divine eschatology, in which God will be glorified. "The glorification of God is the ultimate purpose of creation. . . . To 'glorify' God means to love God for his own sake, and to enjoy God as he is in himself" (*CoG*: 323). "Divine eschatology" amounts to God's self-glorification as he glorifies himself through his creatures. Such thinking requires us to conceive of God's character as including not only selfless love, as in the sacrificial love of Christ, but also self-love that will lead to self-glorification. If we do not allow for both types of love, then there can be no divine eschatology in which God is glorified purely for his own sake (324–26). However, the glorification of God is not entirely an affair of self-glorification, as if other subjects were not involved in a meaningful way. God can be glorified in several distinct ways—"through an interaction between God and the world, God and human beings, or between the trinitarian divine Persons" (330). If there are multiple subjects at work in the process of the self-glorification of God, then God can be involved both actively—as the primary agent without which glorification would not happen—and passively—as the recipient of glorification freely offered by his creatures. This capability of the free offering of worship is necessary in Moltmann's line of thinking, because the freedom to exist harmoniously with God and glorify him are states of being into which created beings are to be liberated in the eschatological moment.

Conclusion

Moltmann's eschatology contains certain themes that give it a distinctive shape. Christian eschatology must be situated between the Scylla of historicized eschatology and the Charybdis of transcendental eschatology. That is, it is historical in that it pertains to the flow of events in the world that lead to a particular *telos*. However, it cannot be reduced to history, because that *telos* has to do with a transformation of the created order that transcends potentialities within history itself.

Eschatology depends on *advent*—the coming of God—and on *novum*—the "new thing." This means that the coming of the Holy Spirit upon human beings at Pentecost is an event of paramount importance. It signals the coming of God into the human situation that alters the landscape of history. It is an event that embodies the category *novum*—God doing a new thing within human beings and human communities by virtue of the indwelling Spirit.

The *telos* of Christian eschatology has specific content for Moltmann— the appearance of the glorified Christ, the resurrection of the dead, the perfecting of all created beings, the renewal of creation, and so on. At the same time, these events are not defined with the detail that is characteristic of apocalyptic thinking, nor are they viewed with the kind of determinism typical of apocalypticism. Like apocalyptic, Moltmann's eschatology features the expectation of a break between this age and the age to come. The Holy Spirit softens the lines of discontinuity for Moltmann. Contradiction is tempered with continuity. Therefore, whereas contradiction posits that future states cannot grow out of present states by some process of development, this must be tempered by the Holy Spirit, who is the first fruits of that future state. As we saw in Pauline pneumatology, there must be both continuity and discontinuity between present and future, and much of the continuity depends on the present work of the Holy Spirit. That is, the Holy Spirit is the eschatological presence of God in the world. If this is so, then we can expect the work of the Holy Spirit to be present in all four arenas of eschatology—personal, historical, cosmic and divine. This certainly creates a broad canvas upon which to paint the eschatological work of the Holy Spirit. Subordination of the Holy Spirit to the activities of Christ or the church is no longer satisfying, nor is the idea of locating the influence of the Spirit primarily in personal experience. In the next three chapters, we will examine Moltmann's pneumatology regarding three of the four arenas of eschatology—corporate, personal and cosmic—to see how his pneumatological positions relate to his eschatology.

6

The Holy Spirit and Human Communities

W ITH this chapter, we begin an extended study of Moltmann's pneumatology. The specific question at hand is how eschatological concepts inform the doctrine of the Holy Spirit as Moltmann develops it. Toward this end, we have set the stage by describing the general character of Moltmann's theology, and then his eschatology. We found that his eschatology contains a system of organization revolving around concentric spheres of divine eschatological activity—personal, historical, cosmic and divine. Because this is a sensible way to organize the eschatological activity of the Holy Spirit, I will retain this structure over the next three chapters. However, I am altering the order in which subjects appear. Just as with Paul, Moltmann considers the communal aspects of the work of the Spirit to take precedence over the individual ones. The individual takes his or her place within the community of faith, which, in turn, is a part of the makeup of the world.

Therefore, in keeping with the organization of the Pauline material, this chapter will focus on the work of the Holy Spirit in human communities, and the next will cover pneumatic activity in individual human beings. Finally, in chapter Eight, I will add some points on the cosmic aspects of the eschatological work of the Spirit, ending with a recap of Moltmann's pneumatology in general.

This chapter contains two major sections. In the first, I will lay out phenomena that operate as preconditions for the life of the church. These preconditions consist of the sending of the Holy Spirit by Christ, and the eschatological turning of the ages. These are theological and historical considerations that set the stage for the subject matter of the second section—the fellowship of the Spirit within the setting of the church.

The Spirit and the Early Christian Community

Early Christian Experience of the Spirit

Moltmann constructs an account of the experience of the Spirit within the early church, claiming that the early Christian experience of the Holy Spirit was expressed in two different ways, both of them relating the Spirit to Christ. One is Spirit-christology, which is reflected in the Synoptic Gospels. The other is a christological doctrine of the Spirit, which is reflected in the writings of Paul and John. Moltmann recognizes that these two perspectives are interrelated. They mutually interpret each other. Consequently, Moltmann works them out in a mutual relationship (SL: 59). Roughly speaking, Moltmann regards the topic of "the Christ of the Spirit" to pertain to the history of Christ before his death, and "the Spirit of Christ" to pertain to the history of Christ after his resurrection.

THE CHRIST OF THE SPIRIT

For Moltmann, the notion of the "Christ of the Spirit" is essential to christology. "Both chronologically and theologically, the operation of the divine Spirit is the precondition or premise for the history of Jesus of Nazareth" (60). The dependence of Jesus on the power of the Spirit begins with the incarnation of the Word by the Holy Spirit and continues through the Spirit-endowment of Jesus at his baptism, his public ministry, his death on the cross, and his resurrection from the dead.

Jesus' ministry, especially his power over sickness and demons, demonstrated that the kingdom of God and the new creation of all things were beginning. "The Spirit makes Jesus 'the kingdom of God in person,' for *in the power of the Spirit* he drives out demons and heals the sick; in the power of the Spirit he receives sinners, and brings the kingdom of God to the poor" (61).

Moltmann next takes the ministry of Jesus and asks what it might mean for the divine Spirit himself. In answer to this seldom-asked question, Moltmann reasons that if we draw on the concept of the *shekinah*, we can perceive that as the Spirit leads Jesus, the Spirit also accompanies him. And if the Spirit accompanies him, then it becomes his companion in suffering as well. "Although the Spirit fills Jesus with the divine, living energies through which the sick are healed, it does not turn him into a superhuman. It participates in his human suffering to the point of his death on the cross" (62).

The death of Jesus on the cross is the point at which the Spirit of God becomes the Spirit of Christ. Moltmann writes, "Through the Shekinah, the Spirit binds itself to Jesus' fate, though without becoming identical with him. In this way *the Spirit of God* becomes definitively *the Spirit of Christ*, so that from that point onwards it can be called by and invoked in Christ's name" (62). Presumably, Moltmann does not intend to claim that the Spirit is not the Spirit of God after the death of Jesus, but rather that the Spirit of God is also the Spirit of Christ.

With these arguments Moltmann hints at the development of a *pneumatologia crucis*.[1] He contends that the Spirit suffers in the death of Jesus, but not in the same way as Jesus. For the Spirit "is Jesus' strength in suffering, and is even the 'indestructible life' in whose power Jesus can give himself vicariously 'for many'" (64). If the Spirit was Jesus' strength in suffering, then the Spirit must also have been Jesus' companion in his suffering. This follows from the indwelling of Jesus by the Spirit, drawing the Spirit into the event in full measure. Moltmann argues that it is important to appreciate the role of the Spirit in Jesus' passion, because if we do not—if we only consider the power of the Spirit and not his own suffering too—then we must admit that the Spirit's influence on the cross is merely external (67).

For Moltmann, the early Christian community saw in Jesus a man of extraordinary power and righteousness. They were led to conclude that these qualities could be traced to the presence of the Spirit of God within Jesus—the same Spirit that came to rest on him at his baptism and continued to operate through him as he demonstrated the inauguration of the kingdom of God. It would have been one thing to revere Jesus as a spiritual leader, but his ministry went beyond leadership to include empowerment, for "the Christ of the Spirit" soon became the sender of "the Spirit of Christ."

The Spirit of Christ

The transition between "the Christ of the Spirit" and "the Spirit of Christ" takes place as Christ transitions from "Spirit-bearer" to "Spirit-sender." The Christ of the Spirit is the Spirit-bearer. He is the promised one who was filled with the Spirit and who brought justice and salvation to Israel. But in the Gospel of John, Jesus promised the disciples that although he was about to die, he would send the Paraclete in his place (John 16:4–15). When this promise was fulfilled, Jesus became the Spirit-sender, and the Spirit became the Spirit of Christ. The question is when Moltmann un-

---

[1] This project has been taken up fully by Moltmann's student Lyle Dabney in his book *Die Kenosis des Geistes*.

derstands this to have happened. As noted above, he specifies the cross as the transitional event. However, he can also claim, "It is only with the resurrection and exaltation of Jesus that the relationship is reversed: the Son sends the Spirit and is himself present in the life-giving Spirit. In this respect pneumatology will be christological pneumatology" (*HTG*: 84). It becomes unclear in Moltmann's remarks whether the transition takes place in the event of the cross, or the resurrection, or the exaltation.

The bottom line is that the transition took place, signaling a complementary relationship between the Christ of the Spirit and the Spirit of Christ. The benefit of approaching christology and pneumatology in this way is that we avoid two pitfalls: the christomonism into which much of the mainstream Western tradition has fallen, and the enthusiastic tendency toward spiritistic pneumatology which has flourished on the fringes of the Western tradition as a reaction to the mainstream tradition (84).

THE EXPERIENCE OF THE EARLY CHURCH

The experience of the first Christian communities with the Holy Spirit finds many parallels with the history of Christ with the Spirit. Just as the being and ministry of Christ depend on the Spirit, so do the being and life of the church.

In the Synoptic Gospels, Jesus is filled with the Spirit at his baptism and addressed as God's "beloved Son." Similarly, the early church associated baptism with Spirit-endowment and adoption as God's children.

The early church considered the Holy Spirit to be the power of Christ's ministry, and by extension, of its own. Paul in particular recognized the Spirit to be the power of love and edification within the body of Christ.

Finally, the early church believed that it was through the Spirit that Christ was raised from the dead. This meant two things for the church. First, followers of Christ can be ushered into the first installment of the resurrection-life through the Holy Spirit. Second, it is through the Spirit that God will someday raise the dead.

In all these ways and more, the early church maintained a close association between Christ and the Spirit. There could be no salvation through Christ outside of the accompanying gift of the Holy Spirit, and there could be no enjoyment of the blessings of the Spirit without discipleship to Christ. Of course, none of this would have been possible without the sending of the Spirit to the believing community. It was by receiving the same Spirit that empowered Christ in his ministry that the church could take up its own ministry of power and righteousness. In other words, in order to become a body of true imitators of Christ, the church needed to be endowed with the necessary divine power in the person of the indwelling Spirit.

The Spirit and the Eschatological Age

THE SPIRIT AND THE INAUGURATION OF THE NEW AGE

In an inaugurated eschatology, the kingdom of God is understood to have begun with the earthly ministry of Jesus and to be continuing in its partial form in the age of the church. In the terms of the previous section, this means that the kingdom was established by "the Christ of the Spirit" and continues with "the Spirit of Christ." The kingdom does not represent merely a change within the heart of the individual believer (Dodd). Rather, it involves the defeat of sin and death in all of its forms, individual and social. The ideas of the kingdom of God, community and the Spirit of Christ converge, for the believing community is the primary context in which the ongoing defeat of sin and death takes place, and it is only accomplished through the power of the Spirit sent by Christ upon that community. Thinking beyond the Christian community, there is nothing more significant in human history than the establishment of the kingdom of God in and through Christ and the Holy Spirit.

The previous comments assume a standpoint of inaugurated eschatology. However, in chapter six I pointed out that Moltmann's eschatological thinking is not consistently of the inaugurated type. It sometimes reflects the views of consistent eschatology. Therefore, in this section we will return to the issue of the ways in which Moltmann considers the present age to be eschatological, but now we will pick it up with specific regard to the Holy Spirit's role in the turn of the ages.

With regard to the Holy Spirit, when and how does Moltmann consider the eschatological age to have begun? We can find various answers to this question in Moltmann's writings. In *Theology of Hope* he emphasized that the resurrection of Christ marked the turn of the ages. In *The Trinity and the Kingdom* he identifies the raising of Christ as the Spirit's first eschatological work (123). This focus on the resurrection of Christ as eschatological comes from his interpretation of the resurrection as the beginning of the new creation of all things (cf. *WJC*: 214).

In contrast, also in *The Trinity and the Kingdom*, Moltmann locates the turn of the ages in the outpouring of the Spirit at Pentecost. This is the date when the church understands Joel's prophecy to have been fulfilled (122). It is with the Spirit that the eschatological age begins for believers. That is, the experience of the outpouring of the Spirit "on all flesh" was interpreted eschatologically by the early Christians (124). Whereas the resurrection of Christ heralds what is to come, the outpouring of the Spirit makes eschatological reality available to present experience. Moltmann writes,

> In the Spirit people already experience now what is still to come. In the Spirit is anticipated what will be in the future. With the Spirit the End-time begins. *The messianic era* commences where the forces and energies of the divine Spirit descend on all flesh, making it alive for evermore. In the activity of the Spirit, consequently, the renewal of life, the new obedience and the new fellowship of men and women is experienced. The marks of the eschatological experience of the Spirit are boundless freedom, exuberant joy and inexhaustible love. In the Spirit the 'new song' is sung. (124)

Moltmann correctly reflects the thought of the New Testament by claiming that the resurrection of Christ and the outpouring of the Spirit are eschatological events. However, Moltmann's interpretation of the biblical texts is both inconsistent and exegetically dubious. He often takes "all flesh" to mean all living things. However, on at least one occasion he claims that to Joel it means first the people of Israel and by extension, being "all flesh," it includes all of humanity. As another possibility, he quotes Hans Walter Wolff, who understands Joel to mean by "flesh" the weak and those without hope and power (*SoL*: 23). Therefore, it is a bit unclear what "all flesh" is to Moltmann. Nevertheless, the vast majority of the time it signifies all living creatures.

The manner in which Moltmann interprets "all flesh" to mean all living creatures violates basic procedures of biblical exegesis. First of all, he interprets Joel 2:28 by way of Gen 9:10. The latter is the record of God's covenant with Noah, in which God makes a promise to Noah and "every living creature" on the ark that he will never again destroy the earth with a flood. This is a radically different kind of promise from the one set forth in Joel, where the prophet foresees a time when God will pour out his Spirit on all flesh, male and female, rich and poor, great and small. The promise in Gen 9:10 is not an eschatological one, for it does not reference a future time of salvation. In contrast, Joel's prophecy is eschatological, for it explicitly looks to the future "day of the Lord" when these things will happen. The wonder of Peter's speech on Pentecost is that he was openly proclaiming that the eschatological age had dawned—the Spirit had indeed been poured out. Thus, when Moltmann takes Joel's prophetic utterance about eschatological events and runs it through the filter of Gen 9:10, he is mixing two categories of divine promise.

In interpreting Joel 2:28 through Gen 9:10, Moltmann is also using the work of one biblical author to interpret the work of another. This exegetical fallacy becomes all the more obvious when one notices that Joel gives no indication of having in mind the plants and animals when he talks about the Spirit being poured out. Joel does not even appear to have in mind all human beings. His words are directed at the "children of Zion," as 2:23 reflects. It is *their* sons and daughters who will prophesy, *their* old men who will dream dreams and *their* young men who will see visions (v. 28). What Peter was proclaiming on Pentecost was the fulfillment of this promise to the people of Israel. Later he would be surprised to find that it would also extend to the Gentiles as well.

Because we cannot agree with the conflation of Gen 9:10 with Joel 2:28 and Acts 2:16–17, we must part ways with Moltmann when he claims that the Spirit has been poured out on all living things. The scriptural testimony conveys that the Spirit has been poured out on the church, but not on all of creation.

Moltmann is right that the Spirit gives life to all creatures, but to go further causes a dilemma in Moltmann's use of the metaphor of "pouring out." On the one hand, if it is an eschatological metaphor, then all of creation and all human beings are enjoying the first fruits of eschatological resurrection-life. However, there is no evidence that things have changed in nature and humanity such that we could make such a claim. It is difficult enough to support such a claim about the church. On the other hand, if outpouring is not an eschatological metaphor, then we can use it to refer to the general presence of the vivifying Spirit in all living things. However, in this case the metaphor loses the meaning Joel and Luke attached to it. In fact, it loses any distinctive meaning at all.

To put the point in another way, what Joel and Luke seem to have in mind by the "outpouring of the Spirit on all flesh" is a special presence of the eschatological Spirit within God's people. Moltmann also teaches that the Spirit is present in particular people, places and times, but he does this by appealing to the idea of the *shekinah*. What Joel and Luke mean by the outpouring of the Spirit is more in line with Moltmann's description of the *shekinah* than it is with his own rendering of the outpouring of the Spirit.

Richard Bauckham criticizes Moltmann for occasionally engaging in faulty exegesis and unfounded speculation, noting that the two faults tend to go together (167). Moltmann's interpretation of the image of the outpouring of the Spirit is an example of these mistakes.

With this difficulty in the background, let us return to the main issue at hand. We have understood Moltmann to hold that the eschatological age began with the resurrection of Christ and the outpouring of the Spirit. In a technical sense, however, this is not true. In *God in Creation* Moltmann differentiates between "messianic time" and "eschatological time." 'Messianic time' is the time of partial fulfillment as the new creation dawns in the midst of the transient time of this world. It is the beginning of the new age under the still-enduring effects of the old. 'Eschatological time' is the time of universal fulfillment of what was promised in historical time and what has dawned in the messianic time (*GC*: 122–24). Finally, there is 'eternal time,' which will be "the time of the new eternal creation in the kingdom of the divine glory" (124). For Moltmann, messianic time is eschatological for all practical purposes, although he prefers to use the term 'eschatology' for events in the age to come. Labeling the present age as 'messianic' is helpful, because it provides a convenient way to talk about the present age without having to invoke circumlocutions such as "the inaugurated eschatological age." At the same time, reserving the label 'eschatological' for the age to come reflects the tendency of systematic theology to regard the present age as only quasi-eschatological, thereby alienating contemporary theology from the thought-world of the New Testament.

Another point at which Moltmann departs from New Testament thought is in identifying the resurrection and Pentecost as the two events that turn the ages. The New Testament authors are clear that the age of fulfillment begins with the coming of Christ. The best example is Matthew, who cites forty-one passages from the Old Testament and claims in thirty-seven of them that Jesus is the fulfillment of those Scriptures. For Matthew, the fulfillment of prophecy reaches back to events that surround the birth of the Messiah—the virgin birth, Jesus' origin in the town of Bethlehem, the sojourn to Egypt and back, and so on. Thus, Matthew understands the eschatological age to begin with the arrival of the Messiah, not the Messiah's resurrection, let alone the day of Pentecost. The difference between Moltmann and Matthew is that the former's ideas about what ushers in the new age are reductionistic compared with the latter's. Whereas Moltmann isolates the turning of the ages to two events in the history of Christ and the Spirit, Matthew takes the history of Christ (and, by extension, of the Spirit as well—cf. Matt 12:28) as a whole and presents the turning of the ages as a matter of the coming of the Messiah. In Moltmann's terms, Matthew understands the turning of the ages to come with Christ himself, not with one event or another out of the history of

Christ. The new age begins with "the Christ of the Spirit" and continues on from there.

THE SPIRIT AND ESCHATOLOGICAL TENSION

A. J. Conyers argues that the Spirit plays a crucial role in Moltmann's understanding of history. For the Spirit is experienced in the tension between the remembered promise and the hope of redemption (126). It is fundamental to Moltmann's theology that there is a tension produced in people who hope for a future that is more desirable than the present. To a certain extent, the Spirit appears in the midst of this longing that people already have. To a much greater extent, the Spirit actually causes the tension to arise and intensify. This is because the experience of the Spirit confirms and encourages hope in the future consummation, all the while pulling believers fully into the struggles of the world in its present state. The upshot is that eschatological tension is a product of the history of the Holy Spirit. It is not simply that eschatological tension and the experience of the Holy Spirit are related; it is that the presence and work of the Spirit actually *produce* eschatological tension.

Thus, Moltmann draws a very close connection between the Holy Spirit and eschatological tension. For him, eschatological tension can take one of three forms. One concerns the energies of the Spirit: "The children of God, who *have already* been seized by the first energies of the Spirit, long for liberty. They are saved, but as yet only in hope. So their faith is simultaneously assurance and pain" (*GC*: 68). A second form concerns the resurrection and the longing of believers for the redemption of the body. "They are already freed from 'the body of sin,' but because of that they suffer all the more under 'the body of death' from which they have not yet been released" (68). The third form concerns the renewal of creation: "In physical terms, believers are bound together in a common destiny with the whole world and all earthly creatures. So what they experience in their own body applies to all other created things" (68).

All three of these forms carry ethical implications. When the church experiences the mediation of the future in the presence of the Holy Spirit, it is also called to mediate the future to the rest of the world. The church is an open church, and it is so only through the power of the Spirit.

For Moltmann, the relationship between the present and the future is intrinsically pneumatological. In and through the Spirit, future eschatology is pressed upon history, and history takes on an eschatological character (127). Phenomena like the formation and life of the church, the communion of the saints, and the forgiveness of sins amount to the history of the future—the future brought into the present through the Holy Spirit.[2] The era of the rule of God has already become accessible for everyone in faith and can be experienced in "the new potentialities of the Spirit" (*CPS*: 220).

On the other hand, the resurrection of the body and the renewal of creation belong to the future of history. This future is only accessible through the Holy Spirit, for the Holy Spirit brings creation into the eschaton (198).

Because the Spirit mediates between present experience and future hope, the presence of the Spirit can be viewed both historically and eschatologically—"as remembered past, present experience, and hoped-for future" (126). The mediation between history and eschatology through the Holy Spirit means that without the Spirit there would be no connection between present experience and future redemption.

The Fellowship of the Spirit

Shekinah: The Presence of God with His People

The fellowship of the Spirit begins with the Spirit's presence among his people. For Moltmann, this is expressed mainly with the idea of the *shekinah*. The doctrine of the *shekinah* comes from Jewish theology, and Moltmann especially borrows from the thought of Franz Rosenzweig and Gershom Scholem (*CG*: xi). The concept of the *shekinah* begins showing up in Moltmann's theology in *The Crucified God*, and it has been a strong element in his pneumatology ever since.

The fundamental idea of the *shekinah* is "the descent and indwelling of God in space and time, at a particular place and a particular era of earthly beings and in their history" (*SL*: 47). *Shekinah* has referred to God's 'tabernacling' or 'dwelling' among his people, first in the transportable ark and then in the temple. During the time of the Babylonian exile the question was raised whether God was still present with his people or whether he had abandoned them. The doctrine of the *shekinah* became a way for Israelites to understand that God was still present among them, even in the land of exile. For the *shekinah* was believed to represent God's presence that accompanied his people in their wanderings. Thus, God's presence was not necessarily restricted to the temple on Zion, but was associated with the worshipping community of God's people (47–48). The

---

[2] Let us keep in mind that the future is not mediated strictly by the Holy Spirit, for Christ's resurrection is also an element of the future that has happened in history.

ongoing identity of Israel depended on the assurance that comes from the *shekinah* concept, that God's permanent dwelling place is not a locality but the people and its history (54).

The *shekinah* is the full and personal presence of God with his people. In the *shekinah* God participates in the history of Israel, and later on, of the church. God makes the sufferings and victories of his people his own (cf. *TK*: 118).

The *shekinah* is not a divine attribute, but rather the presence of God himself. However, it is not God in his essential omnipresence. It is God present at a particular place and a particular time. Therefore, the doctrine of the *shekinah* posits self-differentiation in God. Because the *shekinah* is the very presence of God, God is portrayed as standing over against himself. The *shekinah* is God present in space and time, which is in some ways distinct from God present in eternity. "The descent and habitation of God at a particular place and a particular time among particular people must therefore be distinguished from the very God himself whom even the heavens are unable to contain" (*SL*: 48). Moltmann exploits this contrast to argue that the *shekinah* gives us a way to posit an internal distinction within the Godhead, which is a path from Jewish theology to the Christian doctrine of the Trinity.[3]

Moltmann connects the divine indwelling of the *shekinah* with the Holy Spirit, even though this connection is not typically made in rabbinic Judaism. He argues that the parallels between *shekinah* and *ruach* are unmistakable. Moltmann lists three ways in which the doctrine of the *shekinah* can inform Christian pneumatology (51).

First, the doctrine of the *shekinah* brings out the *personal character* of the Holy Spirit, in that the *shekinah* is the efficacious presence of God himself. "The Spirit is the presence of God in person" (51). But the Spirit is more than just an efficacious presence. He is also God's empathetic presence—"his feeling identification with what he loves" (51).

Second, the concept of the *shekinah* also brings out the *affective dimensions* of God the Spirit. The Spirit indwells, and in doing so, the Spirit suffers when we suffer. The Spirit can be grieved and quenched. The Spirit

---

[3] Moltmann acknowledges that many later rabbinic and kabbalistic thinkers chose to think of the *shekinah* as a hypostasis, an intermediary or go-between, or a divine emanation. However, he argues, following Rosenzweig, that it is better to understand the *shekinah* as God himself in his 'self-distinction.' In other words, rather than being a sub-divine go-between, the *shekinah* is God himself, although it is God present in space and time rather than in the eternal heavens. Rosenzweig provides a way to retain the unity of God while also claiming that God is present in the fullest in the life of his creation (*SL*: 48–49).

also rejoices when we rejoice. Finally, in and through this indwelling in human beings, the Spirit communicates his intense longing to be one with God, and sighs to be at rest in the new, perfected creation (51).

God loves his creation. He binds himself to every one of his creatures in passionate affirmation. "That is why he himself dwells empathetically in every created being, feeling himself into them by virtue of his love. The love draws him out of himself, so to speak, carrying him wholly into the created beings whom he loves. . . . In the self-distinction and the self-giving of love, God is present in all his creatures and is himself their innermost mystery" (50).

However, Moltmann holds that the moment a creature turns away from this divine love, it becomes anxious, aggressive and destructive, because it has become self-seeking. Moltmann interprets all human misery in terms of the miscarriage of love for God. In this case, God chooses to remain with his creatures, rather than to abandon them. But his choice to remain results in a certain alienation of God from himself. He now suffers in the victims and is tormented in the persecutors. In all of this the *shekinah* stays faithfully with wayward men and women, accompanying them with its yearning for God and its homesickness to be one with God. This wooing and homesickness is what we experience in the 'wooing' of the Spirit (50).

The *shekinah's* unification with God depends in part on the actions of human beings.

> With every bit of self-seeking and self-contradiction which we surrender to the will of the Creator who loves us, the Shekinah comes close to God. If we live entirely in the prayer 'Thy will be done,' the Shekinah in us is united with God himself. We live again wholly, and can undividedly affirm life. The wanderings are over. The goal has been reached. We are conscious of God's happiness in us, and are conscious of ourselves in God's bliss. . . . When we once again break asunder and become inwardly disunited, the Shekinah sets off with us again on our odyssey (50).

And so the wanderings of the *shekinah* go.

There are obvious trinitarian difficulties in explaining how the Holy Spirit can be alienated from the Father and the Son in the way Moltmann describes, without his position falling into tritheism. He does not address the issue. We can surmise that the separation between the *shekinah* and God is not absolute, for as well as claiming that his solidarity with us alienates the *shekinah* from God, Moltmann also claims that the same solidarity draws us up into the life of God. This latter assertion can only rest on the assumption of the unity of the *shekinah* with God.

Seeing both sides of this issue reveals a dialectical relationship that would be consistent with Moltmann's general theology. Through the *shekinah*, God enters into human life, and humans enter into the divine life. Through the *shekinah*, God rejoices and suffers with humanity, and humanity suffers and rejoices with God. Both sides of this dialectic are represented in Moltmann's theology, although he does not present them in this way.

Moltmann's account of the suffering of the Spirit in his solidarity with wayward human beings can help us to appreciate the depths of this element of the Spirit's ministry. For if the *shekinah* suffers with us in our falterings, and if the *shekinah* also knows the exultant joy of oneness with God, then the suffering of the *shekinah* is intensified that much more. The *shekinah* experiences not only our foolishness and selfishness, but also the distance from God which is brought on by that foolishness and selfishness.

Third, the idea of the *shekinah* points to the kenosis of the Spirit. Moltmann claims that in the *shekinah* God renounces impassability and suffers with his creatures (51). It is unfortunate that Moltmann does not explain this statement further, for the idea of renunciation (*Verzicht*) implies that God must have been either impassible before this kenosis, at least in the sense that he had not yet suffered with humanity.

The *shekinah* represents God's kenotic presence in the Holy Spirit with human beings. Moltmann points to one particular instance of kenosis in the Spirit's indwelling of Jesus. He argues that at Jesus' baptism the Spirit descends on him, implying that the Spirit has emptied himself to take up his dwelling in "this vulnerable and mortal human being Jesus." The Spirit fills Jesus with authority and power, but not by way of making him a superhuman. Rather, the Spirit participates in Jesus' weakness, his suffering and his death on the cross (93).

In *God in Creation*, Moltmann argues that God is present in all of creation through the Holy Spirit. There is already a kenosis of the Spirit in his dwelling within creation. This means that the idea of the kenosis of the Spirit has several levels for Moltmann. One is the kenosis of the Spirit's dwelling within creation, and another is the kenosis of the *shekinah* with the people of God. A more specific level is the kenosis of the *shekinah* with each individual human being. Inasmuch as the Spirit's descent on the vulnerable and mortal human being Jesus is a kenosis, then there is a similar kenosis each time the Spirit descends to indwell every believer. There is a greater self-restriction of the Spirit's omnipresence when he indwells an individual than there is when he indwells an entire people. These various levels mean that the kenosis of the Spirit is ever new with each fresh situation and has many different levels (in creation, in Israel, in the church, in Jesus, in believers). Thus, when speaking about the kenosis of the Spirit, Moltmann would be better off speaking of a particular instance or type out of the many *kenosi* of the Spirit.

Moltmann means the same thing by *shekinah* whether he is talking about the *shekinah* in relation to Israel, the church or individuals. The *shekinah* is the presence of God the Holy Spirit in a particular place, person/people and time. This leads us to ask the eschatological question: Is there an indwelling of the Spirit in the new age that is different from that in the old? Based on his explanation of the concept of *shekinah*, the distinguishing mark of this manifestation of God's presence in the new age is that it is no longer temporary or sporadic or limited to certain individuals. The presence of God dwells permanently in the body of Christ and all its individual members. Such an understanding would be consistent with Paul's teaching on the eschatological indwelling of the Holy Spirit.

The virtue of Moltmann's appropriation of the concept of *shekinah* is that it gives him a way to speak about the special presence of God in particular people, places and times. This is necessary if one wishes to take into account the New Testament sense that the eschatological Spirit had been poured out and was now indwelling the church and individual believers. The New Testament writers believed that the church is the eschatological community where God is present in a way that he is present nowhere else. The strength of the doctrine of the *shekinah* is that it provides a useful way to explain some of the dimensions of this claim.

The Fellowship of the Spirit

When the Holy Spirit falls on the community of God's people, the result is fellowship. Like many theologians, Moltmann draws on 2 Cor 13:13 to make the point that fellowship is ascribed to the Spirit, while grace is ascribed to Christ and love to the Father. By 'fellowship' Moltmann means "the reciprocal communication of all that one has and is" (*HTG*: 57). Fellowship means sharing with one another and having respect for one another. In the case of the Holy Spirit, he enters into relationship with human beings, both influencing them and allowing them to exert an influence on him (*SL*: 218).

When Moltmann wrote *Theology of Hope* he spoke of lordship in traditional terms. However, by the time he composed *The Trinity and the Kingdom* fifteen years later, he had developed a suspicion of oppressive monarchies "lording" it over people. Driven by this attitude and by his growing interest in pneumatology, he came to speak more and more of fellowship rather than lordship—specifically, the fellowship of the Holy Spirit. Moltmann interprets God's power in terms of love and community-building, rather than in terms of might and brute strength (Claybrook: 211–12).

Moltmann explains that in developing an understanding of the fellowship of the Holy Spirit, the subjective genitive—"the Holy Spirit's fellowship"—will be the primary meaning. The objective genitive—"fellowship with the Spirit"—will be secondary (*SL*: 217–18). This means that the work of the Spirit will show up in the community that creatures have with each other. Moltmann identifies several different manifestations of this community.

The "fellowship of the Holy Spirit" is typically an ecclesio-pneumatological category. This element is present in Moltmann's vision of *community between churches*. He sees the 'fellowship of the Holy Spirit' as something that transcends denominational frontiers. It is what binds all churches to all other churches as members of the great community of God. The fellowship of the Holy Spirit is the foundation for the ecumenical movement, which is "without doubt the most important Christian event of the twentieth century" (*SL*: 4). Participants in ecumenical discussions are actively seeking common ground in the shared experience of the Spirit.

Because Moltmann's pneumatological paradigm is holistic, his notion of the fellowship goes far beyond ecclesiological concerns. Besides the fellowship between churches, Moltmann also envisions *community between generations*. In the human community there is a vital relation between different generations. Human beings are knit together in a "community of time." The consciousness of the flow of time and the development of previous generations is necessary so that younger generations will gain an understanding of the possibilities open to them (237).

Corresponding to the community of the generations is the *community of the genders*. Community between men and women, like community in time, was given to humanity before the church came into being. The fellowship between men and women is not just an ethical issue; it is a pneumatological issue as well, for the Christian faith confesses that in these days the Spirit has been poured out on all flesh, male and female (Joel 2:28–30; Acts 2:17ff.). Thus, fellowship between men and women finds two sources of unity. One is the commonality of being human beings by virtue of creation. The other is sharing in the same eschatological Spirit, who indwells men and women equally. Therefore, when churches and/or the theological community seek greater fellowship between the genders, they are seeking experience of the Holy Spirit (239–40).

Moltmann makes it clear that any concept of the fellowship of the Holy Spirit must include the world of nature. For all human beings are dependent on nature, being embedded in the ecosystems in which they live. Woven throughout all these relationships is the Spirit of life, who binds together all the members of this cosmic community. Seeing this side of community prompts Moltmann to speak of not only the Spirit's activity of the creation of community, but also of the resulting product—the *community of creation* (225). Since the human community and the cosmic community are related via the Holy Spirit, pneumatology provides a way to develop important links between these two aspects of community. To Moltmann such a project is important, because the emphasis on community helps to overcome the isolation of the individual, and also because the link between the two kinds of community directs our attention beyond merely human social systems.

Finally, since to live is to live in relationship, to lose relationship is to die. If this is true, then fellowship is a part of life, and the 'fellowship of the Holy Spirit' is another way of describing the life-giving Spirit. The Spirit of life imparts vitality to creation by conferring on it the gift of fellowship and community. "Life comes out of community, and wherever communities spring up which make life possible and further it, the divine Spirit is efficacious. . . . *The creation of community* is evidently the goal of God's life-giving Spirit in the world of nature and human beings" (219). The fullest expression of Spirit-inspired community will come in the eschaton, when all creatures are in harmony with God and with each other. They will be completely open to each other, because they will no longer have to defend themselves from each other. Therefore, the facets of community we see in today's world point forward to the all-embracing community of the new creation. The fellowship of the Holy Spirit begins in the eschatological community of the body of Christ, but it constantly reaches outside the church to include human society and creation. It is an inclusive fellowship, not an exclusive one.

The Spirit and the Church

The fellowship of the Holy Spirit extends to many spheres of community, but the first place Moltmann identifies it is in the fellowship among believers in the church. As the eschatological and Spirit-endowed community, the church opens up the possibility for a unique type of relationship. "In the fellowship of the Holy Spirit there comes into being a fellowship of men and women without superiors or inferiors, a fellowship of men and women freed through love" (*HTG*: 64). Thus, the fellowship of the Spirit in the church should be characterized by equality among all its parties. Of course, its history does not reveal such equality. Moltmann believes that sadly, the church has too often been the vehicle of monarchical domination rather than a fellowship of equals.

THE SPIRIT AND THE UNITY OF THE CHURCH

If Moltmann is critical of the monarchial concept of church identity, where does he locate the source of ecclesial unity? He finds it in the trinitarian fellowship of God that is reflected in Jesus' prayer for unity in Jn 17:20f. Here the mutual love and open community of the triune are displayed and modeled for the followers of Jesus. In turn, they are called to imitate it and participate in it, and the Holy Spirit enables them to do just that. Thus, the unity of the church is the trinitarian fellowship of the triune God, opened up for human beings by the Holy Spirit.

The gift of the Holy Spirit is one of the primary sources of church unity for Moltmann. This comes by way of analogy with the rest of creation. The Holy Spirit is the source of the unity of all created things, because the Spirit is in all things, just as all things are in the Spirit. In the Spirit all creatures are one. In a similar way, the Spirit is the source of unity for the church because the Spirit is present in the church in a unique way. The difference between the pneumatic unity of creation and the pneumatic unity of the church is that the presence of the Spirit is different for each realm. In creation the Spirit is present by way of his omnipresence, although the Spirit must undergo the kenosis necessary to infuse his presence into time and space. In the church the Spirit is also present, although now as the *shekinah*, meaning that here the Spirit's presence is especially intense and powerful. In the church the Spirit is experienced as the foreshadowing of the future redemption of all creation.

THE SPIRIT AND THE WORD

Institutional Protestant pneumatology sees the relationship between Spirit and Word as a one-way street. The Word is primary, and the Spirit operates only in conjunction with the Word. Moltmann finds fault with this pattern. For him Spirit and Word operate in a mutual relationship, where the Spirit not only operates in conjunction with the Word, but also determines the Word. By this Moltmann means that there can be no Christian proclamation, including that of the Word, without encounter with the Spirit of God. "There are no words of God without human experiences of God's Spirit" (*SL*: 3).

Just as the Word of God presupposes experience of the Spirit, so also do experiences of the Spirit reach beyond the verbal domain. Some experiences of the Spirit are as basic as sensory reality and take non-verbal forms. Furthermore, experience of the Spirit is not limited to the conscious level. It permeates the unconscious and quickens the body. It is a "new energy for living." Therefore, the Word is bound to the Spirit, but the Spirit is not bound to the Word. Moltmann concludes, "To bind the experience of the Spirit solely to the Word is one-sided, and represses these dimensions" (3).

One can see another side of the 'holistic' pneumatology of Moltmann in this formulation of the relationship between Spirit and Word. Moltmann pushes us to recognize the operation of the Spirit not only in Christian proclamation, but also in experience of the Spirit which can be verbalized as well as that which cannot be verbalized, and even in the human unconscious and the human body. This means that the Spirit is at work on far more levels than just the intellectual. The Spirit's influence on the human being is comprehensive and holistic.

THE SPIRIT AND THE SACRAMENTS

Moltmann sets both the ministries of the church and the sacraments within the context of the history of the Spirit. This means that we do not consider the ministries of the church as somehow containing or mediating the presence of the Holy Spirit. "There is no 'Spirit of the sacraments' and no 'Spirit of the ministry,' there are sacraments and ministries of the Spirit" (*CPS*: 289). What happens when we think in terms of the "Spirit of the sacraments" or the "Spirit of the ministry" is that the sacraments and the ministries of the church become reduced to the functions of the church's office bearers. Instead, we must consider the church to be the messianic community, the charismatically living community, that receives its identity not from its own ministries but from its future in the trinitarian history of God (289–90). The church is to be a community marked by the new order of things, including eschatological peace, freedom from sin, law and death, and the rule of Christ (291–93).

This stance means that Moltmann sets *baptism* within the context of the trinitarian history of God's dealings with the world. He writes, "Through baptism in Christ's name believers are publicly set in Christ's fellowship; and through baptism in the name of the triune God they are thereby simultaneously set in the trinitarian history of God" (226).

What is baptism? Moltmann understands it as "the public sign of life in the Holy Spirit, who unites believers with Christ and brings about the new creation" (226). Protestants have traditionally placed baptism in the framework of soteriology. Baptism is one of the "means of salvation." The grace of the Holy Spirit is mediated through baptism and thus subjectively appropriated (226). In contrast, Moltmann sets it within the context of eschatology by stressing its place within the overall history of God's dealings with the world.

For Moltmann, baptism is also pneumatological. He points out that in the Synoptic Gospels, before Easter Jesus was the only one in the circle of his disciples to have been baptized, and he was also the only one who was operating in the power of the Spirit. Combining this with the Synoptic testimony that the Spirit descended on Jesus at his baptism, Moltmann finds a link between baptism and the Holy Spirit in the quintessential example of Christ.

Moltmann sets not only baptism but also *the Lord's Supper* within the context of God's trinitarian history. The Lord's Supper plays a different role, however, in connecting believers to that history. "Just as baptism is the eschatological *sign of starting out*, valid once and for all, so the regular and constant fellowship at the table of the Lord is the eschatological *sign of being on the way*. If baptism is called the unique *sign of grace*, then the Lord's supper must be understood as the repeatable *sign of hope*" (243).

The Lord's Supper combines hope with remembrance, for at the altar "Christ's redeeming future is anticipated and this hope celebrated in remembrance of his passion. In this meal his past and his future are simultaneously made present" (243). This is reflected in 1 Cor 11:23–26, where Paul stresses both the *remembrance* of Christ and the proclamation of his death *until he comes.*

Moltmann links the celebration of Eucharist with the presence of Christ and by extension the presence of the kingdom of God. The bread and the wine "make the kingdom of God present in the form of Christ's body broken 'for us' and Christ's blood shed 'for us.' They make the kingdom of God present in Christ's person and his self-giving. He is both the giver of the feast and the gift itself. The gift, the kingdom of God, is he himself in person" (250). As we saw in Chapter Six, Moltmann's language about the kingdom of God is inconsistent. Most often he speaks of the future kingdom. However, here is one instance in which the tones of a present kingdom in the person of Christ are very strong. Moltmann apparently reverses this course a few pages later in *The Church in the Power of the Spirit* when he explains that in the Eucharist, Christians remember the death of Christ, acknowledge his presence in their midst, and hope with joy for the coming of his kingdom in glory (256). At any rate, it is clear that Moltmann considers Christ to be present in the Eucharist—not just present in a static way, but a historical one, in which believers encounter Christ in his passion, in his resurrection, and in his coming kingdom.

Christ and a foretaste of the kingdom of God are present in the Eucharist through the Holy Spirit. "Through him the fellowship of the table receives the life and the powers of the new creation and the assurance of the coming kingdom" (257). Thus, the Lord's Supper takes the congregation up into the history of God's dealings with the world. And it does so in terms of the trinitarian God, for through the Holy Spirit Christ is present, bringing the rule of God.

The Spiritual Gifts

Consistent with most of his theology, two themes are prominent in Moltmann's explication of the spiritual gifts: their eschatological and universal nature. To begin with, he sees *charismata* as overflowings of the Spirit which has been poured out on the church in the messianic age. Moltmann cites Joel 2:28–29, interpreting it in such a way that the charismatic presence of the Spirit in the church is the beginning of the outpouring of the Spirit on all flesh in the new creation of all things (*CPS*: 294).[4] For Moltmann, the Spirit is the power of the church's being and ministry.

> The Spirit calls [the people of God] into life; the Spirit gives the community the authority for its mission; the Spirit makes its living powers and the ministries that spring from them effective; the Spirit unites, orders and preserves it. It therefore sees itself and its powers as deriving from and existing in the eschatological history of the Spirit (295).

There are two levels of *charismata* for Moltmann. On the more foundational level is the wide array of powers and energies that are possessed

---

[4] As we have seen, this is one way among several that Moltmann uses the Joel 2:28 text.

by every person. Putting these powers and energies in the service of the church classifies them as *charismata*.[5] In support of the view that even 'natural talents' can be viewed as spiritual gifts, Moltmann refers to 1 Cor 7:20, in which Paul writes, "Let each of you remain in the condition in which you were called." Although Paul appears to mean by 'calling' the beckoning of God unto salvation, Moltmann interprets it as an individual assignment, so to speak, for each person's life. So one person is called to be a slave while another is called to be free, one is called to be unmarried while another is called to remain with a spouse and children, and so on. Moltmann then expands the notion of calling to include anything that God leads a person to do throughout his or her life.

The crucial link between calling and spiritual gifts comes when Moltmann adds that spiritual gifts are any abilities, energies or resources one puts in the service of one's calling. That is, when one uses one's God-given abilities for the Christian ministry to which one is called, those abilities become 'spiritual gifts.' It is the act of edification that renders particular actions 'charismatic.' "Individual powers and energies become charismatic in the *relationships* which give form to the shared life-process" (182).

Just like callings, *charismata* are individualized to each person. "Through the powers of the Spirit, the one Spirit gives every individual his specific share and calling, which is exactly cut out for him, in the process of the new creation" (*CPS*: 295). Just as the Spirit's work spreads throughout all of creation, so there is need for unending variations of Spirit-activity as the Spirit gives new life to all things (295–96). Moltmann formulates this principle: "to each his own; all for each other; testifying together to the world the saving life of Christ" (298).

Because 'natural talents' can be thought of as 'spiritual gifts,' Moltmann warns against searching for one's spiritual gifts by looking for what one does *not* have. Spiritual gifts are not miraculous endowments in the sense of suddenly appearing out of nowhere; they are whatever one has at one's disposal to meet the current need (*SoL*: 56). When believers experience "new" endowments of the Spirit, it is due to the fact that they are in new situations and find that they have capabilities of which they were previously unaware (59).

An extension of this basic level of potentially charismatic abilities is the level of *special charismata*. These are gifts "which are newly created by the Holy Spirit, and are therefore experienced for the first time in the

---

[5] Gifts used in the service of the congregation are not different from gifts used in the service of one's family or employer. It is only that the context is different (*SoL*: 59).

discipleship of Jesus. For Paul these are especially the gifts and tasks connected with the building up of the community of Christ's people, which witnesses to the coming kingdom" (*SL*: 183). Here we find the activities that appear on typical lists of spiritual gifts—preaching, teaching, giving, healing, and so on.

Although we can speak of two levels of spiritual gifts, Moltmann refuses to separate the "special" *charismata* from the "natural" talents. One reason is that "practically speaking, what believers do is to put their natural gifts at the service of the congregation" (183). Another reason is that he views *charismata* not as creations of the Spirit but as the Spirit himself poured out in the gifts (195). To separate the gifts would be to separate the Spirit himself.

What about speaking with tongues? Moltmann admits that he has no personal experience with this phenomenon, but he understands it to be "an inward possession by the Spirit which is so strong that it can no longer find adequate expression in comprehensible language, so that it utters itself in glossolalia—just as intense pain is expressed by unrestrained weeping, or extreme joy by jumping and dancing" (185). Moltmann does not doubt that such phenomena are authentic expressions of Spirit-influence. His one question for the charismatics is where their spiritual gifts are in the everyday world. In a related criticism, Moltmann chastises the charismatic community for being too concerned with escapist 'spirituality' and not concerned enough with problems outside of the church (186).

Obviously, not many people in the charismatic community will resonate with Moltmann's concept of spiritual gifts. For them, spiritual gifts are "spiritual" because they are new abilities, not because they are old (or latent) abilities used for a different purpose. What differentiates this position from Moltmann's is that charismatics have a stronger view of the changes that come with the indwelling of the Holy Spirit and the gift of new life than does Moltmann. It is curious that elsewhere, Moltmann's view of rebirth and new life is marked by eschatological optimism. He expects that things will be truly different for the believer ushered into the resurrection-life. However, when he turns his attention to spiritual gifts, the implication is that the person has really not changed all that much; she just has different interests and goals.

Certainly the new interest in Christ and the goal of serving his kingdom play an important role. For Paul, to take up this interest and goal is itself a miracle brought about by the indwelling Holy Spirit. What grows out of this fundamental miracle, be it inexplicable or apparently mundane, is the charismatic operation of the Spirit.

While it has its shortcomings, Moltmann's understanding of spiritual gifts has the virtue of being holistic. That is, he ties the concept of spiritual gifts into a much larger picture. First, *charismata* are for all believers, not just an elite few. This point echoes the Pauline view that the *charismata* are eschatological signs precisely *because* they are universally poured out. Moltmann takes this view in opposition to the common working assumption that the gifted members of the body of Christ are those called to a special life of Christian service. He writes, "The widow who exercises mercy is acting just as charismatically as a 'bishop'" (*CPS*: 298).

Second, spiritual gifts function in all spheres of life. Moltmann wants to expand our appreciation for the scope of the spiritual gifts by adding that the believer is a charismatic not only for the purposes of church gatherings, but also for activities in "the world." That is, in every sphere of life the believer is to live out the liberated existence which the Spirit has opened up for her—a freedom "which overcomes this world and makes the new creation obedient. In principle every human potentiality and capacity can become charismatic through a person's call, if only they are used in Christ" (297).

Third, spiritual gifts are not only for all believers; they are for the entire church. That is, Moltmann has an ecclesial perspective on the issue of *charismata*. He holds that if we want to determine the particular callings within a particular community, we have to proceed from the calling of the community as a whole. Particular forms of service presuppose the general service of the kingdom of God, a calling which is universal to all believers (300). Moltmann is viewing the entire church universal as charismatically gifted and charged with the prophetic proclamation of the coming kingdom (301). This is a sensible opinion, for the church is operating in the power of the Spirit just as Christ did in his earthly ministry, and the church proclaims the rule of God, just as Christ himself did.

This last point—that the entire church is gifted to work for the kingdom of God—reminds us that Moltmann's idea of the spiritual gifts is consistent with his position that the sacraments and ministries of the church must be set within the greater context of the trinitarian history of God's dealings with the world. The church's giftedness makes sense only in its orientation toward the new creation of all things. Similarly, the individual's gifts are the energies of the new, eschatological life (295). Each individual's particular gifting corresponds to his or her exact role in the process of the new creation. For both the church and individual believers, *charismata* point to the future consummation.

The Power of Liberation

Not only is the Holy Spirit the author of authentic fellowship and mutual edification, he is also an agent of liberation. The theme of liberation is deeply important to Moltmann. He claims, "According to the testimony of the Bible, people's first experience with God is the experience of an immense liberation—of being set free for life" (*SL*: 98). Moltmann asserts that for both Israel and Christianity the experience of God and the experience of freedom are so deeply fused that they become almost synonymous. In the Old Testament the story that defines Israel is the Exodus. Similarly, in the New Testament the experiences of God that people have in encounters with Jesus can also be characterized as experiences of freedom—deliverance from sicknesses and demonic possession, from social humiliation and insults, from "the godless powers of this world," and, as Paul stresses, from the powers of sin and death (99). Moltmann lauds Latin American liberation theology for putting a premium on working to change the world, not just interpret it in a distinctive way. How, then, does he define liberation, and how is the Holy Spirit involved in it?

First of all, liberation is complex. It can come in different sectors of life. There is inward liberation, which is freedom from the obstructions of guilt and the melancholy of death. And there is outward liberation, which is freedom from the compulsions of economic, political and cultural repression.

Liberation can also be explained in terms of the three fundamental dimensions of experience of the Spirit: faith, hope and love. *Liberating faith* is more than giving assent to a body of doctrines or participating in the church. It is "a faith that takes us personally captive" (114). It is a faith that we grasp (because we understand it in an existential way) and by which we are grasped. To take up the stance of faith is to experience "liberation for freedom." Freedom involves not personal autonomy or the ability to dominate others. It is the ability to participate in the divine energy of life. This means entering into the creative work of God and his Spirit, who affirm life through loving it in all of its forms.

Liberating love is freedom realized in sociality. That is, individuals are really free only if they are utilizing their freedom in mutually supportive social relationships. Freedom involves mutual respect and acceptance for other people, openness to share one's life with others, and self-giving communication. In this type of condition freedom as sociality goes far beyond any conception of purely individual freedom, for the potentialities in the network of social relationships are more manifold and diverse than the potentialities of any one individual. Besides, a purely individual sense of freedom typically involves exercising one's liberty at the expense of the liberty of others.

Liberating hope goes even beyond social freedom. Inasmuch as Christian faith involves hope for the resurrection, it also frees us to develop a "creative passion for the possible." "It is not like lordship, directed only towards existing things. Nor is it like love, directed only towards community with existing people. It is directed towards the future, the future of the coming God" (119). Moltmann stresses that we do not completely understand freedom unless we include this orientation toward the future—a component of Christian freedom which is often neglected.

The role of the Holy Spirit is essential to true liberation. The very impetus to be free comes from God through his Spirit. In this way freedom has a transcendent foundation—God in his immanence. If God is the principle of true freedom, then there is no end to either the power of liberation, or the number of forms liberation could take.

When God functions as Liberator, he is often called "Lord." Moltmann points out that there is precedent for understanding the Spirit as Lord in 2 Cor 3:17. He understands this verse to point to a double experience of God. First, the verse indicates that "The Lord is the Spirit," meaning that the presence of God which believers experience is the Holy Spirit, who can function in the capacity of Liberator. "In the Spirit people experience God as 'the Lord,' and that simply means that they experience their liberation for life" (120).

Second, the verse adds that "where the Spirit of the Lord is, there is freedom." Moltmann notices that with these words Paul refers experience of the Spirit and the experience of liberty to Christ. It is not merely the Spirit who liberates, but "the Spirit of the Lord."

Taking both parts of 2 Cor 3:17 together, Moltmann argues that liberation involves a reciprocal relationship between the Spirit and Christ. True freedom comes about when Christ is experienced in the Spirit.

> In practical terms this means that *discipleship of Jesus* and *the liberating Spirit* act together, in order to lead people into true freedom. Pentecostal and charismatic experiences of the Spirit become spiritualistically insubstantial and illusory without the personal and political discipleship of Jesus. Personal and political discipleship of Jesus becomes legalistic and arid without the spirituality which 'drinks from its own wells,' to quote Gutiérrez (121).

I argued in chapter 3 that this verse does not refer to Christ. Instead, "the Lord" in 2 Cor 3:17 refers to Yahweh. As the "Spirit of the Lord," the Holy Spirit is the Spirit of God. Therefore, 2 Cor 3:17 does not indicate that there is a reciprocal relationship between the Spirit and Christ, since it is not making any direct claims about Christ at all. Nevertheless, Moltmann's general point is accurate. Liberation involves both Christ and the Spirit. Christians must not pursue either pneumatomonistic liberation without regard for discipleship to Christ, or christomonistic liberation without regard for the life that comes from the Spirit.

The Power of Justice

Moltmann's vision for a full understanding of justification is by no means limited to the Reformation conception of the term as the imputation of righteousness based on the atoning work of Christ. Moltmann's plan of attack is first to speak of justice as a social *desideratum*. Hence, the ideal of justice involves the conversion of people from either oppressor or victim to free servants of divine justice and righteousness. Clearly it involves work in the social sphere. For Moltmann, God's justifying righteousness is also the righteousness that creates justice.

Regarding sin and forgiveness, Moltmann argues that both are universal. What is particular is the way in which God leads individuals to work out their salvation. For some it involves escaping from their apathy as victims, while for others it involves repenting from their unjust deeds. For all it means that God brings justice where it has been lacking (127–28).

What is needed to counteract injustice is atonement, and this atonement has to take place on three different levels. The main concern of most liberation theologies is *God's justice for the victim*. God is on the side of those who cannot defend themselves. Moltmann calls this God's "preferential option for the poor" (129). God suffers along with the disenfranchised. He enters into solidarity with them. On the basis of this suffering and solidarity, God will judge according to what is done to him in the poor and the vulnerable (130).

God's justice for the perpetrators is necessary in order for liberation to happen. In other words, unless the perpetrators are liberated from their own destructive behaviors and habits, the oppressed cannot be liberated. Moltmann tends to discuss oppression in terms of violence committed by some people against others, and by human beings against weaker creatures. "Because violence has these two sides, the road to freedom and justice has to begin with both: the liberation of the oppressed from the suffering of oppression requires the liberation of the oppressor from the injustice of oppression" (132). His basic point that oppressors need liberation is correct, although it remains true that oppression and injustice happen more often in non-violent ways than in violent ones.

God's justice for communities is needed because structural sin is sin that has taken on a life of its own, so to speak. It transcends mere human acts, for it becomes a force dominating human beings. Structures are made by people, but people are determined by structures as well. "Anyone who exists in these structures becomes sin's accomplice, even if he wants only what is good" (139–40). The only answer for structural sin is the action of God creating justice where it has been lacking.

Moltmann splits the Spirit's role in justice into two sides, negative and positive, each corresponding to the three levels of justice that is needed. In negative terms, the Spirit's role regarding the oppressed is as "the Spirit of righteousness and justice who can be sensed in *the pain of people without rights* over their deprivations" (142). This pain drives the cause of justice. The Spirit's role regarding the oppressors is as "the Spirit of righteousness and justice who speaks in *the guilty conscience* of the people who commit violence" (142). The guilty conscience is uneasiness over a feeling of guilt, but in a broader sense it is a state of inner anxiety and fear of one's own self that becomes manifest in aggression towards others. Finally, the Spirit's role regarding communities is as the principle of instability in unjust structures. That is, unjust systems are inherently unstable, for they are built upon oppression and strife. They are thus open to destructive forces from within and without. The Holy Spirit functions in the role of destabilizer in these structures (143).

In positive terms, the Spirit's role regarding the oppressed is as "*the presence of Christ* among the victims of violence. Christ is their brother— they are his family and the community of his people, whether they know it or not. The Spirit is Christ's solidarity with them" (143). The Spirit's role regarding the oppressors is as "*the atoning power* of Christ's substitution among and in the perpetrators" (143). Finally, the Spirit's role regarding communities is as "*the divine love* which holds in life even self-destructive human communities in order to heal them" (143). This means that the fellowship of the Holy Spirit is the antitype of human communities that are built upon injustice and domination, in that the fellowship of the Holy Spirit includes the reciprocal respect of each member of the community for the other. Domination is excluded from such a community.

The Power of the Resurrection

One of the major themes of *Theology of Hope* is resurrection. Christ's resurrection is the lynchpin upon which Christianity either stands or falls. It is also the key event which opens up the future for humanity and all of creation, for it represents the end of suffering and death and the beginning of new and eternal life in God. Moltmann does not reinterpret the resurrection in order to make it more acceptable to contemporary sensibilities, as do many theologians of our era. Instead, he seizes upon it as a foil with which to challenge the contemporary world and open up new possibilities of hope and action. As Bauckham puts it, Moltmann brings the resurrection into "a critical and productive relationship to the modern experience of the world, opening it up to new possibilities" (39).

This is only possible if the resurrection is something other than a fabrication by the apostles or merely a dynamic of our experience of Christ. The meaning and significance of the resurrection can only be retained if the event conveys a great surplus value which directs our attention to a future which transcends either the apostles' experience or our own (cf. Bauckham: 40). This surplus value is the resurrection to new life which directs our attention beyond the person of Jesus to the future of all creation. Once again, in order for this surplus value to be present, the resurrection must be more than a restoration of Christ's previous life. Because it points to an unprecedented future, the resurrection must be an unprecedented event. It has no historical precedent or prototype at all. "It is something completely new in history" (*SoL*: 30).

Moltmann considers it to be basic Christian doctrine that God will raise the dead through his Holy Spirit. The Spirit, as the giver of life, is the power of the resurrection. This comes from Paul. According to Paul, Jesus was raised through the Spirit (Rom 8:11). By extension, the Spirit is the divine power that gives life to the dead (1 Cor 6:14) (*TK*: 122).

The Spirit raised Christ from the dead into eternal life. "That is what is meant by the word resurrection" (123). Thus, the life the Spirit gives is the eternal life of God. More specifically, this is one kind of life the Spirit gives, for he also gives mortal life to all of God's creatures. Therefore, the Spirit gives mortal life on the one hand and immortal, eternal life on the other.

The amazing work of the Spirit is that he brings the eternal future into history. In *The Church in the Power of the Spirit*, Moltmann writes,

> As the power of resurrection, the Spirit is the reviving presence of
> the future of eternal life in the midst of the history of death; he is

the presence of the future of the new creation in the midst of the dying life of this world and its evil state. In the Spirit and through the Spirit's powers the eschatological new thing—'Behold I make all things new'—becomes the new thing in history, reaching, at least in tendency, over the whole breadth of creation in its present wretchedness. That is why the energies of new life in the Spirit are as manifold and motley as creation itself. (*CPS*: 295–96)

Later, in *The Way of Jesus Christ* he echoes the same theme that the Spirit brings the life of the future into present experience.

What men and women fragmentarily experience here and now, even before their deaths, in rebirths to true life in the energies and powers of love, happens in perfected form and right into mortal flesh itself in the resurrection of the dead. The person who is wholly and entirely seized and pervaded by the living power of the divine Spirit becomes immortal, because death loses its power over him. (*WJC*: 257)

The idea of eschatological tension comes across strongly in these two quotes. The Spirit who raised Christ from the dead is also giving new life to believers. Therefore, believers enjoy life on two levels simultaneously. One is the mortal life that all living creatures currently possess. Added to the believer is eternal life that only Christ possesses in full, but that believers possess in part due to the indwelling of the Spirit of the resurrection.

Resurrection means not only the giving of eternal life, but also transfiguration and glorification. Thus, when Christ was raised from the dead he was given life by the Spirit, but he was also transfigured and glorified by the Spirit (*TK*: 123). This transfiguration is a total alteration of the person, including but not limited to one's physical makeup. For Moltmann, resurrection must have this holistic character. He reasons that if the Spirit infuses the whole person—not just a 'soul'—in the present, then the Spirit raises the whole person to life in the future (*CoG*: 71).

Consistent with New Testament thought, Moltmann claims that Christ's resurrection "is the beginning of the new creation of everything" (*SoL*: 30). Thus, Moltmann recognizes that the resurrection of Jesus is eschatological in that it brings new life to human beings, but he also recognizes that an eschatological perspective is a cosmic perspective. In addition, he acknowledges the operation of the Holy Spirit in the resurrection, and in this way he opens up connections between eschatology and pneumatology in the event of the resurrection of Jesus, and by extension, of all human beings. In the next chapter, we will focus attention on the cosmic elements of Moltmann's pneumatology. As the Spirit of life, the Holy Spirit is not only the source of life for all creatures, he also the source of eschatological life and the power of the new creation of all things.

Conclusion

In this chapter, we have focused on the relationship between the Holy Spirit and the believing community. Institutional Protestant pneumatology would set the work of the Holy Spirit within the context of the ministry of Christ or the ministry of the church. Moltmann shows both of these options to be inadequate.

With regard to the Spirit and Christ, the tendency in the theology of Karl Barth—who is merely following the impetus of the *filioque* clause and traditional Western theology—is to subordinate the Spirit to Christ. Moltmann leads pneumatology in a different direction—that of mutuality between Christ and the Spirit. Christian theology cannot speak of "the Spirit of Christ" without first speaking of "the Christ of the Spirit." Christ and the Spirit depend on each other for the execution of their ministries. They are both sent by the Father, and their roles are complementary. One could maintain that John's Gospel teaches that in the time between the appearances of Christ, the Spirit is strictly subordinate to Christ, but I will argue in Chapter Nine that even in the period of the church Christ is dependent on the Spirit and interdependence between them continues.

With regard to the relationship between the Spirit and the church, Moltmann reverses the trend in institutional Protestant pneumatology to subordinate the Spirit to the functions of the church. Rather than thinking of the activity of the Spirit within the context of the ministries and sacraments of the church, Moltmann thinks of the ministries and sacraments of the church within the context of the entire history of the Spirit—which, in turn, we can set within the broader context of the flow of eschatological history, which is a segment of the trinitarian history of God's dealings with the world.

It is generally true that words and concepts gain meaning from the context in which they appear. The same holds true for understanding the work of the Holy Spirit. It gains its fullest meaning when placed within a context larger than christology and ecclesiology—the context of inaugurated eschatology. I have identified this context under the guidance of Paul, although the same basic orientation toward pneumatology is shared by the New Testament witness as a whole. Even though Moltmann is inconsistent in his comments about the eschatological character of the present age, he shows us some ways into this new way of speaking about the Holy Spirit. It is a way of speaking that is new to the Protestant tradition, but by being apostolic, it is actually quite ancient.

7

The Holy Spirit and the Individual

WITHIN the context of social and religious communities comes the individual human being. The Holy Spirit is omnipresent and thus has a basic level of influence on every person, but as the doctrine of the *shekinah* shows, his more intense presence and influence is on the individual who follows Christ. This individual will come to know the Spirit through the Christian community and its authoritative writings, and also through experience. Over the years of a person's life, such experience will cover various modes of Spirit-activity, including justification, rebirth and sanctification. In this chapter, we will examine the views of Moltmann about these aspects of the influence of the Spirit on the individual person—experience of the Spirit and the Spirit's role in justification, rebirth and sanctification. We will be searching out the eschatological aspects of the Spirit's presence and work in all these regards.

Experience of the Spirit

What is Experience of the Spirit?

This is an important question to ask, because as Moltmann sees it, the problem with much of the Christian understanding of the Holy Spirit is that the influence of the Spirit is restricted to the "holy" spheres of life. The narrower notion of experience of the Spirit which Moltmann rejects is an association of the Holy Spirit with what we perceive to be "holy." Presumably, what Moltmann means by 'holy' is worship of God, reading of Scripture, sanctification, the gifts of the Spirit, and the like—where these subjects are defined in terms of a separation between the 'holy' and the rest of life. These are the categories in which pneumatology has usually been pursued. The problem Moltmann sees with such an approach is that the Holy Spirit is thought to be too holy to be concerned with everyday life (x). Most people feel little connection with this pious realm.

Thus, they do not often report having experiences of this Spirit of holiness. Moltmann writes,

> The simple question: when did you last feel the workings of the Holy Spirit? embarrasses us. The Spirit's 'holiness' fills us with religious awe. We are conscious that the Spirit is something apart from secular life, and sense our own remoteness from God. Religious experiences, as we all know, are not everyone's line of country (x).

Moltmann wants to change this pattern. He develops what he calls a 'holistic' pneumatology, which is reflected in the subtitle of *The Spirit of Life*—"*A Universal Affirmation*" (*Eine ganzheitliche Pneumatologie*). This means drawing our awareness of the influence of the Holy Spirit into all spheres of life. In order to draw the Holy Spirit into the flow of everyday life, Moltmann defines 'experience of the Spirit' as "an awareness of God in, with and beneath the experience of life, which gives us assurance of God's fellowship, friendship and love" (17). His correction to a reductionistic concept of 'experience of the Spirit' is conveyed in the words, "in, with, and beneath the experience of life." He defines experience of the Holy Spirit as a part of life in general, and he opens our eyes to the extensive interlacing of the presence of the Spirit throughout the broad variety of everyday events. Going by the narrower "holiness" concept, most of us are unfamiliar with experiences of the Spirit. On the other hand . . .

> It is a different matter if we are asked: when were you last conscious of '*the spirit of life*'? Then we can answer out of our everyday experiences and can talk about our consolations and encouragements. Then 'spirit' is the love of life which delights us, and the energies of the spirit are the living energies which this love of life awakens in us. The Spirit of God is called *the Holy Spirit* because it makes our life here something living, not because it is alien and estranged from life (x).

Not only does Moltmann broaden the domain of 'experience of the Spirit' beyond special "holy" experiences, he also extends it into the unconscious mind. Because of the speed with which our minds conceptualize and process information about the world, Moltmann holds that the great majority of our experiences are never consciously registered. This is true for experiences of the Spirit just as it is true of other types of experience.

Later in *The Source of Life*, Moltmann adds that the experience of the Spirit is not a uniform, static phenomenon that is the same for all people. Rather, "the Spirit of life is present only as the Spirit of this or that particular life. So the experience of the Holy Spirit is as specific as the living beings who experience the Spirit, and as varied as the living beings who experience the Spirit are varied" (*SoL*: 56). This is an excellent way of pointing our attention to the variety of the Spirit's workings. It is refreshing to see such an approach instead of blanket statements about what the Holy Spirit does in all places and contexts.

Moltmann has basic theological grounds for wanting to broaden the concept of experience of the Spirit. These grounds are the doctrines of creation and omnipresence. Based on passages from Job, Psalms and Wisdom, he understands the Spirit of God to be the power of creation and the wellspring of life (35). If the Spirit is present everywhere as the power of creation and the principle of life—that is, if the Spirit's presence permeates every aspect of human existence—then, concludes Moltmann, it must be possible to experience the Spirit "in, with and beneath each everyday experience of the world" (34). It is important to note that Moltmann is not saying that we *do* experience the Spirit in each everyday experience of the world, but only that it is *possible* to do so. Still, he clearly assumes that the possibility of experiencing the Spirit in everyday experiences of the world is realized to a significant degree (although he is not precise about what this degree is). It is also important to note that Moltmann does not dispense with "holy" experiences of the Spirit. Rather, he adds the "everyday" experiences of the Spirit as a category distinct from, but just as valid as, the "holy" experiences (35).

Experience of the Holy Spirit has a trinitarian dimension. In our experience of the Holy Spirit we also experience liberating fellowship with Jesus. That is, through the Holy Spirit believers have experience of the history of Christ (*FC*: 84). But lest one conclude that experience of the Spirit is only an avenue to experience of Christ, Moltmann points out that experience of the Spirit acquires a stature and dignity which is its own (*SL*: 18).

Experience of the Spirit draws us into the trinitarian history of God's interaction with the world. Therefore, experience of the Spirit has a historical character, for it connects us with the presence and action of God that reaches back to creation and forward to the eschaton. Moltmann describes experience of the Spirit as "the intermediate state of every historical experience between remembered past and expected future. The experience, life and fellowship of God's Spirit come into being when Christ is made present and when the new creation of all things is anticipated. These things are resonances of Christ, and a prelude to the kingdom of God" (17). Lending the experience of the Spirit its historical character is an original and important move for Moltmann to make. He finds a way to link religious experience, which is a phenomenon of the present moment, with the broad sweep of salvation-history. On the other hand, Moltmann also points out that experiences of God can be so intense that the past and future are all but obliterated for the moment in an ecstatic experience of the pure present (18). Not all experiences of the Spirit have a deep historical character.

In conclusion, Moltmann expands the notion of experience of the Spirit in ways that are in keeping with recurring themes in his theology. It is holistic, permeating all aspects of human life. Similarly, it is universal, affecting all life in general. Finally, it is trinitarian, involving not just the Holy Spirit but also the Father and the Son. The themes of holism, universality and Trinity are all vital to the overall Moltmannian theological project.

Experience, Scripture, and Moltmann's Pneumatological Methodology

Redefining experience of the Spirit in the way Moltmann does, we might expect that there is an effect on his pneumatological methodology. In fact, in the introduction to *The Spirit of Life*, Moltmann states in strong terms that he plans to construct his pneumatological views on the basis of human experience of the Spirit, *as opposed to* "the objective word of the proclamation, and the spiritual institutions of the church" (17). In the coming paragraphs we will pause to consider Moltmann's theological method vis-à-vis the formation of his pneumatological positions.

There are several reasons why Moltmann advocates an experiential method in *The Spirit of Life*. First, in other works of his corpus he has already founded assertions about the Spirit on Scripture and the creeds, and he intends the pneumatological views set forth in *The Spirit of Life* to complement the views in his other works. However, his use of Scripture in *The Spirit of Life* is not very different from that in other of his works. He does emphasize experience more in *The Spirit of Life*, but that does not amount to the intentional neglect of Scripture.

Second, Moltmann wants to start *The Spirit of Life* from shared experience of the Spirit rather than the proclamation and spiritual institutions of the church, primarily because theology based on the former is 'church theology'—theology for pastors and priests—whereas theology based on the latter is 'lay theology'—theology for every believer (17). This is rhetorical flourish from Moltmann, aimed at legitimizing the typical experiences of average believers as a field of data from which theological positions can be developed. Still, it is dangerous—even irresponsible—rhetoric, for three reasons. It implies a destructive antagonism between clergy and laity; it postulates a false opposition between Scripture and experience that is inconsistent with Moltmann's common stance on the matter; and it associates Scripture and the creeds with clergy, and religious experience with laity—another false opposition.

The third reason Moltmann wants to take the experiential approach—the most important one for our purposes—is that Moltmann also believes that experience of the Holy Spirit is a source of pneumatological data which has been insufficiently mined. The reason is that the work of the Spirit, and thus experience of the Spirit, has been conceived in overly restrictive terms, and that we have theological warrant for expanding these notions. If we do so, there will be much previously unused material with which we will then be able to construct a theology of the Holy Spirit from experience.

A fourth reason is that Moltmann is reacting against Barth's polemic against religious experience. Moltmann reports that Barth understood the Holy Spirit to reveal something to human beings that they never could experience: God's eternity and the life which lies beyond the frontier of death—eternal life. "Barth therefore calls the Holy Spirit 'the Spirit of promise,' because it places human beings in expectation of the 'Wholly Other,' and can hence never be experienced" (7). This means that Barth and Moltmann share common ground in including eschatological elements in their understandings of the Holy Spirit. But Moltmann's openness to religious experience reveals that his theological approach is radically different from that of Barth.

A fifth reason is that it gives Moltmann a chance to quiet his critics who charged that *Theology of Hope* was so one-sided in its stress on the future that it effectively denied all present experience of God (Bauckham: 23).

For these reasons and possibly others, Moltmann relies heavily on experience of the Spirit in *The Spirit of Life*. In doing so, he expresses that he hopes he can develop a pneumatology out of experience of the Spirit rather than "the objective word of the proclamation and the spiritual institutions of the church" without being put down as a "modernist, liberal or pietistic 'experiential' theologian" (17).

Moltmann significantly broadens the territory covered by the concept of the experience of the Holy Spirit by adding several dimensions that deepen the concept for us. It is holistic, trinitarian, both conscious and unconscious, and historical. Based on this expansive notion of the experience of the Spirit, it would seem that he has opened up new possibilities for constructing a pneumatology from experience. However, these possibilities do not materialize. For Moltmann's broader concepts of the Spirit's presence and of experience of the Spirit reveal an epistemological problem. In criticizing the "holiness" concept of experience of the Spirit, he draws attention to the fact that Christians typically do not report having constant, or even frequent, experiences of the Spirit in their everyday lives. In fact, he goes so far as to lament the estrangement from the Holy Spirit that most people feel. However, his position is that Christians frequently do experience the Spirit in everyday life. Does this discrepancy prove Moltmann wrong? Does the perceived lack of experience of the Holy Spirit demonstrate that the Spirit is only involved in "holy" things after all? William Alston gives us good reason to refrain from drawing this conclusion too quickly.

In his book *Perceiving God*, Alston distinguishes three levels of experience of God, all of which constitute a genuine perception of God. First is perception of God in which the subject is aware that it is God with whom she has had an encounter. In order to identify the other two levels, Alston trades on the crucial point that there can be genuine awareness of God that the subject does not take as such. Thus, the second level is perception of God in which the subject is not attending to the matter of whether God was present in the experience, although she would so construe the experience if the question arose. The third level is the experience of God in which the subject is actually perceiving God, even though she would not be disposed to identify the object of the experience as God if the question arose, "just as one can see a cyclotron without realizing that what one sees is a cyclotron" (11).

Incorporating the insights of Alston into Moltmann's position, we can hypothesize that the Holy Spirit is a consistent element in the everyday experience of Christians (Moltmann), but that they either do not notice him (Alston's second level) or they misidentify him as something else (Alston's third level). Based on Moltmann's inclusive notion of experience of the Spirit, we must conclude that, in relation to the Spirit, Christians operate most of the time on levels two or three. But upon closer inspection, level two is less a concern than level three. On the one hand, based on the way Christians talk about their experience of the Holy Spirit, they apparently experience the Spirit even less frequently in non-religious contexts than in "holy" contexts. On the other hand, Moltmann teaches that Christians actually do experience the Spirit in the midst of everyday events. If he is correct, the feeling of estrangement from the Spirit that many Christians have cannot be due to an infrequency of experiences of the Spirit, but rather to an infrequency of recognizing the pneumatic dimensions of their everyday experiences.[1]

Moltmann's line of thinking leads to the conclusion that the vast majority of the experiences of the Spirit that Christians have are on Alston's third level. Because Christians associate the work of the Spirit strictly with "holy" spheres of life, they do not, and would not if asked, identify the pneumatic dimensions of their everyday, "mundane" experiences. We must conclude that just as one would not seek an account of cyclotrons from people who constantly walk by them without knowing what they are, in the same way, one would not seek an account of the Holy Spirit from people who frequently experience the Holy Spirit in everyday life but are not aware that it is the Holy Spirit they are experiencing. After all, of the three levels Alston identifies, the third is the most deficient epistemic position. This situation cuts short the project of constructing a pneumatology from experience. However, let us recall that Moltmann states in *The Spirit of Life* that he plans to do just that, choosing experience *instead of* Scripture and tradition as a basis for a pneumatology. But is this what he actually does?

The most direct way to cure the misidentification of the objects of experience that characterizes Alston's third level is through education. Teaching Christians that certain dimensions of their experiences can be interpreted pneumatically is one of Moltmann's central projects in *The Spirit of Life*. However, one quickly notices that in this case, Moltmann's strategy is no longer to use experience as the basis for pneumatology. Rather, his strategy is to use pneumatology to interpret experience, and then use re-interpreted experience to inform and deepen pneumatology. That is, Moltmann comes to experience with a well-developed pneumatological structure already in place. This structure is built around the central notion of the Holy Spirit as the wellspring of life—a notion which does not come primarily from experience but from Scripture and the creeds. Therefore,

---

[1] John Baillie argues for a similar position in his book *Our Knowledge of God* (New York: Scribner, 1959). His thesis is that we are all confronted personally by God on a continual basis, often without knowing it. We all experience the challenge and conviction of Christ. Often it is in our unconscious minds, as one inner conflict among many. Some of us recognize the presence of God for what it is, but many of us do not. Regarding the atheistic tendency in humanity, he writes, "We may have an awareness of a certain reality without being aware of that awareness. And we may therefore, without ceasing to be aware of such a reality, set about doubting and denying its existence—and all that in good faith" (51). Although it is difficult to conceive of an awareness of which we are not aware, Baillie's point is well taken and in harmony with the general thrust of both Moltmann's and Alston's positions.

when Moltmann states that he will base his pneumatological construction on experience *instead of* Scripture and the creeds, we can conclude that he has either spoken hyperbolically or been inconsistent—probably the former. For he does not set Scripture and the creeds aside through the course of his work in *The Spirit of Life*. Rather, Scripture and the creeds contribute the primary operating assumptions by which experience can be interpreted so that it can serve to enhance pneumatological reflection.

To sum up, Moltmann's expansion of the definition of 'experience of the Holy Spirit' is a welcome move. It is innovative, and it greatly enriches the concept. Even though it runs the risk of making the concept of experience of the Spirit too broad so that it begins to lose its meaning, it is a desirable change, for it destroys the bifurcation of the Christian life into "holy" and "secular" spheres.

Although he claims to take up an extreme method by choosing experience rather than scriptural authority as a basis, his actual working method is quite conventional. Our experience of the Spirit is not a sufficient basis upon which to found pneumatology, but it is invaluable for deepening the pneumatological views developed in Scripture and throughout the Christian tradition. Since attempting to found a pneumatology strictly on experience of the Spirit would run into the epistemological problems identified above, we can conclude that the more modest method Moltmann actually uses—not the radically experiential method he purports to use—is the proper approach to the subject. That is, regarding experience and pneumatological method, we should do as Moltmann does, and not as he says.

Immanent Transcendence: God in All Things

When Moltmann broadens the concept of the experience of the Holy Spirit, he finds that one way he can speak of the pneumatic dimension of everyday experiences is in terms of transcendence. Whereas modern theology has looked for transcendence mainly in the experience of self-consciousness, Moltmann believes that it is possible to discover transcendence in every experience, not only in experience of the self. Moltmann employs the term 'immanent transcendence' for this broader notion of experience of God (*SL*: 34).

He begins with the saying, "God's Spirit fills the world and he who holds all things together knows every sound" (Wisd 1:7). In other words, God is in all things, and all things are in God. This means that God is both immanent in all things (because God is in all things) and transcendent beyond all things (because all things are in God). Specifically, God is present in all things in the person of the Holy Spirit. This is why Moltmann describes the Spirit as "immanent transcendence."

Extending the argument to experience, Moltmann reasons that every experience we have can possess a transcendent side. We can encounter God's Spirit not only the experience of the self, but also in the experience of the 'Thou,' the experience of sociality, and the experience of nature. "It is therefore possible to experience God *in, with and beneath* each everyday experience of the world, if God is in all things, and if all things are in God . . ." (*SL*: 34). He explains, "*To experience God in all things* presupposes that there is a transcendence which is immanent in things and which can be inductively discovered. It is the infinite in the finite, the eternal in the temporal, and the enduring in the transitory" (35). To refer to nature as God's creation is to invoke the idea of immanent transcendence. "*To experience all things in God* means moving in the opposite direction. It means moving from the all-embracing horizon of the world and perception to the individual things which appear against this background. . . . We then perceive the finite in the infinite, the temporal in the eternal, and the evanescent in what endures" (36).

Moltmann's argument is that if God is present in all things, it must be possible to *experience* God in all things. Here his warrant would be that if God is present, we can experience him. This is true as it is stated, especially if we keep in mind Alston's second and third levels, which make it possible to experience objects without immediately identifying them. However, if Moltmann goes on to claim, as he often seems to, that we actually do experience God in all things, such a conclusion cannot be supported. That is, it cannot be supported unless Moltmann goes on to form the bridge between the two propositions that God is in all things and that we experience God in all things. It is one thing for God to be present, but it is another thing for us to *experience* God when he is present. The bridge that must be formed is an epistemological one. Whereas it may be true that we actually experience God in all things (without being aware of it most of the time), Moltmann asserts the idea more than he argues for it.

Moltmann cautions that his idea of immanent transcendence is not to be understood pantheistically, as if all experiences have the same quality of transcendence. Not all experiences of God are the same. The experiential phenomena in the sphere we call 'holy' render a quality of divine encounter that is distinct from other spheres of life. Moltmann wants to make sure we can retain an appreciation of the holy without having to declare everything else profane (35).

The Holy Spirit's Own Experiences

One final note is needed on the subject of experience and the Holy Spirit. Moltmann not only inquires what it means for us to experience the Holy Spirit, he also capitalizes on the idea of immanent transcendence to make the claim that because he is in all things, the Holy Spirit has his own experiences of the world. Of course, the Spirit's modalities of experience will be much different from ours, but Moltmann's basic point must be correct. If the Spirit is immanent in all things—if he truly indwells all things—then he must experience life in the world in one way or another.

The Spirit's Identity and Work in the Individual

In *The Spirit of Life*, Moltmann articulates the experience of the Spirit from several different angles. He constructs a pneumatological *ordo salutis*, covering areas of the Spirit's influence from rebirth to mysticism. I will not attempt to recount all these areas, but I will discuss the ones most germane to an examination of the eschatological dimensions of Moltmann's pneumatology.

Justification

The justification of believers by grace has always been a prominent concept in Protestant theology. Although he comes out of the German Reformed tradition, Moltmann believes that the Reformation doctrine of justification has its shortcomings. One is that it is backward-looking, focusing on the forgiveness of sins coming through the atoning work of Christ; it is not sufficiently trinitarian. Another is that it concentrates on the cross to the exclusion of the resurrection, so that justification ends with forgiveness of one's sins. To correct these reductions, Moltmann sets out to give a more expanded account of justification.

Moltmann proposes three specific alterations in the doctrine of justification. First, justification "must show the saving significance of Christ's death *and resurrection*" (149). Bringing Christ's resurrection into the concept of justification means that being justified involves more than just forgiveness of sins. It also leads to the regeneration of the individual, and then to the renewal of the cosmos.

Second, justification "must from the outset be presented pneumatologically as *experience of the Spirit*" (149). Because it is through the work of the Spirit that the death and resurrection of the particular man Jesus is made universally efficacious, the event of being justified must be a pneumatological event.

Third, justification "must be *eschatologically oriented*" (149). Justification never ends with the individual. To think that it does is to forget the context in which individual redemption takes place: the new creation of all things.

To sum up, Moltmann wants to expand the notion of justification to include other elements besides the cross and juridical pardon. He wants to include such dimensions as the new creation to life, the awakening of love and the rebirth to a living hope (149). We may recall that for Moltmann, experience of the Spirit must be christologically oriented and eschatologically aligned. That is, it must connect one with Christ, and it must also connect one with the trinitarian history of God's dealings with the world. Moltmann's way of looking at justification is consistent with this. Justification is experience of the Spirit that is based on Christ's death and resurrection, and is oriented toward the consummation of all things.

Rebirth

Although justification is a pneumatological experience, when we speak about justification we are mainly pointing to the work of Christ. Regeneration or rebirth is also a trinitarian event, but it is associated particularly with the Holy Spirit. From reading Tit 3:5–7 and 1 Pet 1:3, Moltmann finds the trinitarian nature of rebirth. It is eternally founded on the mercy and love of God the Father; it is historically founded on the resurrection of Christ; and it is brought about by the action of the Holy Spirit (146).

Moltmann observes that for the most part, the Christian tradition has viewed rebirth as a phenomenon affecting the individual human being—an inward experience of the soul (145). However, this is not the way the Jewish apocalyptic tradition has thought about it. For the apocalypticists, rebirth took on eschatological tones, because it meant the rebirth of the entire creation for the eternal kingdom of God. Similarly, the Christian tradition can acknowledge the eschatological nature of rebirth, even when it is primarily talking about the rebirth of the individual. A Christian doctrine of regeneration can bring together eschatology with christology and pneumatology. For the experience of rebirth in the Spirit makes the risen Christ present to the believer and points from the resurrection of Christ to the rebirth of all of creation (147). Although the connection Moltmann makes with eschatology is with future resurrection at the consummation, rebirth is eschatological in itself, for it is an outcome of the believer's endowment with the eschatological Spirit.

Moltmann argues that based on Jewish apocalyptic, Christians can also connect individual rebirth with cosmic eschatology, and this by way of pneumatology. "A coherent process issues from the rebirth of Christ from death through the Spirit, by way of the rebirth of mortal human beings through the Spirit, to the universal rebirth of the cosmos through the Spirit" (153). The rebirth of believers to a new life in the Spirit corresponds to the resurrection of Christ from the dead. Like resurrection, rebirth is the inception of a new form of human life. It is the anticipation of the resurrected life that Christ already enjoys. For this reason, rebirth casts the believer's gaze on the fulfillment of the new life that has begun (*SoL*: 30).

What is the experience of the Spirit in rebirth? Moltmann answers, "If the new life is experienced and lived *in* the Spirit, then the Spirit is not itself the object of experience; it is the medium and space for experience" (*SL*: 157). That is, in rebirth we do not experience the Spirit as a counterpart, but rather as a divine presence who is intimately close with our deepest being. In this type of experience the Holy Spirit can appear to be so mysterious not because he is far away, but because he is so close. All the same, Moltmann explains that theological reflection can proceed from an experience like rebirth and develop ideas about the Holy Spirit in an indirect manner. The dominant image of the Spirit which Moltmann draws from the experience of rebirth is of the Holy Spirit as mother.

The Motherhood of the Spirit

Out of the experience of rebirth in the Spirit arises the issue of the motherhood of the Spirit. The themes of birth and motherhood have an obvious connection, and this connection has been established in the Christian tradition by two particular sources—Makarios and Count Zinzendorf. Makarios was a fourth-century monk from the Syrian tradition who developed a pair of theological arguments regarding the motherhood of the Holy Spirit. First, combining Jn 14:26 and Isa 66:13, he teaches that "the promised Comforter (the Paraclete) will 'comfort you as a mother comforts'" (158). Moltmann does not comment on the exegetical fallacy of conflating these two passages. Second, Makarios points to the experience of being born again and the link in John 3:3–6 between rebirth and the activity of the Holy Spirit. If believers are "born of the Spirit," then they are "children of the Spirit"—the Spirit is their divine Mother (*HTG*: 64–65).

The other theological forefather Moltmann looks to is Count Zinzendorf, founder of the first American community of brothers and sisters in Pennsylvania in 1741. Makarios' *Fifty Homilies* had been translated in Zinzendorf's time, and they were influential with the Count. Zinzendorf reasoned that since the Son is the only-begotten Son of God and our true brother, it follows that the Father of the Son is our true Father, and the Spirit of God is our true Mother (64). What is motherly about the operations of the Holy Spirit can be sensed in the tenderness and sympathy with which she cares for us (*SL*: 159).

Following Makarios and Count Zinzendorf, Moltmann interprets the experiences of rebirth and divine comfort as revealing the femininity of the Holy Spirit. "If believers are 'born' again from the Holy Spirit, then the Spirit is 'the mother' of God's children and can in this sense also be termed a 'feminine' Spirit. If the Holy Spirit is 'the Comforter' (Paraclete), it comforts 'as a mother comforts'" (157).

The motherhood of the Holy Spirit can confirm the relationship we have with Jesus as our brother. For we are all born of the Holy Spirit. Matthew and Luke claim that Mary conceived Jesus when "the power of the Most High" came upon her, and in the creed we state our belief that Jesus was "conceived by the Holy Spirit, born of the Virgin Mary." Thus, the Holy Spirit was the immediate agent of the incarnation of the Word and the birth of the person Jesus of Nazareth. Much like Jesus, believers also experience their own miraculous birth from the Spirit of God. In this case Mary becomes a type for the Holy Spirit, for both of them take on their respective motherly roles in the history of Christ and his disciples (*WJC*: 83–84).

The motherhood of the Holy Spirit plays a prominent role in Moltmann's pneumatology. The image of the Holy Spirit as Mother is so important that Moltmann claims that the personality of the Holy Spirit can be grasped more precisely with this image than with any other. In addition, the fellowship of the Trinity can be better understood with the image of Mother than with other images for the Holy Spirit, because a Mother-figure within the Trinity is a more personal image than Basil's Third Person who proceeds from the Father, or Augustine's non-personal bond of love between Father and Son. Moreover, the symbol of the dove is a feminine symbol. Thus, Moltmann concludes, "In its feminine and motherly characteristics 'the fellowship of the Holy Spirit' has a healing, liberating and sensitizing effect" (*HTG*: 65).

Although he flirts with the idea, Moltmann does not embrace the idea of the Trinity as a "divine family" with Father, Mother and Child.

This is because such an idea leads to subordination of the Son to both the Father and the Spirit. It also sets the Father and the Spirit above human beings as parental figures, and this smacks of a trinitarian model of domination. Nevertheless, the image of the divine family does bring one desired effect. With the Holy Spirit appearing as a Mother-figure, femininity and motherhood are brought into the concept of God, even having equal stature with God's masculinity (*HTG*: 64). The question is whether picturing the Trinity as a divine family is the best way to accomplish this very worthy goal. One may emphasize the femininity, or even the motherhood, of the Spirit without having to construct a family model for the Trinity that is fraught with problems. If we experience the Holy Spirit as a feminine or a motherly figure, that can be enough in itself. It can bring us to appreciate the feminine characteristics of God.

The motherhood of the Spirit is an important pneumatological theme to Moltmann because it gives him a way to open dialogue with feminist theologians. He claims that by introducing femininity into the concept of God, we can move toward overcoming patriarchalism in the image of God and male domination in the church (*HTG*: 65). However, Catherine Keller reports that Moltmann has not succeeded in establishing much of a presence in the feminist theological community. She relates that most of her colleagues show Moltmann either aversion or indifference (Keller: 149). This is because even though he recognizes the femininity of the Holy Spirit, Moltmann's idea of God is still more masculine than feminine. Also, he continues to use the masculine pronoun for God and for the Holy Spirit unless he is specifically speaking about the femininity of the Holy Spirit. In response to the feminist community, Moltmann does not believe that championing the motherhood of the Spirit is the best way to answer the questions of feminist theology. He holds that instead of integrating motherhood into the Godhead, the answer is emphasizing the friendship between God and humanity. Such an approach breaks us out of the authoritarian image of God—an image that is not escaped just by making the Holy Spirit into a Mother-figure for us (Moltmann, 1993: 40).

The motherhood of the Holy Spirit has two instances for Moltmann. One is the Spirit's motherly function with respect to Jesus at his incarnation, and the other is the Spirit's motherly function with respect to believers at our rebirth in the Spirit. Although Moltmann does not make the point, in both of these instances the motherhood of the Spirit is eschatological in nature. For the coming of the Messiah is a happening of the new age of salvation, as is the rebirth of his followers to the first installment of their resurrection-life.

Personhood

Closely related to the femininity of the Holy Spirit is the question of the personhood of the Spirit. Regarding the problem of personhood, Moltmann states, "A more precise discernment of the personhood of the Holy Spirit is the most difficult problem in pneumatology in particular, and in the doctrine of the Trinity generally" (*SL*: 268). This is because it is difficult to pick a proper starting point from which to develop our conclusions. To start from experience of the Spirit has meant finding largely non-personal metaphors to describe the Spirit—divine energy, wind, fire, light, wide space, inward assurance, and mutual love (10). Based on experience of the Spirit, the tradition has rendered a toss-up as to whether the Spirit appears more as a person or a power in experience.

If we instead take our cue from Tertullian's formula *una substantia—tres personae*, then the concept of personhood derived from the Father and the Son are simply transferred to the Spirit. The result is that the personhood of the Spirit is asserted rather than demonstrated (268).

Because it obscures rather than clarifies the personhood of the Spirit, Moltmann sets aside talk about the "three Persons" of the Trinity. Rather than having a somewhat generic divine personhood, the Holy Spirit has his own unique personhood. Even the Eastern perichoretic model of the Trinity is deficient at this point, for it merely socializes the Holy Spirit relationally as the third in a bond of perfect fellowship. It does not arrive at a unique personhood for the Holy Spirit (268–69). Moltmann believes that the Spirit has a particular personhood, as long as this is not understood in terms of an independent personhood reflective of modern individualism.

Moltmann outlines a combined strategy for finding the unique personhood of the Holy Spirit. He first gathers metaphors by which the Spirit has been described in human experience of the Spirit.[2] After that he returns to the perichoretic Trinity and considers the personhood of the Spirit in his inter-trinitarian relations (269).

PNEUMATOLOGICAL METAPHORS

Moltmann explains that the way the pneumatological metaphors have arisen is that people have experienced the Spirit and inferred from those experiences certain characteristics of the Spirit. The process of inference

---

[2] In gathering his pneumatological metaphors, Moltmann returns to previous chapters of *The Spirit of Life*. In them the Holy Spirit has been described as "Lord," "Mother," and so on. What this means is that Moltmann will use not experience alone, but a complex mixture of sources including and stressing experience.

is not completely random, for the Spirit is allowing himself to be experienced in these ways (273). That is, the human subject is not merely the active manufacturer of his or her own experiences. He or she does not go out and "make" experiences happen. There is a strongly passive character to human experience, although it is not strictly passive.

How do we know which experiences particularly reveal the Third Person of the Trinity? On one hand, because the action of the Spirit represents the efficacy of God, every experience of the Spirit can be construed as an experience of God himself, and every metaphor we use for the Holy Spirit can be a metaphor for God as well. On the other hand, the operations of the Holy Spirit are different from the Father's activities in creation and the Son's activities in reconciliation. The unique personhood of the Spirit appears out of these distinctive operations (285–86). In order to make this distinction, a certain amount of theological structure has to be in place so that experiences can be interpreted in trinitarian terms. For Moltmann, this structure is supplied by Scripture and the Christian tradition.

Moltmann takes a variety of metaphors and organizes them in a systematic way, making four groups of three metaphors each. First is the group of *personal metaphors*, wherein the Spirit appears as *lord, mother* and *judge*. The experiences of liberation and rebirth to new life complement one another. Moltmann asserts that freedom and life are the two key aspects of experience of the divine Spirit. "Freedom without new life is empty. Life without freedom is dead" (271). In the experiences of liberation and new life the Spirit takes on the character of the lord who liberates and the mother who gives birth. Although freedom and life need each other, they both need an atmosphere of justice in which to thrive. For it is only in a just and righteous environment that freedom actually benefits life. "So justice brings the two key factors freedom and life down to a common denominator, just as, conversely, freedom and life prepare the broad place which the divine justice is to fill . . ." (271). All three of these dynamics come from the one Spirit, who appears in personal terms as lord, mother and just judge.

Second is the group of *formative metaphors*, wherein the Spirit appears as *energy, space* and *Gestalt*. The experience of the Spirit of God as a divine power or energy goes back to the Hebrew concept of *ruach*. The *ruach* is the "breath of life" which appears and disappears mysteriously, giving to its recipients the energy for living. Beyond the gift of vitality, every creature needs space within which to develop. In other words, creatures need to enjoy the proper conditions in order to fulfill their potentialities. When a creature experiences the presence of these conditions it is experiencing the Holy Spirit. Finally, the development of a creature into its own unique configuration or Gestalt takes place in and through the Spirit. Thus, when a human being experiences her life-force engaging its environment and maturing in unforeseen ways, she is experiencing the presence and work of the Holy Spirit (274–78).

Third is the group of *movement metaphors*, wherein the Spirit appears as *tempest*, *fire* and *love*. Moltmann chooses a group of movement metaphors because they "express the feeling of being seized and possessed by something overwhelmingly powerful, and the beginning of a new movement in ourselves" (278). The basic image for this type of transformation is the Pentecost story, which tells of how the experience of the Spirit turned a group of intimidated disciples of Jesus into bold and free witnesses and apostles. Again we are drawn to the Hebrew notion of God's *ruach*, which is akin to a rushing of wind or water. The tempest of the Holy Spirit picks us up and carries us along in the direction it takes. When the Spirit appears as fire, it is a flame that kindles our enthusiasm. "It consumes us, and we become a consuming flame for other people" (279). Often Scripture describes God's wrath as a "devouring fire." This is not the opposite of God's love. Rather, it is "his love itself, repulsed and wounded." It is not the transformation of God's presence from life-giving into exterminating—only God's absence would accomplish this. Rather, it is God's loving judgment of his creatures. Thus, one cannot separate God's fire from his love. Fire and love are complementary aspects of the experience of the Holy Spirit.

Fourth is the group of *mystical metaphors*, wherein the Spirit appears as *light*, *water* and *fertility*. Moltmann calls these metaphors 'mystical' because "they are concepts charged by mystical experience, and because they express so intimate a union between the divine Spirit and what is human, and between the human spirit and what is divine, that it is hardly possible to distinguish the two" (281). As radiant light, God is both the object of our knowing and its source. But more than knowledge, divine light is also energy which gives warmth. When light and warmth are combined with water, many varieties of life emerge out of the earth. Similarly, when believers are baptized in water they are reborn "from water and Spirit" (John 3:5) into new life. Thus, the metaphor of fertility follows in close connection to the notions of the presence of the Spirit as light and water. In these metaphors the presence of the Spirit is as close as one's own life, for it represents an organic cohesion between the divine and the human (283–85).

From these various metaphors for the Spirit drawn from human experience, Moltmann arrives at a conception of the personhood of the Spirit, as the Spirit relates to humanity. Taking in the range of the twelve metaphors, Moltmann arrives at a complex notion of the Spirit's personhood. It is clear that no one metaphor could ever capture the personhood of the Spirit. Instead, Moltmann works to show how each set of metaphors exists in a mutually dependent relationship. For instance, it is not enough to describe the Holy Spirit as the life-force of all creatures. Each creature needs not only the gift of life, but also the space in which to develop and the experience of actually fulfilling its potentialities. No one aspect of this process can stand alone. It is the character of the Spirit not only to give life but also to empower and lead it to its full potential.

In weaving together several different metaphors and maintaining that we can prefer none of them to the exclusion of the others, Moltmann makes a point of significant import. Anyone who wants to peg the Holy Spirit strictly as "Lord," for instance, is operating with a badly reduced idea of the Spirit's character. Here the danger of simple pneumatological paradigms emerges. Describing the Holy Spirit using one controlling metaphor is pedagogically effective, but Moltmann shows that it is also misleading, for there are eleven more metaphors to take into account. Actually, one could add to Moltmann's list so that there are more than twelve metaphors, but at some point the picture may become too complex to be helpful, other than for showing us just how complex a character the Holy Spirit is.

This concern with paradigms brings us back to Moltmann's own pneumatological paradigm—"the Spirit of life." His treatment of the material is powerful because it is simple. Once one grasps what Moltmann means by 'life,' the picture of the Holy Spirit as the principle and giver of life comes into focus rather quickly. On the other hand, the notion of 'life' functions very much as a controlling metaphor. Moltmann interprets all other metaphors for the Spirit in terms of life. One has to ask, then, how much his own paradigm is ultimately reductionistic and misleading according to his own standards.

PRESENCE AND COUNTERPART

One prominent theme of the Spirit's personhood is that the Spirit can appear as either *presence* or *counterpart*. That is, some aspects of the Spirit's operations entail an experience of the Spirit appearing as close to us as we are to ourselves. At the same time, it is not uncommon for people to experience the Spirit as a counterpart who leads, challenges, encourages and comforts them. Moltmann argues that the personhood of the Spirit takes on further distinctive contours in the interplay between the Spirit's operations as presence and as counterpart (288).

We experience the Holy Spirit as both presence and counterpart. For Moltmann, this is necessarily true, because "it is only in his presence that we can perceive him as counterpart . . ." (287). In other words, perceiving the Spirit as counterpart assumes as a necessary condition that the Spirit is already there as presence. When Christians pray *to* the Spirit, they are already praying *in* the Spirit.

How helpful is the distinction between presence and counterpart? Richard Bauckham rejects it, because it seems "to obscure the experiential basis for making trinitarian distinctions in talk of experience of God" (170, n9). By this he means that the Spirit's distinctive personhood comes from his operation as indwelling Presence. This is the fundamental activity that differentiates the Spirit from the Father and the Son. To claim that the Spirit can also appear in experience as Counterpart "to whom we relate in a person-to-person relationship" only muddies the waters when explaining experience of God in trinitarian terms. For Bauckham, the unique identity of the Holy Spirit is "as a *distinctive* form of divine presence by indwelling" (170). Bauckham's point is well taken, and there is no denying that indwelling human beings as the immediate presence of God is a central aspect of the Spirit's identity and work. However, there is also no denying that Christians often speak in terms of experiencing the Holy Spirit as Counterpart. They pray to the Spirit, and they also talk about being prompted by the Spirit, convicted by the Spirit, led by the Spirit, comforted by the Spirit, and so on. Our trinitarian language must take these phenomena into account, and this is where Moltmann makes a valuable contribution by allowing for the Spirit to appear as both Presence and Counterpart. Whereas Moltmann's duality of Presence and Counterpart gives us the flexibility to explain descriptions of Counterpart-type experiences, it seems that Bauckham has no other option than to reinterpret those experiences by explaining that the Spirit cannot appear as Counterpart. This would resemble Barth's theology, wherein the Holy Spirit is the subjective element that complements the objective elements of the Father and the Son. Moltmann has moved beyond such a model. His solution requires a more complex explanation of the trinitarian aspects of experience of God, but Christian experience calls for this adjustment to be made. Furthermore, scriptural language such as the Johannine metaphor of Paraclete leads toward the notion of the Spirit as Counterpart. In addition to adding greater challenge to explaining Christian experience,

Moltmann's idea of the Spirit's dual modes of interaction with us makes the Spirit's unique personhood all the more interesting.

All the same, Bauckham makes a significant point. He implies that the distinctive personhood of the Spirit lies in the fact that the Spirit does *not* appear in experience as a "personal" counterpart. I am disputing Bauckham's implication that the Spirit does not appear as Counterpart. However, I agree with Bauckham that the personhood of the Spirit is marked by the paradox that appearing to us in nonpersonal ways is fundamental to the Spirit's personhood. Christians can easily assume that because the Spirit does not often appear to them as a "personal counterpart," the Spirit is then less than fully personal. They base their opinions of the Spirit's personhood on whatever ways the Spirit may appear as "personal." They then look at the "nonpersonal" traits of the Spirit as anomalous, since these traits lend a nonpersonal character to the Spirit, when trinitarian theology confesses the Spirit to be personal. This is how the problem of the personhood of the Spirit arises.

Generally speaking, we tend to associate "personal" traits of the Spirit with the Spirit's appearance as a Counterpart to whom we can relate person-to-person. This is largely because the modern concept of personhood includes the element of individual autonomy.

By the same token, we associate "nonpersonal" traits of the Spirit with the Spirit's function as indwelling Presence. The recent work of Moltmann's student, Michael Welker, on the Holy Spirit[3] construes the Spirit as a dynamic force-field of justice, mercy and knowledge of God. The idea of the Spirit as force-field places a strong emphasis on the Spirit as Presence. It does not come as a surprise that the personhood of the Spirit is a weak point in Welker's pneumatology.

Although Welker could do more to strengthen his treatment of the Spirit's personhood, the problem does not lie so much with talking about the Spirit as Presence as it does with adjusting our notion of 'personhood.' If personhood necessarily implies "counterpart," then there is no escaping the problem of the personhood of the Spirit. Since the Spirit's ministry of indwelling will not change, we can only alleviate the problem by adjusting our concept of personhood. In this regard, it may help to reflect on two points.

First, the Presence we know as the Holy Spirit is not a nonpersonal force or power. It is the presence of the personal God. Gordon Fee entitles his massive study on Pauline pneumatology, *God's Empowering Presence.*

---

[3] *God the Spirit.*

With this title he conveys the idea that the Spirit is not just *an* empowering presence; the Spirit is *God's* empowering presence—that is, the personal presence of the personal God.

Second, the primary ministry of the Spirit can be described as forming and nurturing relationships. The Holy Spirit forms and nurtures relationships between human beings and God, between human beings and other human beings, and between human beings and the rest of God's creation. It is in this primary function that the Spirit's unique personhood comes to light. The Spirit acts within us ushering us into relationships, and creating and strengthening our desire and ability to maintain relationships. *There is no more personal activity possible than the formation and nurturing of relationships.* The fact that the Holy Spirit does this in the mode of Presence more often than Counterpart takes nothing away from the deeply personal character of the Spirit. On the contrary, the manifestation of the Spirit as Presence adds to his personhood. For the Spirit is carrying on this ministry from within us, not as a detached outsider. The intimacy of this indwelling relationship only deepens the personal nature of the Holy Spirit's identity.

The Trinitarian Personhood of the Spirit

Human experiences of the Spirit reveal what the Spirit is in relation to human beings, but they do not necessarily speak to the Spirit's relations within the Godhead. Similarly, metaphors drawn from experience of the Spirit can effectively describe the way the Spirit appears to us, but they do not necessarily describe the Spirit as he is in himself.

In pursuing the knowledge of the trinitarian personhood of the Spirit, Moltmann proceeds from four different angles. First is the *monarchical concept of the Trinity*, which has been the dominant trinitarian model in the West. It has tended to subordinate the Spirit, especially through the inclusion of the *filioque* clause in the creed. However, Moltmann points out that once we remove the *filioque* from the Western creed, it becomes possible to see the interdependence between the Spirit and the Son. The origination of the Son presupposes the presence of the Spirit, and the origination of the Spirit presupposes the presence of the Son (this matter will be more fully developed in the next chapter). Not only is their origination an interrelated affair, their work is mutually dependent as well. In the monarchical concept of the Trinity, the Spirit's identity is highlighted by his interrelation with the Son.

Second is the *historical concept of the Trinity*, linking in sequence the times of the Father, the Son and the Spirit in salvation history. In the

Christian tradition creation has typically been associated with the Father, redemption with the Son and sanctification with the Spirit. These three divine works can be aligned in a sequence of creation—redemption—sanctification. Each stage points to the next one. Thus, creation points to redemption, which points to sanctification, which finally points to glorification.[4] "History begins with creation and ends with the transfiguration of the world. It begins in the Father and is consummated in the Spirit" (298). The identity of the Spirit revolves around bringing to completion the work of the Father and the Son.

Third is the *eucharistic concept of the Trinity*, wherein the experience of grace arouses gratitude. Here praise proceeds from the indwelling Spirit, is mediated by the Son and is directed toward the Father. The eucharistic direction of praise teaches that God not only works; he also receives. Whereas the monarchical concept of the Trinity stresses the sending of the Son and the Spirit from the Father, the eucharistic model reverses the direction and talks about praise rising from human beings in the Spirit through the Son to the Father (299–300). Here the Holy Spirit is identified as the originator of praise directed to the Father.

Fourth is *trinitarian doxology*, in which God is glorified for his own sake rather than thanked for what he has done. It is the ultimate destiny of humanity that it will eventually worship and glorify God in this way. The trinitarian doxology describes a phenomenon that will take place in the eschaton. It represents the eternal sight that lies beyond faith. This phenomenon is accessible to us in our present state only in the 'eternal moment'—"an awareness of the present which is so intense that it interrupts the flux of time and does away with transience" (303). The eternal moment is a fleeting state of ecstasy. In the eternal moment the Spirit is discerned in his perichoretic fellowship which he shares with the Father and the Son. He is no longer "third person," and there is no longer a linear progression of sending or return. Instead, the Spirit is one among the Three who live in a circular flow of mutual self-communication (301–5).

Moltmann establishes the contours of the personhood of the Spirit from both experience and trinitarian theology. When examining the outcome, it becomes apparent that the identity of the Spirit proceeding from trinitarian theology should form the context for ideas coming from religious experience. For experience delivers data about the Holy Spirit, but it

---

[4] Moltmann works with the threefold scheme of Joachim of Fiore, who assigned a time of creation to the Father, of redemption to the Son, and of sanctification to the Spirit. To this threefold scheme Moltmann adds a fourth stage, glorification, which is the final goal of all the preceding stages.

is fragmentary and easily misunderstood. This is why the personal nature of the Spirit is such a persistent problem. Although Moltmann is right that we cannot simply solve the problem by simply trotting out a doctrine of the Trinity, it is nevertheless true that the problem is ultimately unsolvable without trinitarian theology.

Finally, it is worth remembering that the problem of the person-hood of the Holy Spirit is a temporary one. For the indwelling ministry of the Spirit, in which the Spirit's personhood is obscured because he is not Counterpart but Presence, is an eschatological ministry. It is a fact of salvation in the new age. As such, it points forward to what Moltmann calls "divine eschatology," which is the doxological glorification of God for his own sake. In the fourth trinitarian model that Moltmann describes— "trinitarian doxology"—the Spirit's personhood comes into focus as one among the three mutually interrelated divine Persons. Here the Spirit is no more or less personal than the Father or the Son. The Presence of the indwelling Spirit points toward is this eschatological understanding of the Spirit.

The Spirit and Sanctification

The concept of rebirth in the Spirit describes the bringing forth of the be-liever into the new existence of eschatological life. To continue the imag-ery, this new life will want to grow and arrive at its intended form. "If the primal experience of the Spirit is called rebirth, this metaphor [of sanctifi-cation] itself implies 'growth' in faith, in knowledge and in wisdom" (*SL*: 161). In other words, if rebirth suggests the image of a child, sanctification pictures the child growing into mature adulthood. Along the way believers will experience progression in areas like knowledge of God, the liberation of the will, and the assurance of the heart (162). Growth and maturation in the resurrection-life under the transforming power of the Holy Spirit is known as sanctification.

However, Moltmann cautions that we must not interpret the growth of sanctification individualistically. We experience growth in the interplay between what is inward and what is outward. This means that our indi-vidual biography is woven into the history of the social groups to which we belong, and into the political history of our era (161). Sanctification takes a different route with each individual, and that route is partly determined by the individual's social and historical context.

Neither must we interpret the growth of sanctification linearly. The perfection of the human person is a complex affair, involving not just the alteration of conscious choices, but the transformation of the entire person, including the unconscious. If the divine project of sanctification is the transformation of the exceedingly complex human person, then it would be foolish to expect this transformation to proceed along a catalog of progressive steps. Nevertheless, we can expect certain things to change for the individual who is being sanctified. This is why Wesley argued that if sanctification is the process of healing the spiritual life of people, it must be possible to discern the stages of growing health (161).

What is common to the work of sanctification in all human beings is the end result of correspondence to God. Moltmann summarizes sanctification in the following way. "God chooses something for himself and makes it his own possession, which means that he lets it participate in his nature, so that it *corresponds* to him. In doing so he sanctifies it, and in its relationship to God it itself becomes holy" (*SoL*: 45).

Moltmann also speaks of sanctification in terms of harmony with God, brought about by the action of the Holy Spirit. A sanctified life "finds its meaning in its participation in God and its correspondence to God in the Spirit" (47). In this vein, the most important thing is seeking harmony with God. "Harmony with God is called *sanctification*" (48). We must seek this anew every morning. But harmony with God often implies conflict with society, since human societies are not typically in harmony with God. The good news is that even while we find ourselves at odds with society, we also find ourselves settling into our own true identity as God's people. Harmony with God means harmony with self. By extension, it also means harmony with any part of creation that is in harmony with God (48).

One of the ways in which we talk about sanctification is in eschatological terms. Moltmann points out that for Paul growth in the Spirit is eschatologically aligned, for the Spirit experienced in the present is the advance payment on our complete sanctification. Therefore, the present experience of the Spirit always points to greater fulfillment. "The Spirit is the great Mover in the direction of the future in which 'God will be all in all.' The protean gifts of the Spirit are 'the powers of the age to come' (Heb 6:5)" (162). This means that the completion of our growth cannot be experienced in the present life. Regeneration is rebirth into eternal life and will be completed only in the resurrection of the dead. "Sanctification is the beginning of glorification; glorification is the consummation of sanctification" (163).

The Spirit as Eschatological Guarantee and Down Payment

The language of eschatological glorification begun and guaranteed brings up the issue of how Moltmann uses Paul's metaphors of first fruits, guarantee and down payment (discussed in chapter two). The fact is that Moltmann does not make use of these metaphors very often. When he does, they carry the kind of eschatological import that is characteristic of Pauline usage. As one would expect from Moltmann, they have connotations of cosmic glorification of God.

For instance, he echoes Paul that the Spirit is the first fruits of total redemption. For Moltmann, the Spirit is the first fruits of the complete transformation and glorification of the entire world. For the church this means that its attention is turned not to itself in appreciation of its own gifts, but rather to the world. What believers experience in the presence of the eschatological Spirit is "the beginning of the world's future" (125).

Similarly, Moltmann writes,

> The parousia of the Holy Spirit is nothing other than the begin-
> ning of the parousia of Christ. That is why the Holy Spirit is called
> the pledge or down-payment of glory (Eph 1:14; 2 Cor 1:22). So
> what begins in the Holy Spirit *here* will be completed and per-
> fected in the kingdom of glory *there*. The kingdom of glory does
> not come unexpectedly and without any preparation. It is already
> heralded in the kingdom of the Spirit, where it already has power
> in the present. The relation is like the relation between spring and
> summer, seedtime and harvest, sunrise and high noon. (*SoL*: 11)

This passage indicates Moltmann's wavering stance with respect to the relation between eschatology and the present. The kingdom of glory is anticipated by the kingdom of the Spirit, which is apparently a phenome-non of the messianic age. The relation between the present kingdom of the Spirit and the future kingdom of glory is like the relation between spring and summer, and sunrise and noon—both images in complete harmony with Pauline inaugurated eschatology. However, mixed in with these im-ages is the relation of seedtime to harvest. This is a misrepresentation of the metaphor of first fruits, in which the relation between the "already" and the "not yet" is like the relation between first fruits and full harvest, not between seedtime and harvest. The difference is significant, for the relation between the seed and the crop is completely different from the relation between the first of the crop and the rest of the crop. Applying this collection of metaphors and remarks to eschatology, Moltmann is simultaneously speaking the language of consistent eschatology and inaugurated eschatology.

Moltmann correctly states that for Paul the raising of the crucified Jesus is the beginning of the eschatological resurrection of the dead and new creation of the world. When Paul uses the metaphors of first fruits and down payment for the Holy Spirit, he means that present experience of the Holy Spirit is a part pointing to the whole as the beginning points toward its completion. Moltmann turns this idea in a unique direction: "Faith in the resurrection is therefore the Christian form of belief in creation" (*GC*: 66). That is, if we believe in the completion we must also believe in the beginning, and vice versa. Creation implies consummation, and consummation implies creation. But for Moltmann, what lies between creation and consummation are christology and pneumatology. It is on the basis of the work of Christ and the Holy Spirit that the consummation will come to pass. Along these same lines, Paul calls Christ the first fruits of the resurrection of the dead, and the Holy Spirit the first fruits of our complete redemption. For Paul also, christology and pneumatology have a necessary connection with the consummation.

Conclusion

As the immanent presence of the transcendent God in human beings, the experience of the Holy Spirit is basic to human existence. Moltmann argues for a notion of the experience of the Spirit that expands beyond conscious encounters with God in "holy" spheres of life to include elements of transcendence in all spheres of life. This can take place in any context and can reside in the unconscious as well as conscious mind. Such a holistic and inclusive notion of experience of the Spirit opens up lines of inquiry that appear only when we get beyond the tendency to equate the Holy Spirit with the operations of the church or with personal sanctification.

Moltmann also widens the scope of personal experience of the Spirit by identifying eschatological aspects of the Christian encounter with the Spirit. Although justification is the application of Christ's work of atonement to each human being by the Spirit, the Spirit's work can hardly be reduced to that. Justification is based on Christ's death and resurrection, and is oriented toward the new creation of all things.

Similarly, rebirth begins with the individual, but it finds its horizon of meaning in the new creation of all things. It is not an individualistic mode of experience. It is participation in the universal rule of God in which sin and death will be finally defeated. In this way, personal experience of rebirth expands beyond the individual and takes in all of humanity, and ultimately, the whole of creation. It also expands beyond the present moment and takes in the past and the future, both in a personal and in a cosmic sense. That is, rebirth is experienced by each individual believer as a new beginning in life, and it thus connects with the past and future of that person's history. This much is common to experiential pneumatologies in the Protestant tradition. However, beyond this, the experience of rebirth draws the believer into a cosmic drama that will conclude only with the rebirth of all creation in the glory of God. Thus, the ultimate horizon of meaning regarding rebirth in the Spirit is not personal sanctification, but rather universal transformation. The rebirth of the individual is only one instance in the overall process of the rebirth of the entire creation.

8

The Holy Spirit and Creation

So far we have explored communal and individual aspects of Moltmann's pneumatology. In this chapter, we will see how he sets these themes into the broader context of the Spirit's presence and activity in creation. The church, and the believer within the church, constitute one privileged segment of creation. They are privileged in that they enjoy the beginnings of eschatological life—a life that will soon spread to the rest of creation. The work of the Holy Spirit in creation will be our concern in the first part of this chapter. The second part will be an extended review of the main themes of Moltmann's pneumatology.

The Holy Spirit and Creation

Moltmann's book, *God in Creation*, deals with the divine presence in nature. He explains that by "God in creation" he means God the Holy Spirit. God is present in all created beings as the giver and lover of life. Thus, Moltmann's doctrine of creation is a pneumatological one (*GC*: xiv).

Moltmann observes that in both Protestant and Catholic theology there is a tendency to view the Holy Spirit solely as the Spirit of redemption. This has led Western Christians to look for the experience of the Spirit only in the context of faith and the church.

Alongside this perceived limitation of the Spirit's efficacy is an incipient individualism within Western Christianity, which Moltmann associates with a continuing influence of Platonism on Christianity. That is, spirit and spirituality are set over against the concerns of the body and the world. They have to do with "the inner experiences of the soul rather than the sensory experiences of sociality and nature" (8). This 'spiritual' sphere comports with the idea of human redemption as inner salvation from the world.

Also at work is the *filioque* clause in the Creed. The result of the *filioque* is that the Spirit comes to be viewed as the Spirit of Christ, and the Spirit of Christ is a Spirit of redemption. Moltmann reminds the Western tradition that the Holy Spirit is also the Spirit of the Father and is thus a Spirit of creation. Furthermore, if Christ is the reconciler of the entire cosmos, then redemption has to be understood to touch the whole creation, not just the human soul (9). For these reasons, Moltmann hopes to redress the understanding of the Holy Spirit's relationship to creation. This relationship takes place in three distinct but overlapping phases—original creation, ongoing creation, and the new creation of all things in the eschaton.

The Spirit and Original Creation

In chapter six, I mentioned that Moltmann considers creation to be a trinitarian process. Since he believes that the Christian tradition has emphasized the first two persons of the Trinity in the act of creation but not the third, Moltmann hopes to highlight the activity of the Holy Spirit in creation. He rejects any view of creation that leaves out the role of the Holy Spirit. This includes not only the act of original creation, but also the preservation of creation and the coming renewal of creation. For Moltmann, all of these phases of the act of creation are dependent on the agency of the Spirit.

The Christian tradition has always held that all divine activity is pneumatic in its efficacy. That is, the Spirit brings the activity of the Father and the Son to its goal and completion. God the Father creates through the Son in the power of the Holy Spirit. "All things are therefore created 'by God,' formed 'through God' and exist 'in God'" (*HTG*: 72). As Basil asserted, in the creation of any being the Father is the origin who underlies it, the Son is the one who creates it, and the Spirit is the one who completes it (*On the Holy Spirit*, §38).

What follows from this basic axiom is that the triune God is unremittingly breathing his Spirit into his creation. That is, existence and life are actualized only through the flowing energies of the cosmic Spirit (*GC*: 9).

The scriptural basis upon which Moltmann builds his concept of the relationship between the Spirit and creation consists of passages from the Old Testament. In Gen 1–2, the creation narrative begins by stating that the Spirit of God hovered over the waters. Moltmann concludes that this account is intended to point out that the Spirit of God is the creative power and the presence of God in his creation (99). The Psalmist writes, "When you hide your face, they are dismayed; when you take away their breath, they die and return to their dust. When you send forth your spirit, they are created; and you renew the face of the ground" (Ps 104:29–30). For Moltmann, this passage indicates that the Spirit is present in all living beings, and that all life depends on the Spirit. Finally, Prov 8 shows that God creates through the Spirit. This passage illustrates the immanent activity of God in the creation process.

Moltmann reads the Old Testament creation accounts with a trinitarian theology in mind, and he concludes that God set forth the original creation through the Holy Spirit. This means that the Holy Spirit is God immanent in his creation, completing the creative process and giving life to creatures.

Constructing a trinitarian account of creation that features the Spirit as immanent transcendence within all things creates a link between theology and ecology. "Creation in the Spirit is the theological concept which corresponds to the ecological doctrine of creation which we are looking for and need today" (12). The link with ecology is important for Moltmann, because he sees humanity's exploitation of nature creating a state of crisis. We simply cannot go on treating nature the way we have been, as an object to conquer and to manipulate strictly for our own needs. Such selfishness and arrogance will eventually lead to catastrophe. Moltmann believes that the idea of the Holy Spirit as God's presence immanent in all things is one answer to this problem. If we can learn to appreciate nature as *God's creation*—the fruit of his labor and the dwelling place of his Spirit—then we may be more apt to treat it with respect. Again, this is one answer to the problem. In Moltmann's mind, the real answer would be for humanity to be liberated from its compulsion to dominate and manipulate its environment—be it natural, social, familial, or other—and instead exist in a relationship of mutuality and equality. This is the destiny of humanity, but it will not be realized until the eschaton.

THE PRESENCE OF THE SPIRIT IN CREATION

Moltmann points out that a trinitarian doctrine of creation recognizes a certain tension in God himself during the creation process. God creates the world *ex nihilo*, thereby being distinguished from it, but he also enters into the world by his indwelling Spirit (15). Moltmann identifies two key concepts which help to unpack this tension in the divine act of creation.

First is the doctrine of the Trinity. "Through the Son, God creates, reconciles and redeems his creation. In the power of the Spirit, God is himself present in his creation—present in his reconciliation and his redemption of that creation" (15).

True to his nature, God exists in a mutual relationship with creation. He created it and exerts influence upon it. At the same time, he allows himself to be influenced by it. This mutuality mirrors the inner life of the Trinity. Moltmann pushes the trinitarian analogy further by positing the mutual indwelling of God in creation and creation in God. This train of thought leads him to speak of the *perichoresis* that exists between God and creation (16–17). Of course, he does not mean that the *perichoresis* between God and creation is of the same type or reaches the same level as the *perichoresis* between the Persons of the Trinity. Neither does he have in mind a form of pantheism, in which God and the world would be indistinguishable. His claim stops short of these ideas, but it is still radical enough to raise the question of whether God retains sufficient transcendence.[1] Still, Moltmann's criticism of modern Western society is on the mark. We tend to think of nature as *our environment* and not as *God's creation*, and we need to exercise much greater care to treat nature with respect, even reverence. Moltmann chooses to emphasize the immanence of God because he believes that to be the most therapeutic message for modern Christians.

The second key concept that unpacks the combination of transcendence and immanence in creation is the doctrine of the *shekinah*. In the last chapter we learned that Moltmann uses the idea of the *shekinah* to explain how it is that God, who is infinite and eternal, can still be present in and with his people, who are finite and temporal. In discussing his doctrine of creation, we can see that Moltmann uses the concept of the *shekinah* for God's immanent presence within all of creation. Therefore, there are multiple levels of God's *shekinah* for Moltmann. The presence of the Holy Spirit in creation is of a different quality than his presence that is eschatologically poured out on followers of Christ.

Thus, God is present in the *shekinah* in his people, and he is also present in the *shekinah* in the whole of creation. In either case it means that God constricts himself so as to be present in beings, objects, processes and events which are circumscribed by linear time and finite space. Moltmann calls this self-constriction the kenosis of the Holy Spirit. The kenosis of the Spirit is foundational for the *shekinah*. Without kenosis, there is no true divine immanence.

For Moltmann, true divine immanence means deep relationship characterized by mutuality and vulnerability. Mutuality between God

---

[1] Stanley Grenz and Roger Olson argue that Moltmann falls into the trap that has snared so many contemporary theologians: emphasizing the immanence of God to the detriment of his transcendence (Grenz & Olson: 186).

and creation was mentioned above. Vulnerability includes the openness of God toward his creatures, so that by being present with them, he is deeply affected by their triumphs and failures. In the *shekinah*, God the Spirit both exults and suffers with every creature. For Moltmann, the ambiguity within creation and the Spirit's willingness to fully experience it are the reasons why Paul says that the Spirit groans along with all of creation (Rom 8:22).

Just as God is immanent in all things, this perichoretic indwelling means that the presence of the infinite imbues everything and the community of all things with self-transcendence (101). The *shekinah* is the principle of transcendence in all things. For as much as Moltmann stresses the immanence of the *shekinah*, it is still the presence of God himself, who remains transcendent beyond creation as its Creator and Sustainer.

The Spirit and Ongoing Creation

ONGOING CREATION AND SALVATION HISTORY

Ongoing creation in the present age is characterized by tension between present difficulties and future promise. The present is neither the pristine past nor the transformed future. Unlike these eras, the present age is scarred by continual violence and destruction. "The Pauline talk of 'creation in bondage' (Rom 8) and the stress on the reconciliation of all things through Christ (Col 1) presupposes that the present reality is no longer the original creation nor yet the new creation. It has come under the power of time and the violence of death and is exposed to destruction" (76). In the present age, the community of creatures with each other is vital. It is a community of suffering. Because creation exists in community and solidarity, any redemption hoped for by one part of creation must be a redemption for all of creation.

According to Moltmann, the Christian tradition holds either that God sustains what he has created or that at every moment he repeats his original Yes to his creation. The former is the idea of the preservation of the world (*conservatio mundi*) and the latter is the idea of continual creation (*creatio continua*). Moltmann asserts that both ideas fall short of a complete understanding of creation, for neither suggests the new creation of all things.

> The original creation and its preservation serve a goal. It is the consummation of creation in the realm of divine glory. All that is created longs to participate in the divine glory. What has been created is preserved for that. That is the goal of the continuation of

creation. . . . Every act which preserves creation from destruction
is an act of hope for its future. (*HTG*: 75)

God preserves creation through his Spirit of life, who continues to
permeate creation, remaining patient and tolerant despite human sin and
cosmic disorder. In addition, the Spirit suffers along with creation and lifts
creation's eyes to the future renewal of all things. As all creation groans in
longing for this future, the Spirit groans along with it.

Moltmann speaks of the Spirit groaning along with all of creation,
but he also speaks of creation groaning for the coming of the Spirit. "If
we are waiting with the earthly creation for the coming of the Holy Spirit,
then we are waiting for both liberation from injustice and violence, and
liberation from time and death" (72). This is the eschatological coming of
the Spirit in the consummation. We saw above that the *shekinah* is God's
presence in creation, but that there is a greater manifestation of the Spirit
still to come. I expressed this idea in terms of multiple levels of the *shekinah* presence of God—the *shekinah* in all of creation as the source of life
and the *shekinah* in the people as the source of eschatological life. Here we
see that even the community of God's people, who enjoy the presence of
the Spirit, still wait for a further manifestation of the Spirit. This suggests
a third level of the *shekinah*—the dwelling of God in creation in all of the
fullness of the consummation.

Moltmann identifies four specific operations of the Holy Spirit in
nature. First, "The Spirit is the principle of creativity on all levels of matter
and life" (*GC*: 100). By creating new possibilities for living organisms the
Spirit is the principle of evolution.

Second, "The Spirit is the holistic principle. At every evolutionary
stage he creates interactions, harmony in these interactions, mutual perichoresis, and therefore a life of co-operation and community. The Spirit of
God is the 'common Spirit' of creation" (100).

Third, the Spirit is also the principle of individuation in which each
creature is unique. Rather than contradicting each other, creatures complement each other.

Fourth, "all creations in the Spirit are in intention 'open.' They are
directed towards their common future, because they are all, each in its own
way, aligned towards their potentialities. The principle of intentionality in
inherent in all open systems of matter and life" (100).

THE "SPIRIT OF LIFE"

The emphasis on life and the association between life and the Holy Spirit begin showing up already in *Theology of Hope*. "The 'Spirit' is according to Paul the 'life-giving Spirit,' the Spirit who '*raised up* Christ from the dead' and '*dwells* in' those who recognize Christ and his future, and '*shall* quicken their mortal bodies' (Rom 8:11)" (*TH*: 211). By the time Moltmann writes *The Spirit of Life*, the paradigm of vivification controls his approach to pneumatology.

According to Bauckham the concept of 'life' serves three primary purposes for Moltmann. First, it breaks pneumatology out of its narrow association between the Spirit and revelation so characteristic of Barthian theology. This, in turn, allows Moltmann to give experience a wider definition as the experience of God in all spheres of life rather than just the revelatory word of God.

Second, a pneumatology of life is holistic in character, and this corresponds to Moltmann's holistic christology and soteriology. As the Spirit of life, the Spirit is related to the whole human being, the whole of human social relationships, the whole world and the whole creation.

Third, the notion of the Spirit as the divine source of life highlights the continuity between God's life and the life of his creation, so that creatures are not distant from God but live out of his own life. It also highlights the continuity of creation and salvation, because the Spirit is the source of both the transient life that ends in death and the eternal life of the new creation (23).

Moltmann bases his understanding of the Holy Spirit as the principle of life mainly on the Old Testament concept of the divine *ruach*. Whereas *pneuma* and *Geist* carry metaphysical connotations of immaterial spirit in antithesis to matter and body, this is not true of *ruach*.

> Whether we are talking Greek, Latin, German or English, by the Spirit of God we then mean something disembodied, supersensory and supernatural. But if we talk in Hebrew about Yahweh's *ruach*, we are saying: God is a tempest, a storm, a force in body and soul, humanity and nature. . . . The word always means something living compared with something dead, something moving, over against what is rigid and petrified. In the transferred sense, when the word is applied to God, the tempest becomes a parable for the irresistible force of the Creator's power, God's killing wrath and life-giving mercy. (cf. Ezek 13:13f.; 36:26f.) (*SL*: 40–41)

Ruach is the divine power to give life, to sustain it by God's mercy, and to take it away in God's wrath. It can be understood to be the breath of life (Eccles 12:7; 3:21). It can also point to the 'personal soul' (*ruach*) as apart from the 'blood soul' (*nephesh*).

Based on these thoughts, Moltmann suggests conceiving of *ruach* in the following ways. First, *ruach* is the divine presence that reaches into the depths of human existence in the event of personal encounter. If we understand *ruach* to be the confronting event of God's presence, we also have to turn the thought around and understand the happenings of God's presence as *ruach*. "Every efficacious presence of God is determined by the *ruach* and, as Calvin said, has to be interpreted pneumatologically" (42).

Second, *ruach* is the power of life in all the living. Here Moltmann makes a strong statement of divine immanence. Whereas the role of God's creative power is the transcendent side of *ruach*, the role of the life-force in creatures is the immanent side of *ruach*. Thus, the *ruach* is present as vivification in everything that lives.

Third, *ruach* can also carry the connotation of breadth, or space. "To experience *ruach* is to experience what is divine not only as a person, and not merely as a force, but also as *space*—as the space of freedom in which the living being can unfold. That is the experience of the Spirit: 'Thou has set my feet in a broad place' (Ps 31:8)" (43). To live 'in' God's Spirit is to have the space to live and develop to one's full potentialities.

Thus, in the concept of *ruach* Moltmann sees both universal and particular pneumatic operations. In order to live every creature needs the presence of God's creative power and the gift of the breath of life. For any creature to have life it requires the efficacious presence of God functioning as life-giver. However, merely giving life to all creatures does not exhaust the functions of the *ruach*, for it also opens up potentialities to creatures which cannot be realized without the enabling help of the *ruach*. These operations are common to all creatures, but the *ruach* also acts in a unique way with each specific creature.

Moltmann notes that *ruach* is also associated with *dabar* (word), so that when God speaks creation into being he does so by means of his breath (*ruach*) and word (*dabar*) together. Moltmann capitalizes on this construction and stresses the idea that God breathes the Spirit of life into every living creature. His idea of divine creation posits a close connection between Creator and creation. Although creation is not "begotten" by God as is the Son, it still bears a closer relationship to God than those reflected in the notions of act/actor and work/master. The metaphor of expresses this relation that is intermediary between act/actor and begetting is the divine breath of life, in which God fills everything with *his own life* by virtue of infusing it with his own Spirit (*TK*: 113).

Another metaphor that Moltmann uses to express the intimate relation between God and creation is the pouring out of the Spirit's energies into all things. God does not merely create *ex nihilo*. He also creates out of the energies of his own Spirit. "It is the powers and energies of the Holy Spirit that bridge the difference between Creator and creature, the actor and the act, the master and the work—a difference which otherwise seems to be unbridged by any relation at all" (113). I have already argued in Chapter Eight that the metaphor of the outpouring of the Spirit is inherently eschatological. To use it in a non-eschatological sense violates the biblical text and drains the metaphor of its meaning. Nevertheless, the point Moltmann is trying to make is a valid one: God not only creates all things, he also enters into intimate relationship with all things. This is a forgotten theme in many accounts of creation.

In summary, Moltmann portrays the Spirit of life as God immanent in creation—vivifying it, experiencing its victories and defeats, leading it to fuller life, pointing it toward its future fulfillment and groaning with it in its longing for that future. As the giver and sustainer of life, the Holy Spirit supports life and is opposed to death in all its forms. This general picture is simple enough to understand, and it is theologically powerful because it picks up so many prominent themes in the Christian tradition's proclamation about the Holy Spirit. However, it does raise an important question. If the Holy Spirit is immanent in creation as Moltmann says and is the principle of life for all creatures, does this not also commit the Spirit to acting as the Spirit of death, at least in this present age? For in order to live, all creatures must eat, and most of them eat what they kill, be it plant, insect or animal. In addition, the planet can only support so much life at any one time. The populations of beings in all ecosystems must be kept in balance in order for those ecosystems to support life. We must conclude that death is necessary for life. If we are to claim that the Holy Spirit is the universal promoter of life, then we must also say that the Holy Spirit is the universal promoter of death inasmuch as death is a vital component of maintaining the delicate ecological balance of our planet. Clearly all life cannot simply go on multiplying, for the planet would not support it. Because death is necessary for ecological balance and the survival of all living things, we must embrace the Spirit's role in killing and in death, inasmuch as it is necessary for creatures to kill in order to live.

This is a most difficult issue, but we must engage it if we are to claim that the Holy Spirit is the promoter of life on earth. To further complicate matters, the details of the ways in which life is perpetuated can quickly become gruesome. Take, for instance, the tarantula wasp. When the wasp is ready to reproduce, it stings and paralyzes a tarantula spider, digs a hole and drags the spider into it. The wasp then lays an egg on the still-living but helpless spider and seals the hole. When the egg hatches, the young wasp slowly consumes the spider and grows on the nutrients of the spider's weakening body. When the wasp is mature, it digs its way out of the hole to live and someday repeat the process. This is only one example of ghastly violence and exploitation that goes on in the world of nature every day. The question becomes, if the Holy Spirit is the perpetuator of life, and if this is how tarantula wasps perpetuate their own life, is the Holy Spirit behind this oppressive behavior? If this is what it takes for the tarantula wasp to live and reproduce, are we to rejoice in the process? If we praise the Holy Spirit in the wonders of creation and the miracle of ongoing life, then we must also be able to take these issues into account. Unfortunately, Moltmann does not address these problems. Based on what we know of his theology, his answer would probably be that the Spirit works to perpetuate life, but that he is forced to do so in the present age in ways that he finds most wretched. This only would deepen the intensity of the Spirit's groaning as he anticipates the new creation of universal peace and love.

REVERENCE FOR LIFE

Moltmann believes that the Reformation's testimony to the freedom of faith was therapeutic to the public sicknesses of medieval ecclesiastical society. Later the Methodist testimony to personal sanctification acted therapeutically on the social maladies of industrial London. Today we are also in need of a notion of salvation that will work toward the healing of present Western culture. What characterizes our culture today? Western industrial society has been marked by the ethic of "produce more—consume more." But now people are seeing that the cost of the production/consumption ethic is becoming too great (*SL*: 171). In addition, the environment cannot sustain ongoing stripping by a society whose hunger for "more" shows no sign of being satiable.

If these are the basic ills of our society, then what can Christianity offer as healing salve? Moltmann outlines four characteristics of a notion of sanctification designed to minister to the ills of our society. First, sanctification must mean rediscovering the sanctity of life and the divine mystery of creation. This will lead us to defend life and creation from destruction and violence perpetuated by our culture.

Second, if life is holy, then Albert Schweitzer was right to take up the stance of a 'reverence for life.' "Reverence links a religious attitude towards life with a moral respect for it—one's own life and the life of other creatures" (172). To reflect such a sensibility Moltmann adapts the double commandment of love, expanding it from an application strictly to human beings to an application to all of creation—"love this earth as yourself, and yourself as this earth! You shall love God and this earth and all your fellow creatures with all your heart, and with all your soul, and with all your might" (172).

Today the reverence for life has a personal dimension: "What am I doing about my consumerism and my refuse?" It also has a social dimension: "How can Christians, in joint discussion and shared worship, arrive at a reverent life-style?" Finally, there is a political dimension: "What laws for protecting the environment and other creatures do we speak out for?" (172).

Third, the ethic of reverence for life requires the renunciation of violence towards life, whether this means conscientious objection and pacifism, or reducing the expenditure of energy (since, according to Moltmann, the use of energy amounts to violence towards nature; 172).

Fourth, sanctification today must include "the search for the harmonies and accords of life." This means that instead of thinking only of our own consumption and happiness, we must remember that we are members of a community, one generation among many, and creatures who share the house of the earth. If we consider that life exists within these contexts, then it can lead us to live less ruthlessly (173).

What all this means is that the Spirit who sanctifies must today be thought of as the Spirit who gives and supports life. Moltmann believes that we must learn to see the *spiritus vivificans* in the *spiritus sanctificans* (178). That is, sanctification includes a concern for the whole of life, not just the "life of the soul." Sanctification, like pneumatology in general, must become more holistic for us.

It could be argued that Moltmann reduces sanctification to reverence for life. What is involved beyond environmental activism and protecting people who are less fortunate? The traditional foci of holiness are absent—things like abstention from sinful activities, maturing in worship of God, developing a more consistent prayer life, loving God and others, and the like. Presumably, Moltmann would see these elements as the 'spiritual' sides of sanctification and would thus leave the conversation about them to others. He has other fish to fry, namely the neglected holistic character of sanctification.

The Spirit and the Consummation of All Things

CREATION AND CONSUMMATION

Moltmann notes that creation, salvation and eschatology are all intertwined in the Scriptures. He contends that creation is determined by soteriology, and soteriology is determined by eschatology. In creation, all things are brought into existence. In salvation, all things—not just human beings—are brought under the umbrella of God's universal plan of redemption. In eschatology, toward which creation and salvation point, all things arrive at their telos—a goal which is definite and universal, yet individualized to each creature (*TK*: 99–100).

What Moltmann does not mention is that in the New Testament, salvation and eschatology are so closely related that salvation can be viewed as a component of eschatology. Salvation that is enjoyed now represents not the stage *before* eschatology, but a beginning stage *of* eschatology.

However, he does make a significant point by linking creation and the consummation. In many ways they are doctrines that mirror each other. Both are universal and have to do with all God's creatures. This applies whether one agrees with Moltmann that salvation will be universal, or whether one takes the traditional position that some creatures will suffer everlasting punishment.

Both doctrines have to do with God's creative activity. In original creation, God brings the world and its inhabitants into existence out of nothing. In the consummation, he will re-create all things and take them up into his eternal glory.

Creation and consummation not only mirror each other; they also depend on each other. For God creates with the telos of the consummation in mind from the beginning. To think of creation and not consummation would be to attribute futility to God's will and work. By the same token, the consummation cannot happen unless creation has taken place and is ongoing. In other words, there cannot be a "consummation of all things" without the existence of "all things."

In Moltmann's way of thinking, creation and consummation are chapters in a story—the history of God's interaction with his creation. It is an ongoing story, for creation is continuous, and the eschatological era is just beginning. This means that when we set out to examine the Holy Spirit's relation to creation, it inevitably leads us beyond original creation and ongoing creation to the Spirit's role in the consummation of all things.

THE CONTENT OF THE CONSUMMATION

What is included in the consummation of all things? Moltmann notes that usually we claim agnosticism about the content of eschatological events, for we do not have any experience of those things. Thus, we string together several negative statements, like "no more crying or pain." However, Moltmann states that we cannot form any concept of the negative without anticipations of the positive. "From the positive experiences of life, love, abiding we form conceptions of hope for the new creation of all things. So we speak of the 'kingdom of God' which will drive away the powers of chaos and death. We speak of the 'eternal life' which overcomes death. We hope for the 'divine righteousness' which will drive injustice and violence from the earth" (*HTG*: 78–79). Therefore, we can make some positive claims about the consummation.

Furthermore, Moltmann does not consider it be completely true that we have no eschatological experience, and he makes this point pneumatologically. In the Spirit we experience the "life, love, and abiding" to which Moltmann refers. In the Spirit we experience the rule of God taking effect in our lives and in the lives of others. In the Spirit we experience a new sense of life and a new hope that death will eventually be completely overcome. In the Spirit we experience "divine righteousness" in which peace, love and justice take hold in the world. The hope that these experiences engenders is not limited to our individual future or even the future of humanity; it is a hope for all of creation. Such universalization of hope is itself a component of experience of the Holy Spirit.

For Moltmann, experience of the Holy Spirit is itself an encounter with the eschatological future. However, he adds that the new creation began before the Holy Spirit was poured out on the church. Christ *proclaimed* the new creation of all things when he brought the kingdom of God to the poor, salvation to the sick and divine justice to sinners. His resurrection *began* the resurrection of all the dead and the new creation of all things. "In Christian understanding, the day of Christ's resurrection is the first day of the new creation" (77). Moltmann also observes that the timing in the Christian calendar of the Easter festival coincides with spring, for spring represents the eternal spring of the new creation of all things. Likewise, the celebration of Pentecost coincides with the beginning of summer, for early summer's greening and blossoming represents the eternal enlivening of all of creation in the breath of the Spirit (78).

Therefore, the new creation lies in the future, but it began with the resurrection of Christ and is anticipated in the Christian experience of the Spirit of the resurrection. All believers who proclaim Christ's resurrection in the power of the Spirit are participating in the coming glorification of God.

THE OUTPOURING OF THE SPIRIT

We saw in the last chapter that Moltmann cites the prophecy of Joel 2:28 and combines it with Gen 9:10 to argue that the outpouring of the Spirit applies to all of creation in a non-eschatological sense as well as the traditional eschatological sense. Moltmann's various comments on the outpouring of the Spirit lead to a three-tiered understanding of the concept. First, the Spirit is poured out on creation, because the Spirit is God immanent in all things. Second, the Spirit is poured out on the church, because it is the charismatic community existing in the messianic age. Third, the Spirit will be poured out in the fullest at the consummation. At this point, creation rather than heaven will be the dwelling place of God.

I argued that use of this metaphor in non-eschatological contexts is not faithful to the scriptural meaning of the metaphor. To Joel, the "outpouring of the Spirit" is an eschatological event. Luke makes it clear in his account of Peter's Pentecost sermon that he considers the outpouring of the Spirit to have happened on that day. Still, it would not violate the message conveyed by either Joel or Luke in their uses of the metaphor to assert that a further outpouring of the Spirit on all of creation will be an event included in the consummation. The idea of the future outpouring of the Spirit implies the following. Just as the Holy Spirit opens up the Trinity for creation and creation for the Trinity (*TK*: 127), so the Holy Spirit brings that openness to its completion in the consummation. At that time, God will be "all in all," permeating all things and living in all things by the fullness of his presence.

Conclusion

Moltmann bears witness that his search for the influence of the Holy Spirit was "a voyage of discovery into an unknown country." The result has been one of the major contributions to the understanding of the Holy Spirit in the modern era. Laurence Wood lauds Moltmann: "His work in pneumatology is no less insightful and impressive than Barth's work in christology" (54). In this conclusion we will revisit the main themes of Moltmann's pneumatology, tying the material of these last five chapters into a brief summary.

Themes in Moltmann's Pneumatology

AN EXPERIENTIAL PNEUMATOLOGY

Breaking out of Barth's suspicion of religious experience, Moltmann leans a great deal on experience to fill out pneumatological positions. All of his work in *The Spirit of Life* revolves around various aspects of the experience of the Holy Spirit. Moltmann begins with an experiential interpretation of the scriptural witness to the Spirit, and he moves into a major treatment of a pneumatological *ordo salutis*. Finally, he finishes with the fellowship of the Spirit and the personhood of the Spirit, continuing to draw from Christian experience of the Spirit for crucial data.

Although he makes remarks in *The Spirit of Life* that disparage Scripture and tradition in favor of experience, Moltmann does not slip into a pure experientialism. Instead, he defines the main layout of the issues by the witness of Scripture, and then he uses experience to deepen and contemporize that account. For this reason, Wood states that Moltmann mines experience deeply, but does so without succumbing to the liberalism of Schleiermacher and the subjectivistic tendencies of Pietism (52).

A HOLISTIC PNEUMATOLOGY

As well as stating the need to recover a full account of experience of the Spirit, Moltmann also expresses the need for a new paradigm in pneumatology in *The Spirit of Life*. He believes that for today's world, pneumatology must be holistic. That is, it must take into account all aspects of religious experience including both conscious and unconscious experiences. It must also take into account experiences of the Spirit in all spheres of life, not just the "holy." Moltmann helps us realize that experience of the Spirit includes not just "Christian" activities like joy in worship and sorrow over sin. It also can include social phenomena, such as outrage over the destruction of the environment and the resolve to do something about it. This in itself is a crucial point to make to Christians who want to better understand the Spirit's complex and often subtle operations.

Furthermore, experience of the Spirit is often an individual affair, but Moltmann sheds light on its collective aspects as well. This shows up in the way he treats the Old and New Testament texts. He reads them as representing the views of the Jewish and Christian communities. For instance, the Old Testament prophetic texts about the Spirit are considered to reflect the hopes and expectations of the Israelites regarding the coming Spirit of God.

Moltmann also wants to get away from any idea that the Holy Spirit is more present among clergy than among laity. One of the reasons he stresses experience of the Spirit so much is that people do not need theological degrees to understand much of the Spirit's work, because they encounter it in their Christian walks.

Experience is an important theme to Moltmann's pneumatology, but it is certainly not limited to human encounters with the Spirit. For with the theme of "immanent transcendence," he portrays the Spirit's presence and influence reaching throughout all of creation. There is a great deal of pneumatic activity going on outside the reach of human experience. Moltmann makes it clear that the Spirit can be found in nature just as easily as he can be found in the lives of human beings.

Moltmann paints pneumatology on a very wide canvas, including what he calls the "trinitarian history of God's dealings with the world." The trinitarian nature of divine activity reveals the specific work of the Holy Spirit. The idea of the history of God's interaction with the world takes everything into account from creation through consummation. Moltmann does not want to exclude any elements.

The following point illustrates Moltmann's universalistic way of thinking. He questions the assumption that Christianity is an anthropocentric religion concerned with the individual human person. This is the way it has been presented in the modern world. "Yet in its original, biblical form Christianity was by no means personal, anthropocentric and historical in the modern Western sense. It was more *a way* and a moving forward, in the discovery of 'the always greater Christ.' Christ is the first-born among many brethren—Christ is the first-born of the new humanity—Christ is the first-born of the whole creation . . ." (*WJC*: 275). This view of the ever-expanding role of Christ leads to the conclusion that even though Christianity calls people to a personal faith in Christ, Christianity is not anthropocentric. In the end, it is cosmocentric. In this vein the work of the Holy Spirit appears as addressing and transforming the human person. Yet, more fundamentally the Spirit transforms the whole of creation, one element of which is humanity.

The holism and universality of Moltmann's pneumatology reminds us of the scope that characterizes Pauline thought about the Holy Spirit. Moltmann develops the holistic nature of the Spirit's work in more detail than Paul, as we would expect a later thinker to do. He is also aided by an era in which we are encouraged to think in global and universal terms. In the late twentieth century we care a great deal about ecology and the diversity among various social groups. Moltmann takes up these concerns in his theology of the Holy Spirit, often making contributions where they have been lacking in the past.

A Unifying Pneumatology

Hand in hand with Moltmann's holism and universalism goes his belief that the Holy Spirit is a force of unification. This idea is well entrenched in the tradition, going as far back as Augustine, who described the Holy Spirit as the principle of unity between the Father and the Son. Moltmann includes this unification of the Father and the Son in the Spirit's role at the cross. However, his perichoretic and social model of the Trinity precludes him from following Augustine very closely.

Besides functioning as a source of unity within the Godhead, a second level of the Spirit's unifying activity consists of bringing creatures together in fellowship. Moltmann speaks of the fellowship of all creatures, which rests on the presence of the Spirit as the principle of life and community that is common to all living beings in the world. Additionally, the Spirit unifies human beings with each other. The *perichoresis* of the triune God becomes a model for human fellowship, in which people come together in relationships defined by commonality, mutuality, equality and open dialogue. The Holy Spirit is the power in which this type of fellowship becomes possible.

A third level of the Spirit's unifying function is to bring creation into fellowship with God. By indwelling creatures, the Holy Spirit draws the fellowship of the Trinity into the life of creatures. By establishing such an intimate relationship with creatures, the Holy Spirit draws them up into the intertrinitarian life of the Father, the Son and the Holy Spirit. This two-way unification is the basis upon which the fellowship of the Trinity can be a working model for human relationships.

His distinctive message lies in the eschatological twist he gives to the theme of unification. For Moltmann, it is in the consummation that God will be glorified—Father, Son and Holy Spirit—for his own sake. This doxological glorification will be the occasion at which the unity of God reaches its zenith, for all things return to God at this point, including the wandering *shekinah*. In the eschaton creation will be completely unified with God, as his rule finally comes to fruition and his fellowship with creatures is made complete. If we carry through Moltmann's thought that God is affected by creation, then it is when creatures are unified with God that he will be most unified with himself. The harmony between creatures and God implies a greater harmony between the divine Persons.

Another way to express the unifying nature of the Spirit's work is to say that for Moltmann, the Spirit's operations can be described as "opening." For the Spirit opens the work of Christ to apply to all human beings and all of creation. The event of the cross is first of all an event between the Father and the Son, as *The Crucified God* shows. The Spirit takes this event and opens it up so that the history of Christ with God and God with Christ becomes the history of God with us and us with God (Conyers: 136). In turn, believers experience themselves opened up to a hope for the promised future.

The Spirit also opens up God to receive creatures into the divine life. In turn, God's openness allows him to be affected by the suffering, hopes, oppression, love, setbacks and possibilities of human history. God is opened to experience the full range of human life through the indwelling Spirit.

The theme of openness corresponds to its opposite of stifling domination. For Moltmann we are living in a twofold "crisis of domination." Many of the complaints Moltmann has with society and human behavior revolve around domination. Oppression is the domination of people over other people, and people over nature. For Moltmann, the crises of the modern world can be explained in terms of domination and oppression.

A TRINITARIAN PNEUMATOLOGY

The social model of the Trinity stresses the fellowship between Father, Son and Holy Spirit. It is a perichoretic fellowship that is characterized by self-communication, sharing, mutuality, cooperation and equality. The idea of trinitarian mutuality shows up in Moltmann's solution to the problem of the *filioque*. He asserts that the ministry of the Son depends on the Spirit, and the ministry of the Spirit depends on the Son. Therefore, the Son is begotten in the Spirit, and the Spirit proceeds through the Son.

The equality that Moltmann strives to maintain in the trinitarian relationships gives him a way to elevate the place of the Holy Spirit in theology—a much-needed corrective to the Western tradition's frequent subordination and neglect of the Spirit. However, it also prevents his theology from becoming pneumatocentric. The Holy Spirit has a unique personhood, and his work has a dignity all its own, but the Holy Spirit is never independent, nor does the Spirit overshadow the Son or the Father. Lyle Dabney is right that Moltmann's "turn to the third article" is really a turn to a fully trinitarian theology.

A HISTORICAL PNEUMATOLOGY

By the word 'historical' I mean that Moltmann's pneumatology is integrated into the flow of events stretching from creation to consummation. The Spirit has a prominent role in original creation, ongoing creation and the consummation of creation. Each of these phases builds upon the previous phase (except original creation, of course), and each implies the others. For instance, the Spirit's presence in original creation already foreshadows the day when God will dwell fully within his creation as its "all in all."

Similarly, Moltmann's ideas about the Spirit's operations in the present Christian community link up with the Spirit's operations in Christ during his ministry, his death and his resurrection, as well as with the Spirit's operations in God's people at the resurrection and the consummation. When the Spirit interacts with people in the present moment, they come into contact with the entire history of the Spirit's work, and this is a great virtue of Moltmann's pneumatology. Wood correctly observes that without placing the doctrine of the Holy Spirit within the flow of salvation history, there is a real danger that pneumatology can bog down in subjectivity (52). Moltmann runs the risk of subjectivity with his emphasis on experience of the Spirit, but his emphasis on the place such experience takes within the greater context of the divine history provides a way out of a subjectivistic quagmire.

In being historical, Moltmann's theology has always had a strong eschatological flavor. However, it has not always been deeply informed by pneumatology. In his early work Moltmann struggled with a radical contradiction between the present and the future. It is pneumatology that has allowed him to escape this problem. Specifically, it is recognizing the Spirit's presence in creation and in the Christian community that establishes the connection that is needed between present experience and future hope. Present reality indicates a closed system in which things can never really get better. The system needs to be opened for God's future, and it is the Holy Spirit who accomplishes this. He does so by offering new potentialities for creation besides the continuation of destructive patterns. If the Holy Spirit is the cosmic Spirit, then the universe cannot be viewed as a closed system. It is "a system that is open—open for God and for his future" (*TK*: 103; Dabney, 1993: 100). The ultimate statement of openness is the eschatological future in which all our greatest expectations and hopes will be filled and surpassed.

Creation will experience ultimate openness in the eschaton. The consummation does not represent a closed system of eternal, timeless, static existence. It is not the transference of reality to one final possibility.

Rather, it means that humanity and the new creation will be taken up into the infinite possibilities inherent in God himself. We will participate in the unlimited freedom of God. We will be able to do this, because we will no longer be bound and shackled by the limitations of sin and death. Eschatological openness is "indeterminate," but not in the sense of being aimless or random. Rather, it is indeterminate in the sense of not being determined by present limitations. Inasmuch as it must consist of the glorification of God, it is still determined in this way. But for Moltmann this is ultimate freedom—the possibility of living in complete harmony with the God of infinite possibilities. Such freedom is only a potentiality for people if they are living in the power of the Holy Spirit. The Spirit alone opens people to God in the present age, and the Spirit will bring this partial openness to its completion in the free and unhindered glorification of God.

I mentioned that Moltmann describes his exploration in pneumatology as "a voyage of discovery into an unknown country." He went looking for something and found it: "the presence of eternity" (x). Moltmann does not mean this in a Barthian sense in which eternity is the antithesis of temporality. Moltmann means it in an eschatological sense in which eternity is the future state of complete redemption. His discovery of the Holy Spirit was a discovery of the eschatological Spirit, the first fruits of our complete redemption.

Moltmann's "Turn to the Third Article"

In order to add perspective to our study of Moltmann's theology of the Holy Spirit, it is appropriate to mention Lyle Dabney's account of the gradual "turn to the third article" in Moltmann's thought. Dabney notes that in his early writings, Moltmann's concern with the Holy Spirit is marginal. In *Theology of Hope* he portrays the Christian God as the God of hope. Trinitarian thinking plays little role in the presentation, but christology takes center stage because of the way the resurrection of Christ defines salvation history. The Spirit is particularly neglected for two main reasons. First, what Moltmann does in *Theology of Hope* is take the Barthian vertical dialectic between time and eternity, and turn it on its side so that it becomes a present-future dialectic. In this case the Holy Spirit becomes shut up in the future, away from the present. The Spirit is the power of futurity and stands over against this "godforsaken" world. In this way, the Spirit's influence is limited to eternity (Dabney, 1993: 94–95). Second, the continental Reformed tradition, and Barth in particular, is marked by its focus on christology to the exclusion of pneumatology. Moltmann is working from within this tradition. Although his approach to eschatology is fresh, the dominance of christology in *Theology of Hope* reflects a clear dependence on Barthian thought.

As we have seen, the theology of *The Crucified God* is little more than binitarian. Dabney agrees that Moltmann's account of the cross describes an event between the Father and the Son. The suffering at Golgotha does not include the Spirit, because the Spirit is the power of life and is thus set at cross-purposes with Christ's death. The Spirit is at odds with the self-surrender of the Father and the Son to the intense suffering and death of the cross (98–99).

Moltmann has been well aware that his pneumatological views lacked development in his early works. With *The Church in the Power of the Spirit* he sought to redress the problem. He explains that the problem of a lack of pneumatology in his first two books comes not from a lack of imagination, but from the models of trinitarian theology that he inherited from the Western tradition. These models characterize all divine activity as originating in the Father and the Son. The Spirit merely brings to completion those actions. The result is that the Spirit is subordinated to the Father and the Son, and pneumatology becomes an afterthought. Dabney argues that Moltmann's acknowledgement of the problem, along with his resolve to correct it, marks the crucial turning point of his approach to pneumatology, and possibly to theology as a whole (99). When Moltmann claims in *The Trinity and the Kingdom* that the action of Christ is incomprehensible without the action of the Spirit, he is breaking out of old patterns and emerging with a truly trinitarian theology (100).

It is not a coincidence that Moltmann's turn to the third article accompanied the transition in his eschatology from a strictly future framework in *Theology of Hope* to the inaugurated overtones that are present in his later work. Much of the inconsistency of Moltmann's remarks concerning eschatology and the present age can be attributed to this evolution in his thought. As he has come to appreciate the vital role of the Holy Spirit in theology, he has also come to appreciate the ways in which the Spirit brings the dynamics of the eschaton into present existence. Thus, for Moltmann, the maturation of his thought has led him toward an inaugurated eschatology and a fully integrated pneumatology at the same time. In this way, he becomes a model of the kind of progress that is possible for the Protestant tradition as a whole.

9

Toward an Eschatological Pneumatology

I N the beginning of this study I claimed that in the Protestant tradition, pneumatology has tended to swing back and forth between two opposing tendencies. On one side is what I have called "institutional" pneumatology, which ties the work of the Holy Spirit to Christ and the functions of the church. That is, the activity of the Spirit primarily consists of applying the atoning work of Christ, revealing God through the Word read and proclaimed, and dispensing grace through the sacraments. The best illustration of this approach is Karl Barth, who regards the Holy Spirit exclusively as the Spirit of Christ. The Spirit unites believers to Christ, and he is the voice of Christ speaking to the church. In Barth's thought, the Spirit's activity is constantly oriented toward Christ. He is the arm of Christ and the power of Christ.

Standing over against this style of theology and arising as a reaction against it is the "experiential" trend in pneumatology. Experiential pneumatology has been perpetuated in a series of movements that can be loosely described as pietistic in character. The experiential approach is well illustrated in the writings of John Wesley. Wesley considered his understanding of the inner witness of the Holy Spirit to be Methodism's unique contribution to the Christian community. He identifies three different forms of the witness of the Spirit—the *direct* witness of the Spirit to *justification*, the *direct* witness of the Spirit to *entire sanctification*, and the *indirect* witness of the Spirit to *justification*. Personal experience is a prominent attribute of all three of Wesley's forms of the witness of the Spirit. Furthermore, Randy Maddox has reported that in correspondence with John Smith, Wesley insisted that if the Spirit fills a person and is at work within her, she cannot help but perceive a change in affections. Such claims earned Wesley the charge of enthusiast.

Both Barth and Wesley—and their respective followers—have made valuable contributions to the field of pneumatology. Institutional pneumatology provides a thorough treatment of the connections between the Spirit and Christ, and the Spirit and the church. Experiential pneumatology deepens our understanding of the pneumatic aspects of human experience.

Nevertheless, the two contrasting approaches contain significant drawbacks. Barth's pneumatology is underdeveloped and marked by subordination of the Spirit to Christ. Also, when Barth continually refers to the Spirit as the power of Christ, he perpetuates a problem that Christian have long had—appreciating the personhood of the Spirit. The thrust of Wesley's pneumatology is personal experience of the Spirit. This drives his theology of the Third Person in an individualistic direction. It also concentrates on what is going on in the present moment, largely leaving the past and future activity of the Spirit out of the picture.

I have suggested that these difficulties are not intrinsic to pneumatology. It is possible to alleviate them, if we can escape the swinging pendulum of tendencies in Protestant pneumatology. Fortunately, we can escape that pendulum by recovering the original center of Christian pneumatology: eschatology. Over the last seven chapters, we have been investigating the eschatological aspects of the pneumatological thought of Paul the apostle and Jürgen Moltmann, and we have seen that the doctrine of the Holy Spirit needs to be painted on a much larger canvas than those used by either the institutional or the experiential approach. A contemporary eschatological pneumatology will need to take advantage of the advances made in theology over the centuries since Paul. This is where Moltmann comes in. No current or recent theologian has done more to integrate pneumatology and eschatology. Still, his eschatology is not always consistent, especially in maintaining a sense of tension between the "already" and the "not yet," and this affects his pneumatology. Further work is necessary in the development of an eschatological pneumatology. Thus, the task of this concluding chapter is to present the contours of a contemporary eschatological pneumatology, drawing on the insights of Paul and Moltmann. In order to do that we must first be clear about what we mean by 'eschatological.' Consequently, the first section of this chapter will lay out the eschatological framework that must support pneumatology. In the second section I will articulate the contours of an eschatological pneumatology. In the final section I will appraise the ability of an eschatological pneumatology to overcome the problems that pneumatology has faced in the Protestant tradition.

An Eschatological Framework

In Paul and Moltmann we have two very different thinkers who nevertheless share an important sense about the Christian faith: it is inherently
eschatological. Not surprisingly, both Paul and Moltmann have significant
contributions to make to the discussion of eschatological matters. For this
reason, I will draw on their thought in forming the framework of eschatology that will support an eschatological pneumatology. Because this is a
study of pneumatology, I will not attempt to lay out a detailed eschatology. However, it is necessary to construct a basic framework in order for the
distinctive contours of an eschatological pneumatology to come to light.

Paul's Eschatology

Pauline theology *is* eschatology. He perceived himself to be living in the
age of the fulfillment of Jewish hopes for a coming age of messianic salvation. The Messiah had come, the resurrection had begun, the Spirit had
been given to all of God's people, the Gentiles had been adopted into
God's family, and so on. When Paul proclaims the gospel, he cannot help
but make eschatological claims. The figure of Christ is eschatological, the
charismatic Spirit is eschatological, the church is eschatological, even salvation itself is eschatological. Running through Paul's understanding of
the gospel and the life of the church in the present age is the theme of
eschatological tension.

Paul's understanding of the new age of salvation was fundamentally
altered when he came to faith in Jesus as the Messiah. Paul views the new
age in two ways. On one hand, he holds a standard apocalyptic distinction
between this age and the age to come. On the other hand—and this is
what distinguishes Paul from typical Jewish apocalyptic—he understands
the phenomena of this age to be the beginning stages of a set of processes
that will be completed in the future age. In other words, the new age has
become not one age but two—this age and the age to come. The two ages
are continuous in that the qualities of the consummation are already present in this age, yet they are discontinuous in that the present age represents
only a foretaste of the consummation. In other words, the eschatological
age has been inaugurated though not consummated.

The themes of inauguration and eschatological tension are so central to Pauline thought that it is not overstating the case to hold that
an appreciation of them is necessary for a proper understanding of the
apostle's writings. To fail to take the themes of eschatological inauguration
and tension into account will result in a distortion of the gospel message.

Furthermore, unless the gospel message has fundamentally changed, these themes are still necessary for contemporary theology. We are living in the dawn of the eschatological age, which means that the present age is itself eschatological in an inaugurated sense.

Moltmann's Eschatology

Although Paul's pneumatology and eschatology have cosmic scope, Moltmann works out the universality of eschatology in much more detail. Eschatology impacts reality in four ever-widening circles. It is individual (life and death, the intermediate state, resurrection), historical (the kingdom of God, messianic millenarianism), cosmic (the end of time and space, the new creation of all things), and divine (the eternal glorification of God). It is to Moltmann's credit that he integrates all of these arenas together. The individual human life does not appear to be significant in the cosmic picture, yet the resurrection of one man signals the beginning of the new creation of all things. By extension, whenever any believer acts in the power of the Spirit to affirm life, he is bringing the dynamics of the new creation into the present. All four of these arenas of eschatology interact in similar ways.

Moltmann is, of course, keenly interested in the future of humanity, both individually and socially. However, he integrates the future of humanity with the future of creation, and vice versa. The end of individual, historical and cosmic eschatology is the eternal glorification of God, where creatures worship God purely for his own sake, and not for the things he has done on their behalf. By holding a cosmic perspective, Moltmann shows that Christianity is far from being anthropocentric. It is cosmocentric.

This universal vision for eschatology is complemented by Moltmann's historical perspective. For him, eschatology is not only universally effective, it also reaches throughout time. Creation has an eschatological orientation for Moltmann. That is, his doctrine of creation is forward-looking. God creates for the sake of the sabbath of creation. Both creation in the beginning and ongoing creation are oriented toward the sabbath of creation—the destiny of all things in the presence of God.

Moltmann expresses the range of divine activity from creation through consummation with the phrase, "the trinitarian history of God's dealings with the world." Obviously, this history includes more than human history, since it begins "in the beginning" (Gen 1:1). It also emphasizes the trinitarian character of divine action, showing that the history of God's dealings with creation is not conducted by a monadic deity but a triune one. Moltmann observes that the trinitarian character of God's dealings with the world comes to light when we contemplate the gospel, for the gospel is the message about reconciliation between humanity and God through Christ in the Holy Spirit. Projecting back onto the Old Testament, Moltmann declares that all of God's dealings with the world, going as far back as creation, are triune. The history of God's dealings with the world is a trinitarian history. Not all of this history is eschatological, but the eschatological periods of it are woven together with the noneschatological periods.

Two ideas that figure prominently into Moltmann's eschatology are "advent" and "*novum.*" The idea of advent stresses that nothing decisive can happen in creation without the inbreaking, definitive arrival of God. The coming of Christ is the classic example of advent, although the outpouring of the Holy Spirit at Pentecost and Cornelius' house is equally decisive for the future of humanity. The idea of *novum* communicates the necessity for a "new thing" to be done in the world. The changes in reality that make up the eschatological landscape cannot arise out of the flow of history, for history does not have the potentiality to transform itself. Therefore, advent and novum together communicate that *God* (advent) must do a *new thing (novum)*. In a nutshell, eschatology is about God doing a new thing, although as it has happened, the new thing stretches across human history from Christ on into eternity.

An Eschatological Framework

Drawing on Paul and Moltmann, we can now lay out eschatological concepts that can form the framework of a paradigm for pneumatology. The Pauline gospel stresses the themes of *inauguration* and *eschatological tension*. These themes are present in Moltmann's work, although, as we have seen, he gives them inconsistent treatment.[1] Therefore, from Paul we can draw the understanding that the ages have turned—that this is the first installment of the eschatological age of salvation that represents the hopes of Israel and all of creation.

Moltmann contributes several key ideas that are consistent with Pauline thought, but are not systematically developed by Paul. First is the *universality* of the eschatological activity of God. We can understand eschatology to have four concentric circles: personal, historical/social, cosmic and divine. All these circles direct our attention to a distinct arena of

---

[1] See sections entitled "The Timing of the Kingdom" in chapter five and "The Spirit and the Eschatological Age" in chapter seven.

eschatological phenomena. Second is the *historical character* of the divine eschatological activity. Eschatology is inherently concerned with time, and Moltmann's notion of the trinitarian history of God's dealings with the world helps us place particular events within the big picture of ongoing divine action. Third is the pair of ideas—*advent* and *novum*—that reveal the key to eschatology: the expectation that God is doing and will do a new thing in order to redeem humanity and creation. Moltmann's well-known theme of hope stems from a trust that God will do a new thing in the parousia of Christ and the new creation of all things.

With these six ideas—inauguration, eschatological tension, universality, historical character, advent and *novum*—our framework is beginning to take shape. Eschatology is a process that began in the past with the coming of Christ and is continuing in the present with the history of the Spirit and the church. Yet the realities of this age, although they are essentially eschatological in nature, will give way to the greater manifestation of the glory of God in the future consummation. The universality of eschatological dynamics is progressive. God's grace was made known first to the Jews and then to the Gentiles (Rom 1:16–17). At present it reaches primarily to all who follow Christ, although the influence of divine grace reaches outside the church walls. Finally, at the consummation all of creation will be transformed as God comes in all of his glory to take up habitation in his creation.

A model for eschatology must take into account the network of people and events described in the New Testament. This network is rather like a symphony in two important respects. First, it is *complex*. The New Testament depiction of the new age is not the simple history of Christ. As Matthew shows us, the process of eschatological fulfillment began long before Jesus began his ministry. As Luke shows us, it continued long after he ascended into heaven. Included in this complex process is a great diversity of figures from John the Baptist to Jesus, from Mary his mother to Mary Magdalene, from Simeon to Saul who would become Paul. All of these people have a part to play in the great symphony of eschatological fulfillment. In addition, there is complexity of a sort within the Godhead. As Moltmann observes, trinitarian theology grew out of the church's need to deal with the relationships between the Father, the Son and the Holy Spirit in its reflection on the history of Christ. Inasmuch as it is sparked by an attempt to understand the revelation of the Son and the intensified activity of the Holy Spirit, trinitarian theology is inherently eschatological theology.

As diverse as the list of figures is the array of events that began the new age. Although all events described in the New Testament carry their own significance, there are some that stand out as major fulfillments of Old Testament promises—the coming of the Messiah, the establishment of the new covenant, the resurrection of Christ, the outpouring of the Spirit, the inclusion of the Gentiles, and the formation of the church as the body of Christ and the charismatic community.

Along with being complex, eschatology shares another trait with symphonic productions—it is *harmonious.* The list of figures and events is long and diverse. Any one of these figures or events by itself would have its own value and beauty, but it would not inaugurate the eschatological age of redemption. Even the incarnation of the Son only acquires its meaning and significance within the context of the overall movement of eschatological events. All of the figures and events work together harmoniously. To leave out some of these elements, or to overemphasize whichever of them happens to be our favorite, will destroy the overall structure of the whole and distort the gospel message.

Understood in these terms, eschatology is complex, but it has definite boundaries. As the Gospel writers show us, the ages turn in the decisive coming of God in Jesus Christ. Clustered in and around the history of Christ is a network of people and events through which God announced and inaugurated the new age. The book of Acts and the New Testament epistles show us that the new age did not end with the death of Christ. Rather, it picked up momentum as Christ was resurrected and the Spirit fell on believers. Therefore, the New Testament message is that the new age continues on in the activities of the church. However, the New Testament writings are also consistent in their hope for the coming of Christ in glory and the transformation of all things. This is a hope that can be generally described as apocalyptic, in that there is a decisive break between this age and the age to come caused by the advent of God.

Portraying eschatology in this way alerts us to its vastness and complexity. Having taken up this view of the ages, it is jolting to return to the conception of eschatology at work in modern systematic theology. Today's theologians have shown a tendency to lose sight of the big picture. They reduce eschatology strictly to future events, thereby eroding the continuity between ongoing eschatological events and future ones.

Theologians are also prone to identify one particular figure or event as the key to the story of salvation, and the impact on theology is deleterious. In *Theology of Hope*, Moltmann singles out the resurrection of Christ as the event that began the new creation of all things. Because Christian hope rests in the future resurrection and new creation, the resurrection of Christ becomes the key to eschatological hope. However, in highlighting this one event, Moltmann loses sight of another key event—the giving of the Holy Spirit to the followers of Christ. The result is an anemic pneumatology in *Theology of Hope*.

Theologians also single out key figures and build the gospel story around them. It is appropriate to state that Christ is the key figure of the New Testament. However, Christ takes his place within a greater narrative. Barth shows a tendency to lose sight of this narrative by his persistent practice of defining all other realities in christological terms. Eschatology is certainly about Christ, but it is not exclusively about him. We even overstate the case when we make Christ the hub of eschatology, with all other events and figures connected to him like spokes on a wheel. In Paul's theology, inasmuch as there is a hub, it is God the Father, for he sends Christ and the Holy Spirit to redeem all of creation for the sake of his own glory.

Therefore, the imminent danger in dealing with eschatological matters is reductionism in one form or another. Reductionism is a failure to keep the greater context of the eschatological narrative in mind. As we will see, the institutional and experiential approaches in pneumatology are each reductionistic in their own ways.

Contours of an Eschatological Pneumatology

The Historical Context of Pneumatology

An eschatological pneumatology is one in which every work of the Spirit is considered within its proper context. One dimension of that context is historical in nature. That is, every work of the Spirit takes its place within the overall flow of pneumatic activity, which, in turn, is set within the grand narrative of eschatology. Eschatology, in turn, must be set within the trinitarian history of God's dealings with the world.

With this notion of context in mind, let us return to two key ideas in Protestant pneumatology: the Spirit's relation to Christ and human experience of the Spirit. As Moltmann points out, the Holy Spirit is "the Spirit of Christ" in that he is sent by God through Christ, and he leads people to God through Christ. "The Spirit of Christ" is the main theme of Barth's pneumatology. However, the perspective of salvation-history corrects this idea in two ways. First, the functional subordination of the Spirit to Christ is a reality, but it applies only to the church age. As Moltmann points out, during the period of Christ's earthly ministry, he was "the Christ of the Spirit" in that in his incarnation, earthly ministry, death and resurrection, he was dependent on the Spirit. Thus, Moltmann rightly concludes that in the history of Christ and the Spirit, the relationship between the two is bidirectional, not unidirectional.

Second, the dependence of Christ on the Spirit cannot be limited to the period of Christ's earthly ministry. Even now Christ is dependent on the Spirit. If Christ is still human, then he is human through the Holy Spirit. By the same token, Christ was raised through the Spirit, and his ongoing resurrection-state remains pneumatic in this regard. These two points show that even while the Spirit is functionally subordinate to the Son during the church age, the Son remains reliant on the Spirit, just as he was and always will be.

Experience of the Spirit is of great importance to believers, and this is natural, if the Spirit is the source of new, eschatological life. However, experience of the Spirit must also take its place within a larger context. For every present encounter with the Spirit is one instant in a long history of pneumatic activity. Forgetting this point results in an overblown evaluation of the significance of experiences of the Spirit. It also results in those experiences losing much of their meaning. The Spirit encountered today is the same Spirit that spoke through the prophets, empowered Jesus and the apostles, and will someday bring about the complete transformation of all things. It is the eschatological Spirit. To experience the Spirit is to be drawn up into this pneumatic movement. Therefore, any experience of the Spirit must take its meaning from this larger historical context.

Along these lines, Moltmann describes what he calls a "historical experience of the Spirit." Such an experience is ". . . always tensed between the remembrance and the expectation which frame that experience. Remembrances of God and expectations of God make the experienced presence of God a historical present" (SL: 39). What Moltmann means is that a historical experience of God is one that is set within the greater context of the trinitarian history of God's dealings with the world. All too often, experience of the Spirit tends to lose its historical character. One of the main reasons for this is that believers are not often aware that their experiences have any context beyond that of their individual life and possibly the life of their church communities. They have lost a sense of context for these experiences. The eschatological history of divine action supplies this context.

The Three-Tiered Presence of the Spirit

The eschatological history of God's dealings with the world gives us a temporal sense of context. But context can also come in spatial terms. Here the issue for pneumatology is the presence of the Spirit. In the eschatological age, God is present on more than one level. In chapter eight, I expanded on Moltmann's concept of the *shekinah* and claimed that it must have three levels. The first level is God's universal presence in creation through the Spirit. For Moltmann, God is in all things, and all things are in God. He elucidates this in pneumatological terms. The Holy Spirit is the immanent transcendence that imbues all things with divine presence. The Spirit is "God in all things."

This universal presence of the Spirit is the context in which the second level of the *shekinah* fits—the presence of the eschatological Spirit in God's people. The presence of God in particular people, events or places was sporadic in the Old Testament. However, in the new age, the Spirit rests on all followers of the Messiah regardless of who or where they are, and this is not a temporary but a permanent endowment. This is the phenomenon that Joel foresaw when he wrote that someday God would "pour out" his Spirit on all of his people. Paul expresses this phenomenon in terms of the "indwelling" of the Spirit.

The metaphors of "pouring out" and "indwelling" are a fascinating pair. One suggests the sending of the Spirit by the Father. He is the one who pours out his Spirit. The image of the Spirit being poured out also connotes the profusion of Spirit-presence in God's people. The Spirit is not just dripping or trickling on God's people; he is pouring all over them, soaking them through and through. This image also brings to mind the collection of God's people as a whole. God pours out his Spirit on all of them, regardless of who they are.

The indwelling of the Spirit, on the other hand, suggests the destination of the eschatological giving of the Spirit. He comes to rest within his people, meaning that the Spirit's influence will not be limited to the religious spheres of life, but will reach to all spheres. Although we as modern Western Christians tend to think in terms of the infusion of the Spirit's presence within the individual, Paul understands the Spirit to indwell both individual believers and the believing community. To quote Vos, the Spirit dwells within "the entire circle of believers, and within the life of every believer over the entire range, subconscious and conscious, religious and ethical, of this life" (1952: 58). The image of the Spirit-indwelt community connects with the image of the community soaked with the Spirit that has been poured out in the eschatological age.

In general, the early Christian community understood the outpouring and indwelling of the Holy Spirit to be phenomena of the eschatological age. Today we take such blessings for granted. As the eschatological overtones of the reception of the Spirit have faded over time, much of the theological significance of this event has drained away. In the Protestant tradition, Christians are much more likely to interpret the reception of the Spirit in terms of salvation or an infusion of personal empowerment for living a holy life and ministering to others. They associate the reception of the Spirit with faith in Christ and personal conversion rather than with the fulfillment of ancient promises and the execution of God's vast plan of redemption. The difference in perspective is significant. Whereas the typical believer today thinks in terms of the Holy Spirit entering her life, the more significant aspect of the event of the reception of the Spirit is that *she is entering into the life of God.* That is, she is being taken up into the trinitarian history of God's dealings with the world, which in this age are eschatological in nature.

The infusion of the Spirit into the believer's life is a phenomenon of eschatological blessing that is shared by all followers of Christ. It is universal to all believers, but it is not universal to all human beings. However, it is the first installment of an even greater outpouring when God's *shekinah* reaches its third level: the fullness of God's presence permeating all of renewed creation in the eschaton. This is the state of God's being "all in all." Therefore, when a believer experiences rebirth to new life, she can look at it as an occasion for rejoicing and also groaning. She rejoices because she experiences the indwelling Spirit as a fulfillment of her most basic existential hopes, and she groans because she longs for all of creation to enjoy the same gift.

The three levels of the *shekinah* correspond to creation, salvation and consummation.[2] They are all distinct, yet they imply each other. Moltmann holds that creation looks forward to salvation, and salvation looks forward to consummation. The link between creation and consummation is not indirect, however. For creation implies consummation, and consummation implies creation. The doctrines are related in two ways. First, they mirror each other. One is a doctrine of the beginning; the other is a doctrine of the end (which is also a new beginning). Both are discussed

---

[2] The second level has noneschatological instances in the Old Testament, but it is mainly exhibited in the eschatological community of the new age of salvation.

in Scripture, but both are conveyed in highly symbolic, mythical language. Both are difficult to support by experience, for experience of the world does not necessarily imply creation by an intelligent designer, nor does experience of new life necessarily imply that new life will lead to complete transformation. Second, creation and consummation imply each other. Creation is ongoing. It began with creation in the beginning, continues with ongoing creation, and it will be completed in the new creation of all things at the consummation. It could be said that the Spirit's presence that permeates all of creation is the first installment of the Spirit's presence that will completely saturate all of creation.

Despite these similarities and mutual relations, the two doctrines are not treated equally by critical thinkers. Creation is a matter of philosophical debate in natural theology. Eschatology is not. In fact, eschatology would be seen as an embarrassment in the philosophical community. What is worse, it is an embarrassment for many Christians. Creation is more "acceptable" among modern-day believers than eschatology.

Taking an eschatological point of view means overcoming this reticence toward eschatology. It means thinking through the interrelations between the presence of the Holy Spirit as reflected in the three levels of the *shekinah*. It also means looking to the present indwelling of the Spirit within believers and imagining a world in which that phenomenon is universalized and intensified. Finally, it means holding such a vision not as wishful thinking but as real hope.

The Spirit and Eschatological Tension

Having discussed two axes of context within which pneumatology must be placed—time and space—I will now take up some specific pneumatological doctrines that demonstrate the contours of an eschatological pneumatology. First is the eschatological tension that marks Christian pneumatology. I stated above that Christian eschatology combines elements of discontinuity and continuity. The dualism of a Christian understanding of history comes from this discontinuity. There is dualism between this age and the age to come, just as there is dualism between partial fulfillment and total fulfillment, or between first fruits and general harvest. In short, some kind of break in history must be expected. For the Christian, there has already been one major break in history—the coming of Christ. If history broke once, there is reason to believe it can break again. Nevertheless, it is not uncommon to see theologians who will speak of the revolutionary character of Christ's ministry but who are hesitant to speak of any kind of futurist eschatology. The latter reeks of apocalyptic mythology and speculation. However, pure speculation about the future is not necessary. This is because although there is dualism in Christian theology, it is *mitigated* dualism. The mitigation comes from the continuity between the ages.

The more continuity we find between this age and the age to come, the more mild the dualism becomes. In pneumatology we find the most accessible source of this continuity. The Holy Spirit is the first fruits of complete redemption in the age to come. This not only means that our present existence with the Spirit forms an *analogy* to our future existence, but also that there is *identity* between the two existences, even though present existence is an incomplete form of future existence.

The question regarding eschatological dualism is: What is the proper stance to take regarding the eschaton? One option is detailed speculation about events surrounding the end of time. Another option, largely influenced by the failures of the first option, is to hold back from speculation and claim ignorance about the future. This is widely accepted as the course of prudence in the theological community. However, such reserve is generally accompanied by a strictly futurist eschatology. An inaugurated eschatology leads us to a third option between these two extremes. In this option, Christians can actually speak of what they *know* about the eschaton—at least some aspects of it. This knowledge is not based on the exegesis of difficult apocalyptic texts, but on experience.

James Ross has argued that we can have pragmatic knowledge of the eschaton if our expectations about it are found to be fulfilled. It is necessary to leave room for a certain amount of surprise upon finding the actual state of things in the consummation, for we simply cannot imagine such things in sufficient detail to support a straight correspondence theory of truth. Ross expects that believers will have a mixed reaction to the consummation. They will exclaim that "this is just what I expected," although at the same time they will marvel that things are "beyond all expectation" (282). We can add to Ross' account that many of these expectations will be founded on present experience of the Holy Spirit.

The present experience of the Spirit includes phenomena expressed by the language of rebirth to new life, living according to the Spirit, exhibiting *charismata* and the fruit of the Spirit, and so on. The resurrection is the completion of the transformation begun in the rebirth to new life that accompanies conversion. Resurrection-life is life according to the Spirit *par excellence*. We now feel an inner impulse to let the fruit of the Spirit govern our behavior, although we struggle mightily toward this goal. In the resurrection-life, this fruit will not change. Rather, we will change, so that the struggle is removed and our character is completely defined by love, joy, peace, and so on. Today we sporadically experience the Spirit working through us for the edification of others in the believing community. In the eschaton there will not be the same need for edification, for the destruction caused by sin and death will no longer be present. However, the Spirit will continue to work through the people of God to further his glorification throughout all of creation. This is a short list of well-founded expectations we can have about future resurrection-life based on present experience and the concept of the Spirit as the first fruits of our complete redemption. It is far from exhaustive.

Edward Schillebeeckx argues that hope grows out of insights of faith regarding the past and present dealings of God with his people. "Although the future has an element of 'not yet' in it, we cannot neglect the element of 'already'" (50). It is the already that forms the basis for our expectations of the not yet. "The post-terrestrial *eschaton* is but a question of the manner in which what is already growing in the history of this world will receive its final fulfillment" (53). Whereas Schillebeeckx is on target with these comments, it is significant that he does not establish the connection between present and future in terms of pneumatology.

Although Moltmann is the greatest theologian of hope and a major contributor to contemporary pneumatology, he does not define hope in pneumatological terms either. In *Theology of Hope*, the volume that catapulted eschatological hope onto the theological landscape, Moltmann based hope on the resurrection of Christ and the faithfulness of God. These are two essential bases for hope. We should neglect neither. However, in this early work, Moltmann did not link hope to the experience of the Holy Spirit.

Later, when he wrote *The Spirit of Life*, Moltmann focused his creative energies on explicating the dimensions and meaning of the experience of the Holy Spirit. Ironically, hope is not a significant element of the discussion. He does not neglect altogether the idea of hope in his investigation of the experience of the Spirit, but neither does he take advantage of the opportunity to give hope a deeper foundation. Although Moltmann does not make this argument, it remains true that experience of the Holy Spirit is a key to hope, because experience of the Spirit is our most direct experiential link with the "not yet" of the eschatological future. Our experience of the Spirit is pleasant, and we are left wanting more of the Spirit's blessings. These desires are not in vain, for our future resurrection-life is marked by the fruit of the Spirit and complete harmony with God. More of the Spirit's blessings is exactly what we will have.

Moltmann's theology of hope would have been more powerful had he worked out the connections between the present gift of the Spirit and our hope in the future. It is significant that early on, Moltmann's theology was deficient in the two areas of eschatological tension and pneumatology. His eschatology was strongly futuristic, and his theology was basically binitarian. As he has "turned to the third article," as Dabney says, Moltmann's eschatology has taken more of an inaugurated tone. This is far from coincidental.

For Paul, the link between the Spirit and hope is strong. Victor Furnish points out that in several passages the Spirit is a specific ground of hope for believers. In Rom 15:13, Paul invokes the power of the Holy Spirit in order that his recipients may abound in hope (1968: 132). In this case, the Spirit is the power of hope. He is the means by which believers may share in the hope given by God. In Rom 5:1ff., the hope of sharing in God's glory survives because of the Holy Spirit. "Precisely because God's love is already powerfully present and active in his Spirit, there is hope for something more, namely, the fulfillment of salvation, the completion and perfection of God's redemptive activity" (132). Finally, in 2 Cor 3:7–8, the Spirit gives validity to, and actually constitutes, the hope of a future glory (132). These passages indicate that Paul considers the Holy Spirit to be the power that gives rise to hope. The Spirit causes hope to grow and endure in believers. In addition, the experienced influence of the Spirit can be a grounds for expectation that something greater is in store for the followers of Christ. Because of connections like these, Shires states, "It is therefore the Holy Spirit who raises most acutely the issue of the meaning of the present and the future in the life of the Christian" (152).

The Spirit and the Future

We have seen that the gift of the Spirit is both a matter of fulfillment of prophetic promises and an indicator pointing toward still greater fulfillment in the future. The eschatological Spirit was hoped for in the previous age, but belongs to the present age and the age to come. Neill Hamilton has argued that in the New Testament, and specifically in the Pauline letters, "the Spirit is related primarily to the future, to eternity, to the time of the consummation of the redemptive process" (17). What Hamilton means is that "on the basis of the [past] work of Christ, the power of the redeemed future has been released to act in the present in the person of the

Holy Spirit" (26). In other words, we might say that Christ is the power of the past, and the Holy Spirit is the power of the future.

This is a way to emphasize the eschatological character of the Holy Spirit in Pauline thought. Hamilton is correct insofar as he directs our attention to the fact that the Spirit's work will not be completed in this age but in the age to come. What we experience now of the Spirit is only the first fruits or the down payment, which is to say, only a small part of the future whole. In this way, the Holy Spirit belongs primarily to "the future, the not-yet-fulfilled, the promised" (27).

At the same time, we must be cautious in associating the Holy Spirit's work primarily with the future age. Although Hamilton's intention is to highlight the eschatological nature of the Spirit, his language runs the risk of eroding the eschatological tension inherent in Pauline thought. Paul does not conceive of the present as secondary to the future. Certainly the future age is to be preferred because of its greater glory, but for Paul the two ages are complementary and necessary to each other. In one sense the future is primary, for it is the time of the completion of God's work. But in another sense the present is primary, for the future consummation of our redemption is a continuation of God's grace as it is already manifest in the work of his Son and his Spirit.

The great danger for twentieth-century Christians in identifying the Spirit primarily with the age to come is that it reinforces our tendency to see the future age as the real eschatological age. By implication, the present age becomes only quasi-eschatological, or eschatological in a secondary or derivative sense. This is the way many think today, but it is not what Paul taught. The apostle, like other early Christians, was convinced that the present age is the Messianic age, and the Messianic age is an eschatological age. God has not yet completed his plan of salvation, but that does not take away from the eschatological nature of the present epoch. This very tenet is what is distinctive about Christian eschatology. Making the claim that we are living in the age of fulfillment immediately set the early Christians apart from the Jews.

Thus, although we can say that in a very important sense the Spirit belongs primarily to the future age, we need to keep in mind that such a claim in no way takes away from the eschatological nature of the present age. In other words, we must be careful to maintain an appropriate eschatological tension when we talk about the present age or the present work of the Holy Spirit. Presumably, Hamilton would not disagree with any of these caveats, but he does not make them explicit as they should be for today's Christians.

The Spirit and Christ

The coming of the Messiah is a vital element of the eschatological symphony. According to Paul, we await the Messiah's return, but that does not mean that the Messiah is absent. For Christ is present in the church and in believers via the Holy Spirit. Thus, here is another eschatological aspect of the ministry of the Holy Spirit—being the means by which the resurrected Christ, the eschatological man, is present in the Christian community. When speaking of "the Spirit of Christ," it is vital that we avoid the assumption that the Spirit's main role is as a surrogate paraclete, filling in for Christ in the interim between his earthly appearances. Keith Green's popular song *There is a Redeemer* reflects this view. The chorus contains the lines, "Thank you, O my Father, for giving us your Son; / and leaving your Spirit 'til the work on earth is done."

In more academic terms, Christiaan Beker has claimed in one of his early works that in Pauline thought

> the Spirit has its movement and location within history. Its occurrence is bound by two events and it operates within these boundaries. As historical reality it was not *before* Christ (cf. only as promise in the O.T. era); and it will not continue *after* the Christ event has been fulfilled in the kingdom. The boundary, then, is that of the 'past,' i.e., the death and resurrection of Jesus Christ, and the other one is that of the 'future,' i.e., the visible manifestation of God's kingdom. (1958: 7)

For both Green and Beker, the widespread activity of the Spirit is temporary. At the parousia, the Spirit will move aside to make room for the coming of God. One wonders what function the Spirit will have after the parousia, if any. The statements of both Green and Beker are subordinationistic. Although the Spirit's presence is necessary in the epoch between the appearances of Christ, the ministry of the Spirit takes on hints of being something with which Christians make do while they wait for the really important figures, the Son and the Father. They are also eschatologically reductionistic in that they cut off the Spirit from continuing his eschatological ministry after the parousia. To the contrary, I have argued that just as God raised Christ through the Spirit, so will he raise all the dead through the Spirit. Furthermore, the Spirit's ministry does not end there. The resurrection-state of believers is the quintessential life according to the Spirit, in which the saints will live in complete harmony with God through the power of the Spirit. Clearly, the Spirit is not just an interim surrogate for Christ.

Moltmann nips subordinationism in the bud by positing a mutual relationship between "the Spirit of Christ" and "the Christ of the Spirit." I have added that the dependence of Christ on the Spirit continues in Christ's present risen state. The dependence of Christ on the Spirit is not temporary but permanent.

There is one final point to make concerning the relation between Christ and the Spirit in eschatological perspective. It is commonplace in theology to find that Christ represents both promise and fulfillment. He is the promised One—the fulfillment of prophetic foresight. However, his life, death and resurrection point to the promise of still greater things. He is the first born of all the dead (Col 1:18). What is not so commonly taught is that the Holy Spirit also represents promise and fulfillment. Like Christ, the Spirit is the promised One—the expected presence of God within his Messiah and all of his people. And like Christ, the Spirit points to still greater things, as our current ways of living according to the Spirit foreshadow our future resurrection-life, in which we will be in complete harmony with God. In other words, the greater promise is that we will live completely in accord with the Spirit, and in doing so we will be like Christ.

Unity in the Church

In the early church the issue of the identity of the eschatological people was critical and explosive. Could the Gentiles be welcomed into the messianic fellowship? If so, under what conditions? For Paul, the Gentiles were not only welcomed, they were sought with every ounce of energy he had. The conditions of their inclusion into God's family were the acceptance of divine grace in Christ. The same conditions held for all human beings, no matter what ethnic background they had. Thus, the church is unified because it is the one and only eschatological community—the body of Christ living in the power of the Spirit to serve and glorify God. We saw in Chapter Three that Paul and his school link church unity to the Spirit in two ways. One is unity of source and the other is unity of purpose.

The church has unity of source because it is indwelt by the same Holy Spirit. Thinking eschatologically, the Spirit unifies all believers by being poured out on them all. I have explained this in terms of the second level of the *shekinah*. The Spirit is permanently present in a powerful way in all of the church. Thus, the second level of the *shekinah* represents an eschatological level of Spirit-presence. However, since it is the same Spirit indwelling the church that also infuses all of creation now and will saturate all of creation in the eschaton, the presence of the Spirit points the church to the outside world. For the Spirit is a unifying force, drawing all members of creation into a relationship of mutual solidarity. The Spirit will thus compel the church to care for creation, including both humanity and nature. Because the church is being influenced by the Spirit in a unique way, it will be especially conscious of the need to reach out. The conscious motivation may simply be outreach, or it may be Moltmann's brand of approximating the future eschatological state of universal justice and peace in the present. Regarding nature, the church will desire not to recklessly dominate and consume nature, but rather to carefully cooperate with it and preserve it. Regarding humanity, the church will take on characteristics of the eschatological ministry of the Spirit—comforting, nourishing, providing a sanctuary for the weary and wounded, but also being willing to judge impropriety wherever it is found.

The function just described shows that the unity of source naturally blends with the unity of purpose. The church that is unified by the Spirit will tend to behave according to the Spirit. Living according to the Spirit, in turn, leads believers to recognize and strengthen the unity they have with each other (Eph 4:13). In Paul's day, division in the church was rampant. The most persistent cause of schism was the question of the status of Gentile believers. However, in Corinth, the cause of division was the question of which Christian leader with which to identify.

Today the Jew-Gentile question continues, although in a different form, since the church is now primarily Gentile. In addition, the lines of division also run along religious and sociological markers. Communication is problematic between racial groups, socio-economic groups and gender groups, not to mention denominations and churches. Therefore, the problem of church unity is at least as pressing as it was in the first century. Yet despite this theological climate, the convictions of Paul still stand. Underlying all the very real and complex issues of religious and sociological identity there remains the more fundamental level of Christian identity. Moltmann expresses this idea in terms of living "under the cross." He realizes that ecumenical dialogue is a long and painstaking process, but he also recognizes that a common willingness to live out our discipleship to Christ together with all other believers is a necessary first step to open fellowship. I would add that it is the one Holy Spirit, received by all believers in all places at all times, that will give rise to the desire to live under the cross with compassion and understanding for our fellow saints. Of course, this does not mean that anything goes in the church, as if the Spirit will lead believers toward unification regardless of the circumstances of division. The Spirit actively convicts humanity of its sins. True unity in the church starts with a willingness to confront sin first in our own movements and then in the movements of others. This can be a healthy process, if it is carried out "under the cross."

Diversity in the Church

Paul uses the concept of spiritual gifts to illustrate proper diversity within the church. While noting that the simultaneous operation of spiritual gifts is itself a unifying element for the churches, the concept of spiritual gifts is an apt way to describe the unique and diverse operations of the Spirit within the eschatological community. *Charismata* are the "manifestation of the Spirit," as Paul says in 1 Cor 12:7. This means that *charismata* can take as many different forms as there are people and circumstances. The Spirit supplies what is needed to edify a particular community in a particular situation. The *charismata* are not limited to the religious sphere of life (if there is one), any more than *charis* itself might be. Neither are the *charismata* limited to the lists developed in the Pauline letters. *Charisma* is simply the operation of God's grace through a person for the benefit of other people. Thus, the range of possibilities for the manifestations of the Spirit is unlimited.

In Chapter Seven I took issue with Moltmann's definition of the spiritual gifts as including 'natural' abilities put into the service of the believing community. An eschatological pneumatology provides us with another way to discern the meaning of *charismata*. The category *novum* shows us that something new has happened in humanity through the advent of the Holy Spirit. The indwelling Holy Spirit makes for a decisive difference between human life inside and outside of the faith. In terms of the *novum* of the new age and the advent of the Spirit, what has happened in the formation and empowering of the Christian community is miraculous. It is something that could not have come out of the potentialities of human communities in and of themselves. Based on this ecclesiological claim, it is entirely consistent to conclude that the manifestations of the Spirit within the community are miraculous as well.

Experience of the Spirit

I have documented the important relation between experience and pneumatology for Moltmann. In the modern context where experience has assumed such a prominent role in the formation of theological understanding, it is necessary to think through the meaning of the experience of the Spirit. In this project, I am approaching pneumatology not from an experiential point of view, but from an eschatological one. On the face of it, when 'eschatology' is understood as pertaining only to the "not yet," it appears that present experience would not pertain to an eschatological pneumatology. Eschatological pneumatology would be forced to rely completely on the problematic exegesis of apocalyptic texts. By definition, the "not yet" lies outside the realm of present experience. However, in conceiving of eschatology as pertaining not only to the "not yet" but also to the "already," I have shown that present experience of the Spirit is, in fact, a vital part of the discussion. This is because *experience of the Spirit is eschatological experience*. This conviction comes from Paul. For him, the Christian encounter with the Spirit is an immersion in realities pertaining to the eschatological age of salvation.

We have also seen that Moltmann expands the concept of the experience of the Holy Spirit beyond "holy" experiences to include experiences from all spheres of life. His theological grounds for making this move are the doctrine of creation and the omnipresence of the Spirit. The Spirit is present everywhere as the power of creation and the principle of life. If this is so, then, Moltmann reasons, it must be possible to experience the Spirit in all aspects of life. Paul may be inclined to make a similar claim, but he would probably do it on different grounds. In Paul's way of thinking, it is possible for the believer to experience the Spirit in all aspects of life because the Spirit indwells the believer. When the Spirit indwells human beings, his influence reaches to every corner of human existence.

Thus, Paul comes to a similar conclusion as Moltmann. However, it is noteworthy that the Pauline idea of the indwelling of the Spirit is an eschatological idea, whereas Moltmann's reasoning from the omnipresence of the Spirit in all of creation is not. The difference between the two approaches may be significant for our understanding of the experience of the Spirit. For if it is possible to experience the Spirit in everyday life because one is a member of the community of living creatures, it is reasonable to assume that it must be more possible to experience the Spirit because one is a member of the eschatological community of Spirit-endowed people. Is this really the case? It would appear so, given the frequent reports that come from believers who undergo a perceptible alteration in the way they approach life. It is not uncommon to hear a recently converted Christian report that she "sees things in a whole different light." What she means is that there are things going on inside her that were not going on before—as far as she is aware. What she is describing is experience of the Spirit that she did not previously have. She is experiencing "God doing a new thing" in the advent of the Holy Spirit.

In classifying present experience of the Spirit as eschatological, present experience of the Spirit also becomes tied into the greater narrative of the trinitarian history of God's dealings with the world. In doing this, the eschatological approach sets experience of the Spirit within its proper context. The existence the believer had before following Christ is "life according to the flesh." It is the "old life"—the non-eschatological life. The present existence of the believer is marked by "living according to the Spirit." This is the "new life"—the eschatological life that reflects the fruit of the Spirit. However, as every believer knows all too well, the new life that we enjoy in this age is incomplete. Our experience of new life in the Spirit is a welcome departure from old, destructive patterns, but we know that life is still not all it can be. In this way, experience of the Spirit points forward to the completeness of the resurrection-life to come.

In the mixture between the already and the not yet, present experience of the Spirit includes both rejoicing and groaning. Believers rejoice because they relish their victories over the former slavery to sin and death. On the other hand, experience of the eschatological Spirit is not triumphalist. Paul teaches in Rom 8 that believers groan *as those who have the first fruits of the Spirit.* The first thing to notice here is that believers groan. As is conveyed all throughout the New Testament, suffering is a part of the Christian life. Conditions are not what anyone would like them to be, for the world is scarred by ongoing violence, manipulation, and oppression. Things are bad enough to lead all of creation to groan, and believers groan as part of creation. On top of this, followers of Christ are sometimes called upon to suffer for the sake of their master. Just as Christ suffered, we must also share in his sufferings. Finally, as Moltmann points out, our groaning is intensified because we have a vision of something better. "When freedom is near, the chains begin to hurt." For the Christian, freedom is not only near; it is already present in the gift of the eschatological Spirit.

The combination of rejoicing and groaning in the Christian life is echoed by the Spirit himself. Because he is immanent in creation, the Spirit groans along with it. To view it from another angle, creation participates in the Spirit's groaning on its behalf. By the same token, because the Spirit is immanent in creation, he also rejoices over the eschatological blessings that are even now being lavished on the world. If it gives God joy to create the world, it also gives him joy to renew it and prepare it for its re-creation.

Therefore, groaning and rejoicing are facts of life in this age. All people groan, and all of creation groans. As human beings and as members of creation, believers will groan. However, there is a crucial difference between groaning in misery and groaning in anticipation. All creatures groan in misery because suffering is universal. But only believers who are in touch with eschatological hope will groan both in misery and in anticipation for the completion of redemption in Christ. Both the groaning and the anticipation are products of the ministry of the Holy Spirit.

Today many theologians are groaning in solidarity with those who have been oppressed and whose voice has been suppressed in the Christian community for centuries. This frustration is proper and even vital in an eschatological worldview. The Spirit groans with them and for them, and because he indwells human beings, they will also turn their attention to these issues of justice, inasmuch as they cooperate with the leadings of the Spirit. However, an eschatological worldview will also point these movements beyond their own hope for liberation to anticipation of the universal liberation of all people in the consummation. This kind of universal solidarity is not always present in the writings of liberation theologians.

Rebirth and New Life in the Spirit

When believers speak of being reborn in the Spirit they are alluding to the experience of gaining a fresh energy for life in communion with God in Christ. They begin to see things in a different light, and they are introduced to new abilities they have not previously had. For instance, the believer may find a fresh reserve of patience for his or her spouse. Such experience is a cause for rejoicing over this wonderful gift, on the one hand, and for groaning that all of creation is not Spirit-indwelt in the same way, on the other. But this groaning is also a groaning for the future when the wish for the universal saturation of the Spirit will be fulfilled. In other words, it is a groaning in anticipation. This is because rebirth in the Spirit is initiation into the eschatological history of God's dealings with the world. Moltmann writes,

> Whoever is reborn in the Spirit lives in hope in the coming glory. But such a person lives in the world and with the world and for the world which shall become the theater of God's glory. For this reason anyone who is reborn cannot be anxiously preoccupied with himself or herself. Rebirth in the Spirit does not isolate us but brings us into community with other human beings. It places us in the communal movement of the Holy Spirit which will be 'poured

out on all flesh.' The rebirth in the Spirit thus combines a small, limited, and in itself insignificant human life with the promise of God for the whole world and thereby gives our transitory life an eternal meaning. *(PL: 40)*

Moltmann conveys the wonder of rebirth that only an eschatological worldview can deliver. Without such a view, one is apt to perceive rebirth in the Spirit as the Spirit coming into one's life or as a new step in self-actualization. These interpretations are true in a sense, but they must be set within the context of the history of divine activity. Then rebirth to new life becomes the immersion of a human being into the living flow of eschatological redemption.

Sanctification and Resurrection

For Paul, the phrase "life according to the Spirit" denotes eschatological life that is lived in accord with the leadings of the presence of God within the believer. As I explained in Chapter Three, this life is made possible only by the empowering Spirit, but it still requires great effort on the part of the believer. This effort is necessary because failure in this age is very much a possibility and, in fact, a reality. Failure to live according to the Spirit means living according to the flesh—according to desires that run counter to the will of God.

Nevertheless, the very possibility of living according to the Spirit is an eschatological reality. Eschatological behavior amounts to true righteousness—a condition that is not possible within the "natural" abilities of human beings, but is possible now that the Holy Spirit has been poured out. For Paul, righteousness includes the practice of *agape*, which is the self-giving love for God and for others. *Agape* arises because of the presence of God among his people. The practice of *agape* is God demonstrating his own righteousness among the believing community through the indwelling Holy Spirit.

The realization of *agape* comes from an inner impulse within believers, combined with their own willful efforts to practice it. The impulse is an eschatological reality, for it represents the Law being written on their hearts through the Holy Spirit. It is one of the major changes noticed by people who become believers and experience new life.

An eschatological view of the Holy Spirit and the Christian life frames a proper amount of moral confidence. On one hand, even in this eschatological era, believers are not rid of the lingering effects of sin and death, for this is still the age of the "not yet." Smugness or arrogance about one's own righteousness can only come from denial of the depths of the unrighteousness that accompanies it. Paul's irritation with the Corinthians was kindled in large part by their pretentious assumption that the fullness of salvation had come, and they were the proof of it. His response was scathing, as he pointed out that their shortcomings were so deep that he could not even call them "spiritual" people (1 Cor 3:1).

On the other hand, righteous behavior is always within the realm of possibilities, for God can be expected to enact his own righteousness within and among his people. Ironically, believers are all too forgetful that they are indwelt by God himself in the person of the Holy Spirit. Although moral behavior is complex, Christians should take up an appropriate amount of confidence in their ability to choose the good. Not only are they indwelt by God, they are indwelt by the eschatological Spirit of the resurrection. This is the same Spirit who will one day raise them up and transform them into the image of Christ. Many believers hope in this transformation, but they sit and wait for it. In these cases, an eschatological worldview can translate into quietism. Believers would be well served to follow Moltmann in focusing their energy on bringing the realities of the future into the present, whether it is within oneself, in the Christian community, in society in general, or in nature.

An appropriate moral confidence can come from recognizing our place within the context of eschatological redemption. As the first fruits of complete redemption, the Holy Spirit is the Spirit of resurrection. In the gift of the indwelling Spirit, the qualities of the resurrection-life become manifest in the present. Viewed in this way, sanctification becomes a process of growth into that resurrection-life. *Resurrection is but one stage in the process of sanctification.* The initial steps we make in becoming holy in this life are actually our first tastes of the resurrection. 'Resurrection' denotes a new way of living. It is a new type of existence that includes changes in body, mind, and every aspect of human existence. The changes we experience in what we call 'new life' are the beginnings of this new eschatological existence. Although it often seems like the goal of complete righteousness will never be reached, the ideas of the Spirit as first fruits and down payment imply a guarantee that what we now experience will surely come to fruition in future resurrection-life. In this way, the Spirit becomes his own promise. That is, his presence functions as a divine promise that sanctification will be completed in the resurrection-state.

Sanctification and resurrection both point beyond the individual to the whole of creation. Sanctification and resurrection entail the renewal of all things. Because holiness is the destiny of not only human beings but also of all of creation, believers are the first fruits of creation. They are the first of all of God's creatures to be redeemed in the eschatological plan of salvation. As they live out their sanctification, they will be led and empowered to bring the light of eschatological glory to every corner of the world.

The Protestant Tradition and Eschatological Pneumatology

Having given some idea of the characteristics of an eschatological pneumatology, the next question is what such a model will contribute to the Protestant tradition's treatment of pneumatology. I will quickly examine the eschatological model according to two criteria. First, how faithful is an eschatological pneumatology to the biblical witness? Second, how well does it handle the problems that persistently accompany the institutional and experiential models? I will be judging it against the institutional and experiential approaches in both of these regards.

Faithfulness to the Biblical Witness

Regarding the question of faithfulness to the biblical witness to the Holy Spirit, the institutional and experiential approaches are both based on important biblical themes. However, the themes of the Spirit's relation to Christ and the church and his presence in human experience are subsidiary to the primary theme of the eschatological character of the gift of the Spirit. This means that what has happened in Protestant pneumatology is that subsidiary themes of New Testament pneumatology have become primary themes for most theologians, while the primary theme of eschatology has become subsidiary.

The immediate effect of such a divergence in approaches is the loss of a sense of context for pneumatological concepts. The actualization of the transforming ministry of Christ within his followers is a vital theme of New Testament thought. The details of the identity and role of the Holy Spirit in this action were expressed only after some time. As trinitarian theology has developed, the Christian community has needed to ask what it means when we understand this actualizing power to be the third Person of the Trinity. What, then, is the relation between the Spirit and Christ considered as two Persons of the Godhead? Barth answers that the Spirit is the Spirit of Christ. The Spirit is subordinated to the Son every way but ontologically. With Moltmann's help, I have argued that the relation between the Spirit and the Son is more complex and bi-directional than Barth understands it to be. Additionally, the functional subordination of the Spirit to the Son—which is real but less severe than Barth states it—is a phase of divine activity that must be set within the wider narrative of the eschatological dealings of God with the world. The biblical witness to the eschatological age of salvation centers around Christ, but it involves a complex network of figures and events. The mutuality and bi-directionality of the relationship between the Spirit and the Son comes from the New Testament writings.

Turning to experience of the Spirit, Wesley is right to hunger for a personal encounter with God. An experience of the power of the Holy Spirit was a turning point for many people in the New Testament communities of belief—the group gathered at Pentecost, Cornelius and his family, the Corinthians, and so on. Luke in particular points to the role such "power encounters" had in early church evangelism. However, Luke's view of the Holy Spirit sets such experience within the context of an overall view of salvation-history. The time after Pentecost is the church age, in which the Holy Spirit works through believers to spread the gospel to the ends of the earth. This is the destiny of the Spirit-empowered church as foretold by Jesus (Acts 1:8). Personal experience of the Spirit fits within this mission plan.

For Paul, personal experience of the Spirit is also important. As we have seen, pneumatic influence can reach to all areas of the life of the believer and the community. Therefore, pneumatic experience can take a wide variety of different forms. However, Paul also has an understanding of the eschatological flow of history toward the goal of the parousia and the resurrection. Experience of the Spirit is a small part of this flow of history.

When Wesley and especially his less perspicuous followers in the pietistic strains of Protestantism define pneumatology primarily in terms of individual experience, they lose touch with the biblical context in which experience fits. In contrast, I have argued that experience of the Spirit actually takes on deeper meaning if it rejoins its context of salvation-history.

Theological Salutarity

There have been many instances in the history of theology when a secondary theme of Scripture became the primary theme for a theologian or movement. The effect is generally negative. In Protestant pneumatology, this is the case. The institutional approach has led to subordination of the Spirit to Christ and the church, and general neglect of pneumatology within theological construction. Furthermore, the personhood of the Spirit becomes confused when the Spirit is seen as the power of Christ. The experiential approach has led to individualism as the Spirit's work is connected to the individual believer. In its worst forms, it can deteriorate into egocentrism. The question becomes what the Spirit can do "for me," rather than how I might fit into the overall movement of the Spirit. The experience of the Spirit also focuses attention on the present moment, often to the exclusion of the Spirit's activity in the past or future of salvation-history. Finally, as the pietistic strains of Protestantism have arisen in protest to the institutional churches, they have sometimes become pneumatocentric, cutting pneumatology loose from its necessary connection to Christ.

SUBORDINATIONISM AND PNEUMATOCENTRISM

How does the eschatological model fare regarding these persistent difficulties? It is neither subordinationistic nor pneumatocentric, for it recognizes the mutual and bi-directional nature of the relation between Christ and the Spirit. There is functional subordination of the Spirit to the Son in the era of the church, but even during this period, Christ is still dependent on the Spirit. Viewing the ministry of the Spirit within the broad narrative of eschatological history does not create a need to favor any Person of the Trinity over the others. It creates the ideal context for a perichoretic concept of the Trinity such as we see in Moltmann's work. Because of this trinitarian balance, the eschatological model escapes the swinging of the pendulum in Protestant pneumatology between the opposite poles of the institutional and experiential tendencies.

PERSONHOOD

In the eschatological model, the Holy Spirit appears as one key figure in the divine drama of cosmic redemption. In the Spirit, God moves within his people to draw them to himself and transform them into his own likeness. The Spirit thus has his own eschatological ministry. Hendrikus Berkhof writes,

> The Spirit is far more than an instrumental entity, the subjective reverse of Christ's work. His coming to us is a great event in the series of God's saving acts. He creates a world of his own, a world of conversion, experience, sanctification; of tongues, prophecy, and miracles; of mission; of upbuilding and guiding the church, etc. He appoints ministers; he organizes; he illumines, inspires and sustains; he intercedes for the saints and helps them in their weak-

nesses; he searches everything, even the depths of God; he guides into all truth; he grants a variety of gifts; he convinces the world; he declares the things that are to come. In short, as the Johannine Jesus says: 'he who believes in me will also do the works that I do; and greater works than these will he do, because I go to the Father.' (14:12) (23)

This is a beautiful statement of the eschatological ministry of the Holy Spirit. If it seems amazing that such remarks would come from Berkhof, who has constructed one of the most radical of the christocentric accounts of pneumatology, one only needs to read on. He admits that these ideas have a scriptural basis, but he rejects them because he perceives a debilitating weakness: the inability of such a view to maintain an intimate connection between the Spirit and Christ. What he has in mind is the complete subordination of the Spirit to Christ—a solution that he claims is demanded by the New Testament texts. However, if his reading of the New Testament was normative in the early centuries of the church, Christianity might have a binitarian theology and not a trinitarian one. The position of the eschatological model presented in this study is that one can maintain christology and an independent ministry of the Spirit at the same time. The choice between them is a false one.

In a view of the Holy Spirit in which he "creates a world of his own," the personhood of the Spirit comes through in vivid colors. As the creator of this world of eschatological grace, he becomes personal in his intentional activity, his mercy, his leadership, his comfort, his convincing, his judging, and so on. Whereas Berkhof fears that if we attribute "independent" activities to the Spirit then the Spirit becomes disconnected from the Son, the attribution of such independence is necessary in order to conceive of the Spirit as personal. Of course, all pneumatic activities are to be qualified by the doctrine of appropriations, but we must also maintain that the Spirit is not the Son, and the Son is not the Spirit. Neither is the Spirit merely the arm or the power of the Son. He is a center of divine intentionality, creating "a world of his own" in concert with the Son and the Father and for the sake of their glory.

THE INDIVIDUAL AND THE PRESENT MOMENT

Because the eschatological symphony of events and figures is complex, each figure takes his or her place within the whole flow of history. The sense of context that an eschatological worldview offers will prevent individualistic interpretations of the Spirit's activity.

Since the Spirit indwells individuals, they experience him as intimate Comforter. He is as near to us as we are to ourselves. He is so near that we often experience him not as Counterpart but as Presence. One of the reasons Christians fail to identify the Holy Spirit in their pneumatic experiences is this nearness. The Spirit becomes so familiar to the seasoned believer that over time many aspects of his influence come to be taken for granted. The gift of this intimacy with God for all believers is an eschatological phenomenon. It is one of the wonders of the new age. However, it is just that—*one* of the wonders. It must be integrated with the Holy Spirit's work in believing communities, in the church as a whole, in human society and history, in the world, and ultimately in the cosmos. It must also be integrated with the Spirit's work over time. Clearly the activity of the Spirit within the individual is important—it is paramount to each one of us—but that activity takes its meaning within the context of the whole of the Spirit's eschatological work.

Just as the Spirit's interaction with the individual is part of a greater context, so is the Spirit's manifestation in the present moment. During those moments when the presence of the Holy Spirit is particularly palpable, one is not concerned with the past or the future. Instead, one is so enraptured that one hopes the experience will not end. The eschatological model places even these experiences within the context of the history of divine activity. They echo the experiences of God's people in the past, possibly including Jesus himself, and they foreshadow the future ecstasy of resurrection-life in which all of creation will dwell in the unhindered presence of God. It is in this way that knowledge of the aspects of pneumatic experience in the present moment can form a basis for limited knowledge of what future bliss will be like.

When we see experience in this light, our own experiences of the Spirit gain an importance beyond our personal enjoyment of them. We get the sense that we are personally part of something that is grand and wonderful. It is this sense of involvement in something much greater than ourselves or our social group or even humanity in general that can motivate people to do "greater works than these" (John 14:12) on behalf of the gospel.

REDUCTIONISM

In developing the eschatological model, I have emphasized the importance of a sense of context for particular themes of pneumatic activity. When we view the movement of the new age as a complex network of figures and events, both the institutional approach and the experiential approach appear to be reductionistic. The institutional approach focuses on the Spirit's mission of applying the atoning work of Christ to believers, revealing Christ to humanity through the Word, and conveying grace through the sacraments. There is no denying the importance of these themes, but when they define pneumatology, the enterprise suffers because so many other important themes are pushed aside in order to make room for the imminent figure of Christ. In the institutional approach, the role of the Spirit becomes circumscribed in clear and well defined boundaries, thus making the identity of the Spirit simpler and easier to grasp. While this is a nice heuristic device, it has serious drawbacks. It domesticates the Spirit and brings him under human control. However, any attempt to delimit the activity of God in this way is futile, for God the Spirit is mysterious and acts in surprising ways.[3]

One of the motivating forces of experiential pneumatology is the expectation that the Spirit's presence is surprising and somewhat unpredictable. It is this dynamic that makes the experience of the Spirit continually fresh and interesting. However, experiential pneumatology suffers under its own brand of reductionism, for it tends to center the work of the Spirit around the experience of the individual. As we have seen, experience is not a sufficient gauge of Spirit-activity for two reasons. First, much of the Spirit's work is not available to human experience, for it spreads across a range as wide as the cosmos and as long as history itself. Second, as we have seen with the help of William Alston, even the pneumatic activity that is available to human experience is often not identified as being pneumatic.

Eschatological pneumatology eliminates these two forms of reductionism in pneumatology by way of the concept of context. However, is an eschatological pneumatology not guilty of its own form of reductionism? An eschatological pneumatology picks out a segment of the trinitarian history of God's dealings with the world and makes it the paradigm for pneumatology. Christian eschatology covers only the period since the coming of Christ. What, then, of the Spirit's role in divine history before the eschatological age?

There is a two-sided response to this issue. On one hand, because the trinitarian history of God's dealings with the world is a continuous process the elements of which are all intertwined, eschatology leads back to creation and the time of Israel. Eschatology implies creation, just as creation implies eschatology. Creation in the beginning is meant to be the abode of God in his glory. Therefore, creation looks forward to consummation.

---

[3] This has been argued effectively by Eduard Schweizer in his book *The Holy Spirit*.

By the same token, consummation is a transformation of existing creation, not the generation of a whole new cosmos.

In a similar way, the encounter of Israel with the Spirit of God pointed forward to a time when that Spirit would be poured out permanently on all of God's people. By the same token, when we experience the Spirit today as followers of Christ, we do so against the backdrop of the history of Israel. What makes certain events eschatological in character? It is advent and the category *novum*—God doing a new thing. The *novum* can only be perceived against the *antiquum*—that which has gone before. Therefore, eschatological pneumatology is necessarily related to the noneschatological encounter with the Spirit in ancient Israel and Israel's hope that God would do a new thing in and through his Spirit. Without this backdrop, the eschatological model of pneumatology loses its meaning.

On the other hand, the interest of this study is to present a paradigm for a *Christian* pneumatology. It is to give the best possible account of the Christian encounter with the Holy Spirit. The fact is that Christian pneumatology is *eschatological* pneumatology. The Christian encounter with the Holy Spirit is an *eschatological* encounter. Lyle Dabney has written,

> In order to answer the question about the Holy Spirit, contemporary pneumatology must turn to the center of the gospel, namely the New Testament witness to the death and resurrection of Jesus Christ. There one discovers the original language of pneumatology, where the crucial pneumatological question for the early Christians was the question about the relation between the Spirit of God and the humiliated, crucified and resurrected Jesus Christ. (1997: 105; my translation)

Dabney is right that the issue of the Spirit's relation to Christ was a major pneumatological question early on. However, the question about the Spirit's relation to Christ can only be asked, let alone answered, from within an eschatological conceptual framework. Therefore, the original language of pneumatology was not christology but eschatology.

An eschatological approach presents the present and future work of the Spirit as a fulfillment of expectations about the Spirit. It thus concentrates its attention primarily on the present and future periods of salvation-history. However, it is the present age in which we live by God's grace and the future age to which we will be raised. This is central to the gospel. Inasmuch as it is reductionistic, the eschatological approach is so in order to reflect the heart of the New Testament message. In returning to its original language, Christian pneumatology is in effect coming home. In its homecoming, pneumatology is free from the unnecessary reductions and imbalances it has suffered in the Protestant tradition.

Postscript: "A Slice of Heaven"

A drug addict interviewed on a television talk show once remarked that hopelessness is the worst feeling a human being can have. The Christian gospel is meant to give people hope not primarily in themselves but in the God who graciously reaches out to them in the person of Christ and in the power of the Holy Spirit. Christian hope ultimately refers to the wiping away of all tears in the eschaton. It is not enough, however, to point to the eschaton as the realm in which our hopes will finally be fulfilled. People also need hope anchored in the present. The aspect of existence that can give rise to this kind of hope is the presence of the Holy Spirit. Whereas the current ministry of the Spirit is not in itself a panacea for all that ails creation, it is the first taste of the universal liberation that we crave. The fact that God is here now gives us hope that God will be here in the future. If we understand God to be one who keeps his promises and completes what he begins, then our hopes regarding the eschaton can reach as far as our imagination can carry them. Such hope is not a flight of fancy, if it is based on divine promises written in Scripture and on experience of the Spirit. According to the principles of Christian eschatology, the Spirit is a promise in and of himself. He is the first fruits of the eschaton. No matter what their circumstances happen to be, all people who perceive the gentle touch of the Holy Spirit can lift up their heads in expectation, for each encounter with the Spirit is a little slice of heaven.

Abbreviations

ATJ	*Asbury Theological Journal*
CD	Karl Barth, *Church Dogmatics.* Edited and translated by Geoffrey Bromiley. Edinburgh: T. & T. Clark, 1975–92. German ed., *Kirchliche Dogmatik*
CG	Jürgen Moltmann, *The Crucified God.* Translated by R. A. Wilson and John Bowden, 1974. Reprinted, Minneapolis: Fortress, 1993. German ed., *Der gekreuzigte Gott: Das Kreuz Christi als Grund und Kritik christlicher Theologie,* 1972
CoG	Jürgen Moltmann, *The Coming of God: Christian Eschatology.* Translated by Margaret Kohl. Minneapolis: Fortress, 1996. German ed., *Das Kommen Gottes: Christliche Eschatologie,* 1995
CPS	Jürgen Moltmann, *The Church in the Power of the Spirit: A Contribution to Messianic Ecclesiology.* Translated by Margaret Kohl, 1977. Reprinted, Minneapolis: Fortress, 1993. German ed., *Kirche in der Kraft des Geistes: Ein Beitrag zur messianische Ekklesiologie,* 1975
EG	Jürgen Moltmann, *Experiences of God.* Translated by Margaret Kohl, 1980. Reprinted, Philadelphia: Fortress, 1984. German ed., "Der Gott, auf den ich hoffe," 1979, and *Gottesfahrungen: Hoffnung, Angst, Mystik,* 1979
EH	Jürgen Moltmann, *The Experiment Hope.* Translated by M. Douglas Meeks. Philadelphia: Fortress, 1975. German ed., *Das Experiment Hoffnung: Einführungen,* 1974; essays published 1966–74
FC	Jürgen Moltmann, *The Future of Creation: Collected Essays.* Translated by Margaret Kohl. Philadelphia: Fortress, 1979. German ed., *Zukunft der Schöpfung: Gesammelte Aufsätze,* 1977
GC	Jürgen Moltmann, *God in Creation.* Translated by Margaret Kohl, 1985. Reprinted, Minneapolis: Fortress, 1993. German ed., *Gott in der Schöpfung: Ökologische Schöpfungslehre,* 1985
HIC	Jürgen Moltmann, editor, *How I Have Changed: Reflections on Thirty Years of Theology.* Translated by John Bowden. London: SCM, 1997
HTG	Jürgen Moltmann, *History and the Triune God.* Translated by John Bowden. New York: Crossroad, 1991. German ed., *In der Geschichte des dreieinigan Gottes: Bieträge zur trinitarischen Theologie,* 1991, essays published 1980–90
JTS	*Journal of Theological Studies*

NIDNTT   *New International Dictionary of New Testament Theology.* Edited by
Colin Brown. 3 vols. Rev. ed. Grand Rapids: Zondervan, 1986

PL   Jürgen Moltmann, *The Passion for Life.* Translated by M. Douglas
Meeks. Philadelphia: Fortress, 1978. German ed., taken from *Neuer
Lebenstil: Schritte zur Gemeinde,* 1977

SL   Jürgen Moltmann, *The Spirit of Life.* Translated by Margaret Kohl.
Minneapolis: Fortress, 1992. German ed., *Der Geist des Lebens: Ein
gan zheitliche Pneumatologie,* 1991

SoL   Jürgen Moltmann, *The Source of Life: The Holy Spirit and the
Theology of Life.* Translated by Margaret Kohl. Minneapolis: Fortress,
1997. German ed., *Die Quelle des Leben: Der heilige Geist und die
Theologie des Lebens,* 1997; essays published 1990–96

TDNT   *Theological Dictionary of the New Testament.* Edited by Gerhard
Kittel and Gerhard Friedrich. Translated by Geoffrey Bromiley. 10
vols. Grand Rapids: Eerdmans, 1964–75

TH   Jürgen Moltmann, *Theology of Hope.* Translated by James W. Leitch,
1967. Reprinted, Minneapolis: Fortress, 1993. German
ed., *Theologie der Hoffnung: Untersuchungen zur Begründung und zu
den Konsequenzen einer christlichen Eschatologie,* 1964; 2d ed., 1965

TK   Jürgen Moltmann, *The Trinity and the Kingdom.* Translated by
Margaret Kohl, 1981. Reprinted, Minneapolis: Fortress, 1993.
German ed., *Trinität und Reich Gottes: Zur Gotteslehre,* 1980

TT   Jürgen Moltmann, *Theology Today: Two Contributions Toward
Making Theology Present.* Translated by John Bowden. London:
SCM, 1988. German ed., *Was ist heute Theologie? Zwei Beiträge zu
ihrer Vergegenwärtigung,* 1988

WJC   Jürgen Moltmann, *The Way of Jesus Christ: Christology in Messianic
Dimensions.* Translated by Margaret Kohl, 1990. Reprinted,
Minneapolis: Fortress, 1993. German ed., *Der Weg Jesu Christi:
Christologie in messianische Dimensionen,* 1989

WTJ   *Wesleyan Theological Journal*

Bibliography

Aune, David E. "Eschatology (Early Christian)." In *Anchor Bible Dictionary,* edited by David Noel Freeman, 2:594–609. New York: Doubleday, 1992.

Barrett, C. K. "New Testament Eschatology: Jewish and Pauline Eschatology." *Scottish Journal of Theology* 6 (1953) 136–55.

Barth, Karl. *Church Dogmatics.* Translated by Geoffrey W. Bromiley. Edinburgh: T. & T. Clark, 1975–92.

Bauckham, Richard. *The Theology of Jürgen Moltmann.* Edinburgh: T. & T. Clark, 1995.

Beasley-Murray, George. *Baptism in the New Testament.* Grand Rapids: Eerdmans, 1962.

Becker, O. "ἀρραβών." In *NIDNTT* 2:39–40.

Behm, Johannes. "ἀρραβών." In *TDNT* 1:475.

Beker, J. Christiaan. "Aspects of the Holy Spirit in Paul." *Union Seminary Quarterly* 14 (1958) 3–16.

———. *Paul the Apostle: The Triumph of God in Life and Thought.* Philadelphia: Fortress, 1980.

———. *Paul's Apocalyptic Gospel: The Coming Triumph of God.* Philadelphia: Fortress, 1982.

———. *Suffering and Hope: The Biblical Vision and the Human Predicament.* Philadelphia: Fortress, 1987.

———. *The Triumph of God: The Essence of Paul's Thought.* Translated by Loren T. Stuckenbruck. Minneapolis: Fortress 1990.

———. "Recasting Pauline Theology: The Coherence-Contingency Scheme as Interpretive Model." In *Pauline Theology,* Volume 1: *Thessalonians, Philippians, Galatians, Philemon,* edited by Jouette M. Bassler, 15–24. Minneapolis: Fortress, 1991.

Berkhof, Hendrikus. *The Doctrine of the Holy Spirit.* Atlanta: John Knox, 1964.

Betz, Hans Dieter. *Galatians.* Hermeneia. Philadelphia: Fortress, 1979.

Blaser, Klauspeter. "Immanente Tranzsendenz oder plurale Emergenz des Geistes?" *Evangelische Theologie* 53 (1993) 566–76.

Braaten, Carl E. *The Future of God.* New York: Harper & Row, 1969.

Bruce, F. F. *Paul: Apostle of the Heart Set Free.* Grand Rapids: Eerdmans, 1977.

Bultmann, Rudolf. *Theology of the New Testament.* 2 vols. Translated by Kendrick Grobel. New York: Scribner, 1951–55.

Claybrook, Donald Adrian. "The Emerging Doctrine of the Holy Spirit in the Writings of Jürgen Moltmann." Ph.D. dissertation, Southern Baptist Theological Seminary, 1983.

Conyers, A. J. *God, Hope and History: Jürgen Moltmann and the Christian Concept of History.* Macon, GA: Mercer University Press, 1988.

Cullmann, Oscar. *Königsherrshaft Christi und Kirche in Neue Testament.* Zollikon-Zürich, Evangelische Verlag, 1946.

———. *Christ and Time: The Primitive Christian Conception of Time and History.* Translated by Floyd V. Filson. Rev. ed. London: SCM, 1962.

Dabney, D. Lyle. "The Advent of the Spirit: The Turn to Pneumatology in the Theology of Jürgen Moltmann." *ATJ* 48 (1993) 81–107.

———. "Jürgen Moltmann and John Wesley's Third Article Theology." *WTJ* 29 (1994) 140–48.

———. *Die Kenosis des Geistes: Kontinuität zwischen Schöpfung und Erlösung im Werk des Heiligen Geistes.* Neukirchener Beiträge zur systematischen Theologie 18. Neukirchen-Vluyn: Neukirchener Verlag, 1997.

Dayton, Donald W. *Theological Roots of Pentecostalism.* Peabody, MA: Hendrickson, 1987.

Delling, Gerhard. "ἀπαρχή." In *TDNT* 1:484–86.

Dodd, C. H. *The Parables of the Kingdom.* Rev. ed. London: Collins.

Dunn, James D. G. *Baptism in the Holy Spirit.* Naperville, IL: Allenson, 1970.

———. "Spirit and Kingdom." *Expository Times* 82 (1970) 36–40.

———. *Jesus and the Spirit.* Philadelphia: Westminster, 1975.

———. "Spirit in the NT." In *NIDNTT* 3:693–707.

———. *Romans.* 2 vols. Word Biblical Commentary 38A, 38B. Dallas: Word, 1988.

Epp, Eldon Jay. "Mediating Approaches to the Kingdom: Werner Georg Kümmel and George Eldon Ladd." In *The Kingdom of God in 20th-Century Interpretation,* edited by Wendell Willis, 35–52. Peabody, MA: Hendrickson, 1987.

Fee, Gordon D. *God's Empowering Presence: The Holy Spirit in the Letters of Paul.* Peabody, MA: Hendrickson, 1994.

Fitzer, Gottfried. "σφραγίς." In *TDNT* 7:939–53.

Furnish, Victor Paul. *Theology and Ethics in Paul.* Nashville: Abingdon, 1968.

———. "Theology in 1 Corinthians." In *Pauline Theology,* Volume II: *1 & 2 Corinthians,* edited by David M. Hay, 59–89. Minneapolis: Fortress, 1993.

———. "Where Is 'the Truth' in Paul's Gospel? A Response to Paul W. Meyer." In *Pauline Theology.* Volume 4: *Looking Back Pressing On,* edited by E. Elizabeth Johnson and David M. Hay, 161–77. Atlanta: Scholars, 1997.

Grenz, Stanley J., and Roger E. Olson. *20th-Century Theology: God & the World in a Transitional Age.* Downers Grove, IL: InterVarsity, 1992.

Gunton, Colin. Review of *The Spirit of Life* by Jürgen Moltmann. *JTS* 45 (1994) 787–90.

Hall, Christopher A. "Stubborn Hope" [interview with Jürgen Moltmann]. *Christianity Today* 37 (Jan 11, 1993) 30–33.

Hamilton, Neill Q. *The Holy Spirit and Eschatology in Paul.* Edinburgh: Oliver and Boyd, 1957.

Hendry, George S. *The Holy Spirit in Christian Theology.* Philadelphia: Westminster, 1956.

Heron, Alisdair. *The Holy Spirit.* Philadelphia: Westminster, 1983.

Hiers, Richard H. "Pivotal Reactions to the Eschatological Interpretations: Rudolf Bultmann and C. H. Dodd." In *The Kingdom of God in 20th-Century Interpretation,* edited by Wendell Willis, 15–34. Peabody, MA: Hendrickson, 1987.

Hollenweger, Walter J. *The Pentecostals.* Peabody, MA: Hendrickson, 1969.

Isaacs, Marie E. *The Concept of Spirit.* London: Heythrop Monographs, 1975.

Johnston, George. "Major Themes in the New Testament Doctrine of the Holy Spirit." *Canadian Journal of Theology* 1 (1955) 82–88.

Keck, Leander. *Paul and His Letters.* Rev. ed. Proclamation Commentaries. Philadelphia: Fortress, 1988.

Keller, Catherine. "Pneumatic Nudges: The Theology of Moltmann, Feminism, and the Future." In *The Future of Theology: Essays in Honor of Jürgen Moltmann,* edited by Miroslav Volf, Carmen Krieg, and Thomas Kucharz, 154–63. Grand Rapids: Eerdmans, 1996.

Kerr, A. J. "ἀρραβών." *JTS* 39 (1988) 92–97.

Korsch, Dietrich. "Gottes Geist—der Geist des Lebens: Aussichten und Schwierigkeiten gegenwärtiger Pneumatologie." *Theologische Rundschau* 58 (1993) 203–18.

LaCugna, Catherine Mowry. Review of *The Spirit of Life,* by Jürgen Moltmann. *Theological Studies* 54 (1993) 755–57.

Ladd, George E. *The Presence of the Future.* Rev. ed. Grand Rapids: Eerdmans, 1974.

———. "The Holy Spirit in Galatians." In *Current Issues in Biblical and Patristic Interpretation,* edited by Gerald F. Hawthorne, 211–16. Grand Rapids: Eerdmans, 1975.

———. *A Theology of the New Testament.* Rev. ed. Grand Rapids: Eerdmans, 1993.

Lampe, Geoffrey. *The Seal of the Spirit: A Study in the Doctrine of Baptism and Confirmation in the New Testament and the Fathers.* 1967. Reprinted, Eugene, OR: Wipf & Stock, 2004.

———. *God as Spirit.* Bampton Lectures 1976. London: SCM, 1977.

Link, Christian. "Points of Departure for a Christian Eschatology." Translated by G. W. Locher and P.-M. Béguin, in *Eschatology in the Bible and in Jewish and Christian Tradition,* edited by Henning Graf Reventlow, 98–110. Journal for the Study of the Old Testament Supplement Series 243. Sheffield: Sheffield Academic, 1997.

Link, H.-G. "ζωή." In *NIDNTT* 2:476–84.

———, and Colin Brown. "ἀπαρχή." In *NIDNTT* 3:415–17.

Macquarrie, John. "Eschatology and Time." In *The Future of Hope: Theology as Eschatology,* edited by Frederick Herzog, 110–25. New York: Herder and Herder, 1970.

Martin, Ralph P. "The Spirit in 2 Corinthians in Light of the "Fellowship of the Holy Spirit." In *Eschatology and the New Testament: Essays in Honor of George Raymond Beasley-Murray,* edited by W. H. Gloer, 113–28. Peabody, MA: Hendrickson, 1988.

McPherson, Aimee Semple. *The Holy Spirit.* Los Angeles: Challpin, 1931.

Meyer, Paul W. "The Holy Spirit in the Pauline Letters: A Contextual Approach." *Interpretation* 33 (1979) 3–18.

Moltmann, Jürgen. *Theology of Hope: On the Ground and the Implications of a Christian Eschatology.* Translated by James W. Leitch, 1967. Reprinted, Minneapolis: Fortress, 1993. German ed., *Theologie der Hoffnung: Untersuchungen zur Begründung und zu den Konsequenzen einer christlichen Eschatologie,* 1964; 2d ed., 1965.

———. *The Crucified God: The Cross of Christ as the Foundation and Criticism of Christian Theology.* Translated by R. A. Wilson and John Bowden, 1974. Reprinted, Minneapolis: Fortress, 1993. German ed., *Der gekreuzigte Gott: Das Kreuz Christi als Grund und Kritik christlicher Theologie,* 1972.

———. *The Experiment Hope.* Edited and translated by M. Douglas Meeks. Philadelphia: Fortress, 1975. German ed., *Das Experiment Hoffnung: Einführungen,* 1974; essays published 1966–74.

———. *The Church in the Power of the Spirit: A Contribution to Messianic Ecclesiology.* Translated by Margaret Kohl, 1977. Reprinted, Minneapolis: Fortress, 1993. German ed., *Kirche in der Kraft des Geistes: Ein Beitrag zur messianische Ekklesiologie,* 1975.

———. *The Passion for Life: A Messianic Lifestyle.* Translated by M. Douglas Meeks. Philadelphia: Fortress, 1978. German ed., taken from *Neuer Lebensstil: Schritte zur Gemeinde,* 1977.

―――. *The Future of Creation: Collected Essays.* Translated by Margaret Kohl. Philadelphia: Fortress, 1979. German ed., *Zukunft der Schöpfung: Gesammelte Aufsätze,* 1977.

―――. *Experiences of God.* Translated by Margaret Kohl, 1980. Reprinted, Philadelphia: Fortress, 1984. German ed., "Der Gott, auf den ich hoffe," 1979, and *Gottesfahrungen: Hoffnung, Angst, Mystik,* 1979.

―――. *The Trinity and the Kingdom.* Translated by Margaret Kohl, 1981. Reprinted, Minneapolis: Fortress, 1993. German ed., *Trinität und Reich Gottes: Zur Gotteslehre,* 1980.

―――. *God in Creation: A New Theology of Creation and the Spirit of God.* Translated by Margaret Kohl, 1985. Reprinted, Minneapolis: Fortress, 1993. German ed., *Gott in der Schöpfung: Ökologische Schöpfungslehre,* 1985.

―――. *Theology Today: Two Contributions Toward Making Theology Present.* Translated by John Bowden. London: SCM, 1988. German ed., *Was ist heute Theologie? Zwei Beiträge zu ihrer Vergegenwärtigung,* 1988.

―――. *The Way of Jesus Christ: Christology in Messianic Dimensions.* Translated by Margaret Kohl, 1990. Reprinted, Minneapolis: Fortress, 1993. German ed., *Der Weg Jesu Christi: Christologie in messianische Dimensionen,* 1989.

―――. *History and the Triune God.* Translated by John Bowden. New York: Crossroad, 1991. German ed., *In der Geschichte des dreieinigen Gottes: Bieträge zur trinitarischen Theologie,* 1991; essays published 1980–90.

―――. "Knowing and Community." In *On Community,* edited by Leroy S. Rouner, 162–76. Notre Dame, IN: Univ. of Notre Dame Press, 1991.

―――. *The Spirit of Life: A Universal Affirmation.* Translated by Margaret Kohl. Minneapolis: Fortress, 1992. German ed., *Der Geist des Lebens: Ein ganzheitliche Pneumatologie,* 1991.

―――. "Talk-back Session with Jürgen Moltmann." *ATJ* 48 (1993) 39–47.

―――. *The Coming of God: Christian Eschatology.* Translated by Margaret Kohl. Minneapolis: Fortress, 1996. German ed., *Das Kommen Gottes: Christliche Eschatologie,* 1995.

―――, editor. *How I Have Changed: Reflections on Thirty Years of Theology.* Translated by John Bowden. London: SCM, 1997. German ed., *Wie ich mich geändert habe,* 1997.

―――. *The Source of Life: The Holy Spirit and the Theology of Life.* Translated by Margaret Kohl. Minneapolis: Fortress, 1997. German ed., *Die Quelle des Leben: Der heilige Geist und die Theologie des Lebens,* 1997; essays published 1990–96.

Montague, George T. *The Holy Spirit: Growth of a Biblical Tradition.* New York: Paulist, 1976.

Nickelsburg, George W. E. *Jewish Literature between the Bible and the Mishnah.* Philadelphia: Fortress, 1981.

Olson, Roger. "Is Moltmann the Evangelicals' Ally?" *Christianity Today,* 37 (Jan. 11, 1993) 32.

Otto, Randall E. *The God of Hope: The Trinitarian Vision of Jürgen Moltmann.* Lanham, MD: University Press of America, 1991.

Outler, Albert C., editor. *John Wesley.* New York: Oxford University Press, 1964.

Pannenberg, Wolfhart. "Can Christianity Do without an Eschatology?" In *The Christian Hope,* edited by G. B. Caird, 25–34. London: SPCK, 1970.

Parratt, J. K. "The Holy Spirit and Baptism." *Expository Times* 82 (1971) 266–271.

Pinnock, Clark H. *Flame of Love: A Theology of the Holy Spirit.* Downers Grove, IL: InterVarsity, 1996.

Rad, Gerhard von. *Old Testament Theology.* Volume 2: *The Theology of Israel's Prophetic Traditions.* Translated by D. M. G. Stalker. New York: Harper & Row, 1965.

Rosato, Philip J. *The Spirit as Lord: The Pneumatology of Karl Barth.* Edinburgh: T. & T. Clark, 1981.

Ross, James. "Eschatological Pragmatism." In *Philosophy and the Christian Faith,* edited by Thomas V. Morris, 279–300. Notre Dame, IN: University of Notre Dame Press, 1988.

Schillebeeckx, Edward. "The Interpretation of Eschatology." Translated by T. L. Westow, in *The Problem of Eschatology,* edited by Edward Schillebeeckx and Boniface Willems, 42–56. Concilium 41. New York: Paulist, 1969.

Schippers, R. "σφραγίς." In *NIDNTT* 3:497–501.

Schweizer, Eduard. "πνεῦμα." In *TDNT* 6:396–455.

———. *The Holy Spirit.* Translated by Reginald H. and Ilse Fuller. Philadelphia: Fortress, 1980.

Shires, Henry M. *The Eschatology of Paul in the Light of Modern Scholarship.* Philadelphia: Westminster, 1966.

Smail, Thomas. "The Doctrine of the Holy Spirit." In *Theology beyond Christendom: Essays on the Centenary of the Birth of Karl Barth, May 10, 1886, e*dited by John Thompson. Princeton Theological Monograph Series 6. Allison Park, PA: Pickwick, 1986

Soskice, Janet Martin. *Metaphor and Religious Language.* Oxford: Oxford University Press, 1985.

Staples, Rob L. "John Wesley's Doctrine of the Holy Spirit." *WTJ* 21 (1986) 91–115.

Thompson, John. *The Holy Spirit in the Theology of Karl Barth.* Princeton Theological Monograph Series 23. Allison Park, PA: Pickwick, 1991.

Travis, Stephen H. *Christian Hope and the Future.* Downers Grove, IL: InterVarsity, 1980.

Vos, Geerhardus. "The Eschatological Aspect of the Pauline Conception of the Spirit." In *Biblical and Theological Studies,* 211–59. New York: Scribner, 1912.

———. *The Pauline Eschatology.* Grand Rapids: Eerdmans, 1952.

Wainwright, Arthur W. *The Trinity in the New Testament.* London: SPCK, 1962.

Weiss, Johannes. *Jesus' Proclamation of the Kingdom of God.* Translated and edited with an introduction by Richard Hiers and David Larrimore Holland. Lives of Jesus Series. Philadelphia: Fortress, 1971. German 2d ed., 1900.

Williams, Colin W. *John Wesley's Theology Today.* Nashville: Abingdon, 1960.

Willis, Wendell. "The Discovery of the Eschatological Kingdom: Johannes Weiss and Albert Schweitzer." In *The Kingdom of God in 20ᵗʰ-Century Interpretation,* edited by Wendell Willis, 1–14. Peabody, MA: Hendrickson, 1987.

Witherington, Ben. *Jesus, Paul and the End of the World.* Downer's Grove, IL: InterVarsity, 1992.

Wood, Laurence W. "From Barth's Trinitarian Christology to Moltmann's Trinitarian Pneumatology: A Methodist Perspective." *ATJ* 48 (1993) 49–79.

Lightning Source UK Ltd.
Milton Keynes UK

174405UK00001B/294/P